I0497576

THIS BOOK BELONGS TO

....

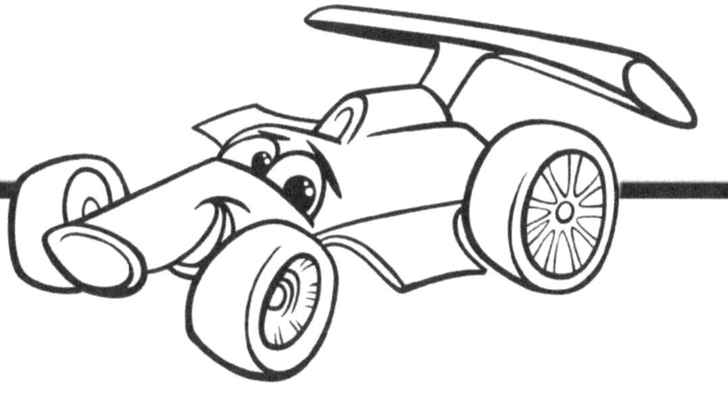

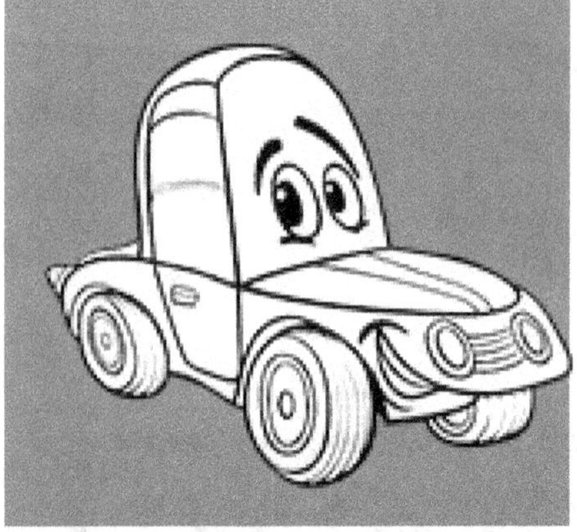
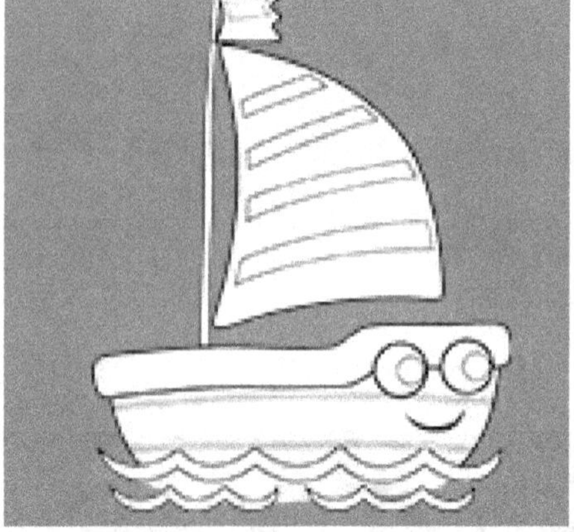
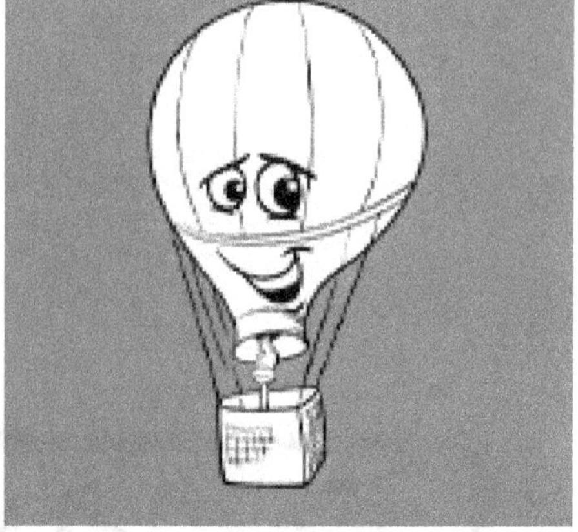
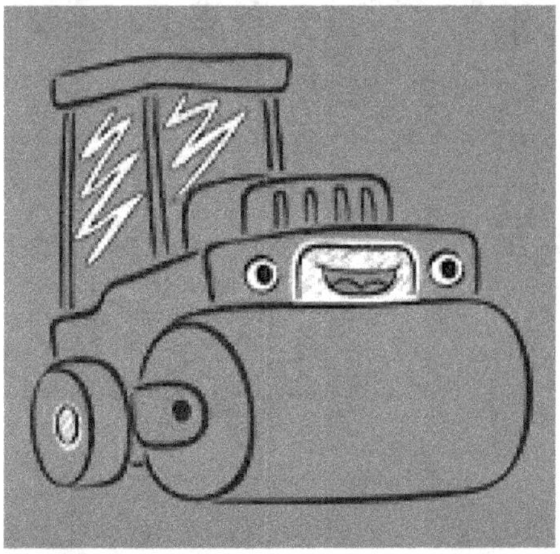
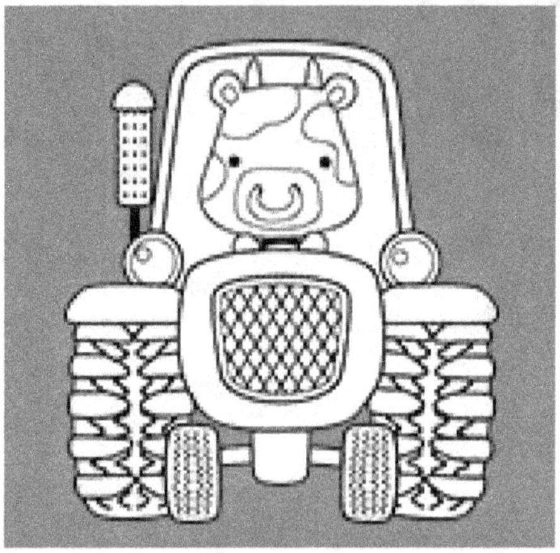
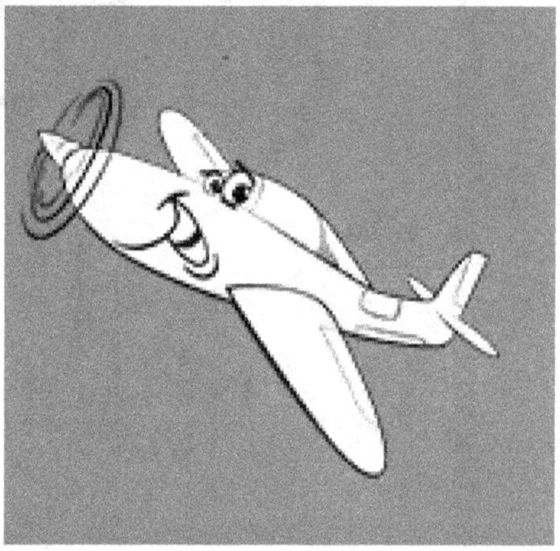
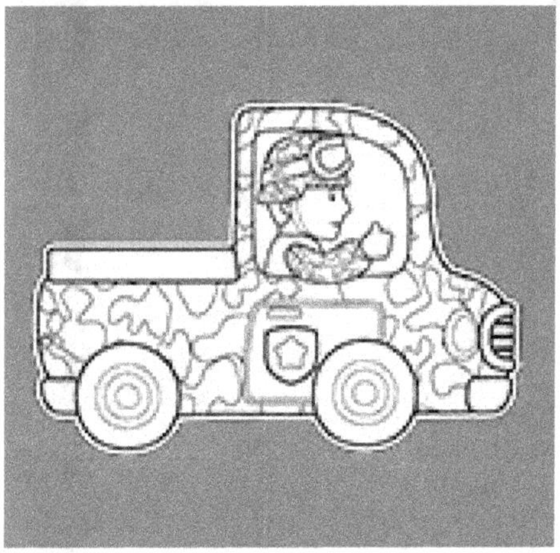
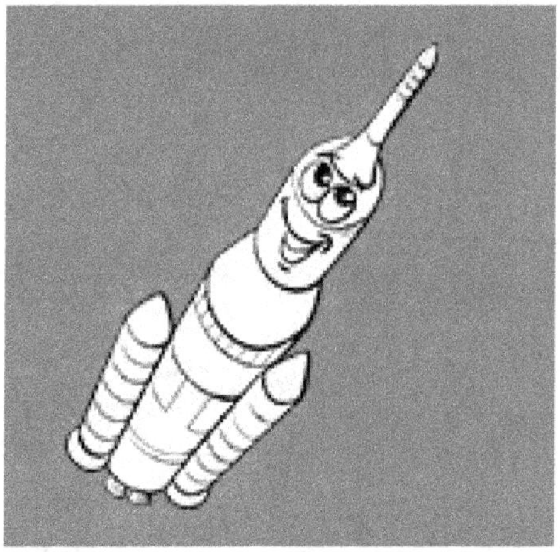
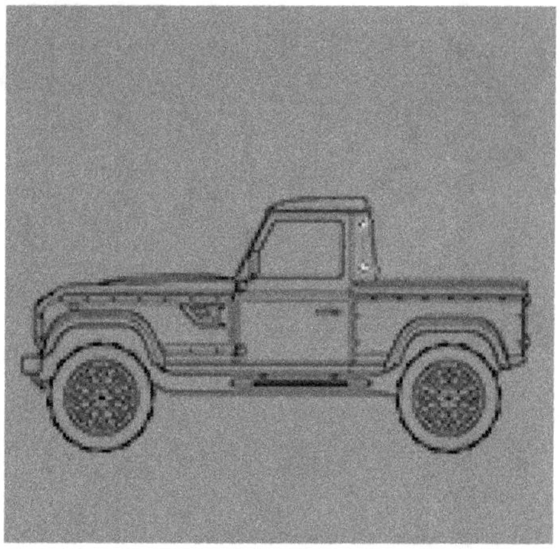
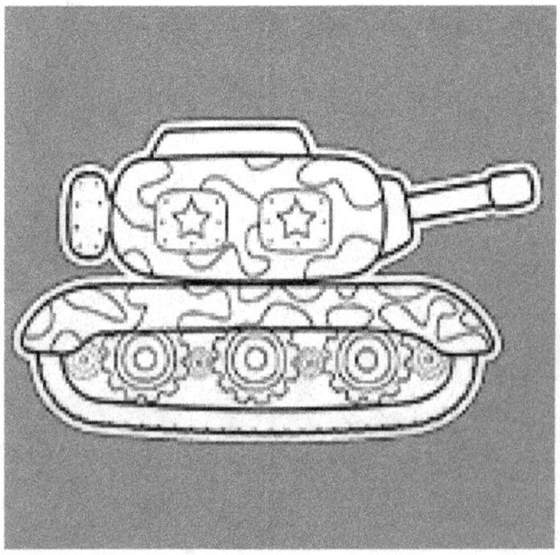
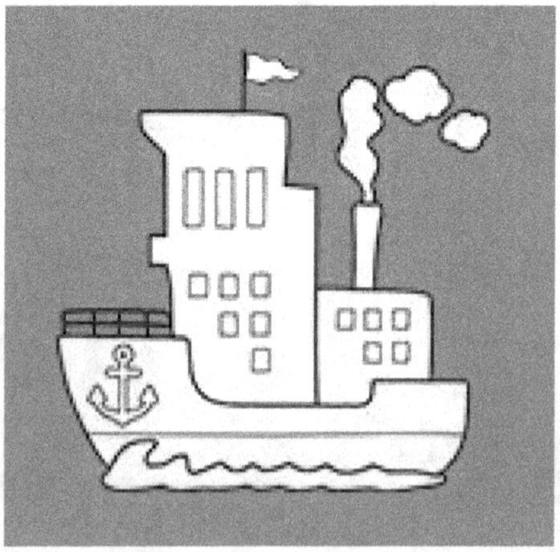

100 DRAWINGS FOR COLORING

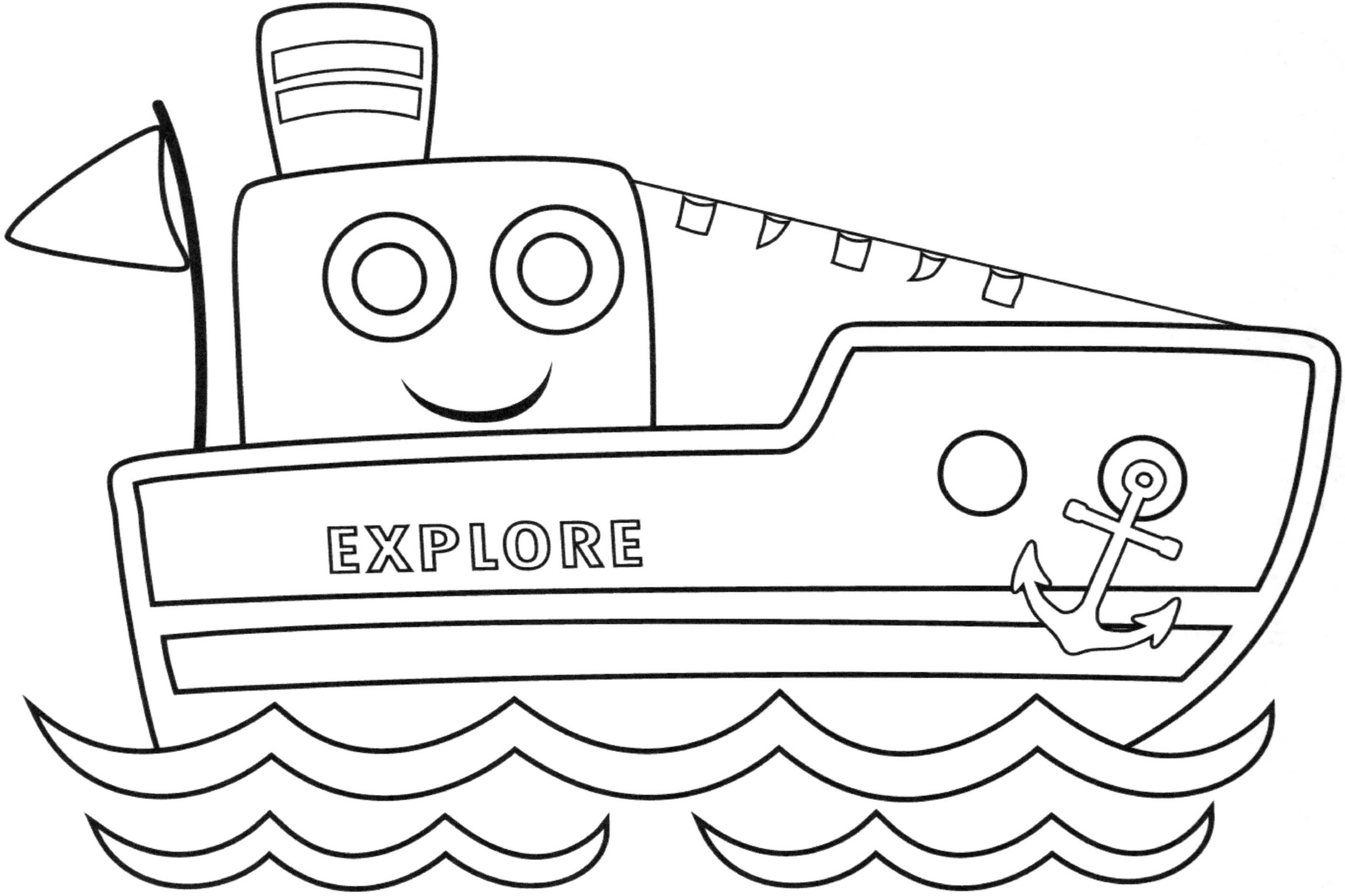
EXPLORE

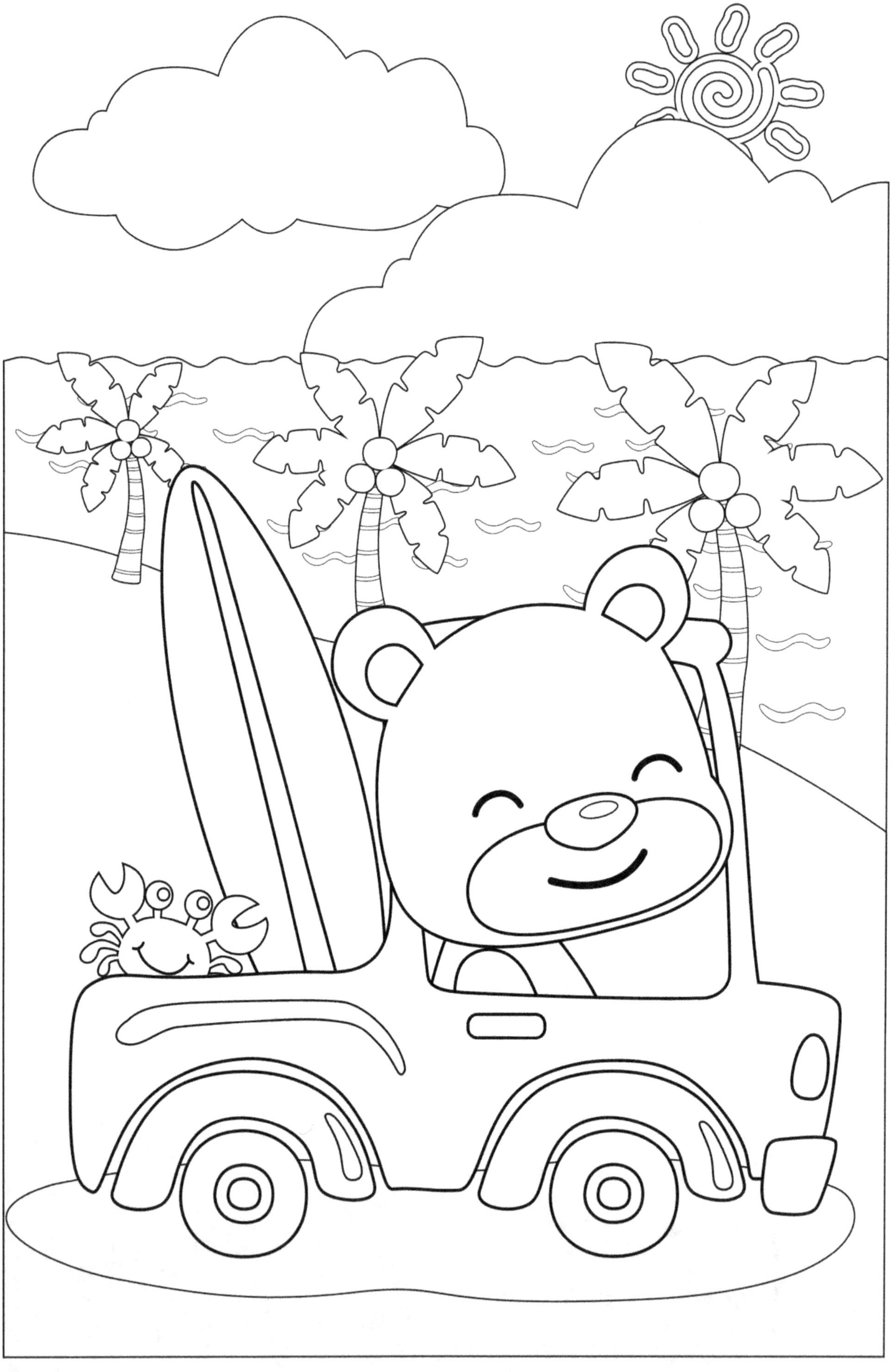

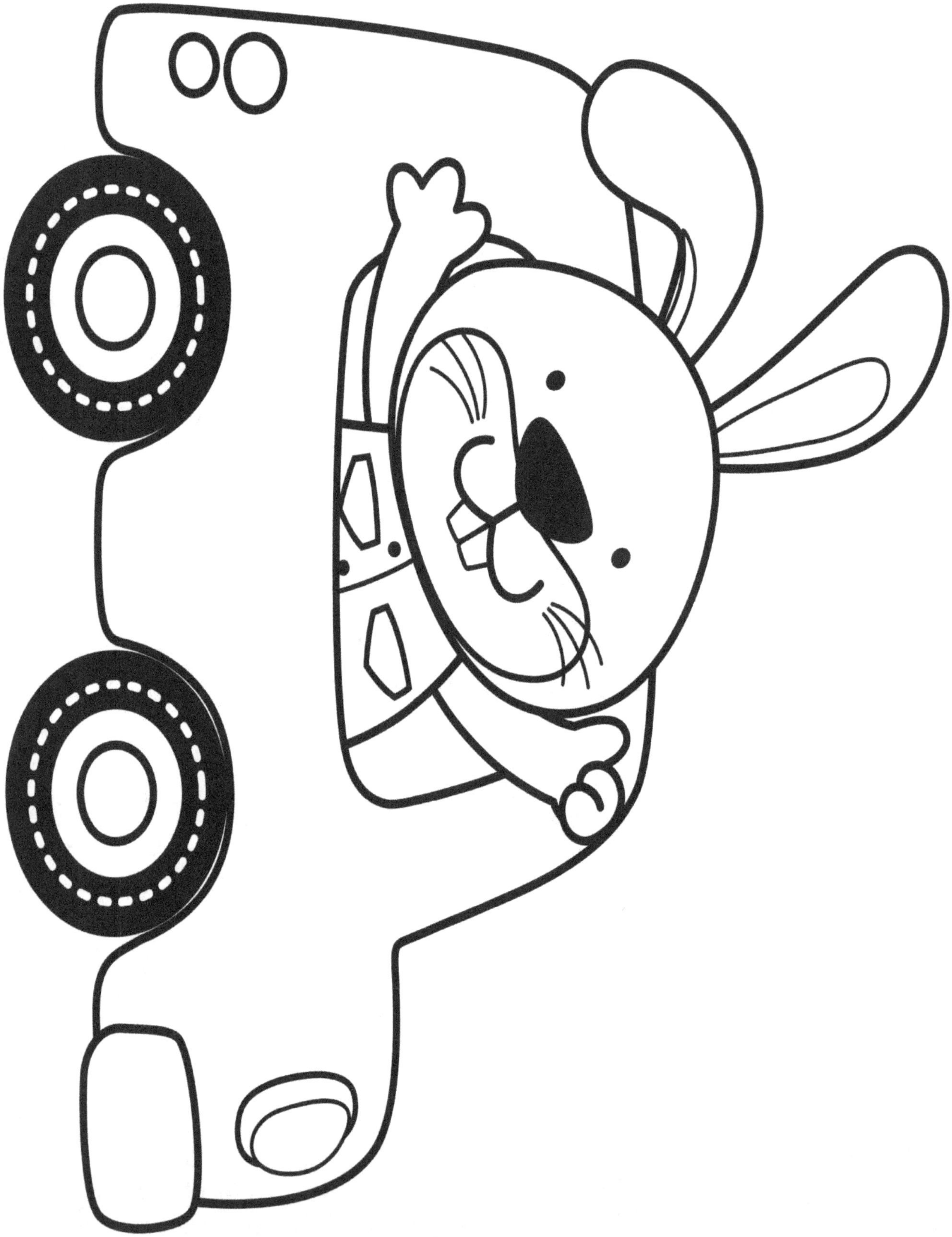

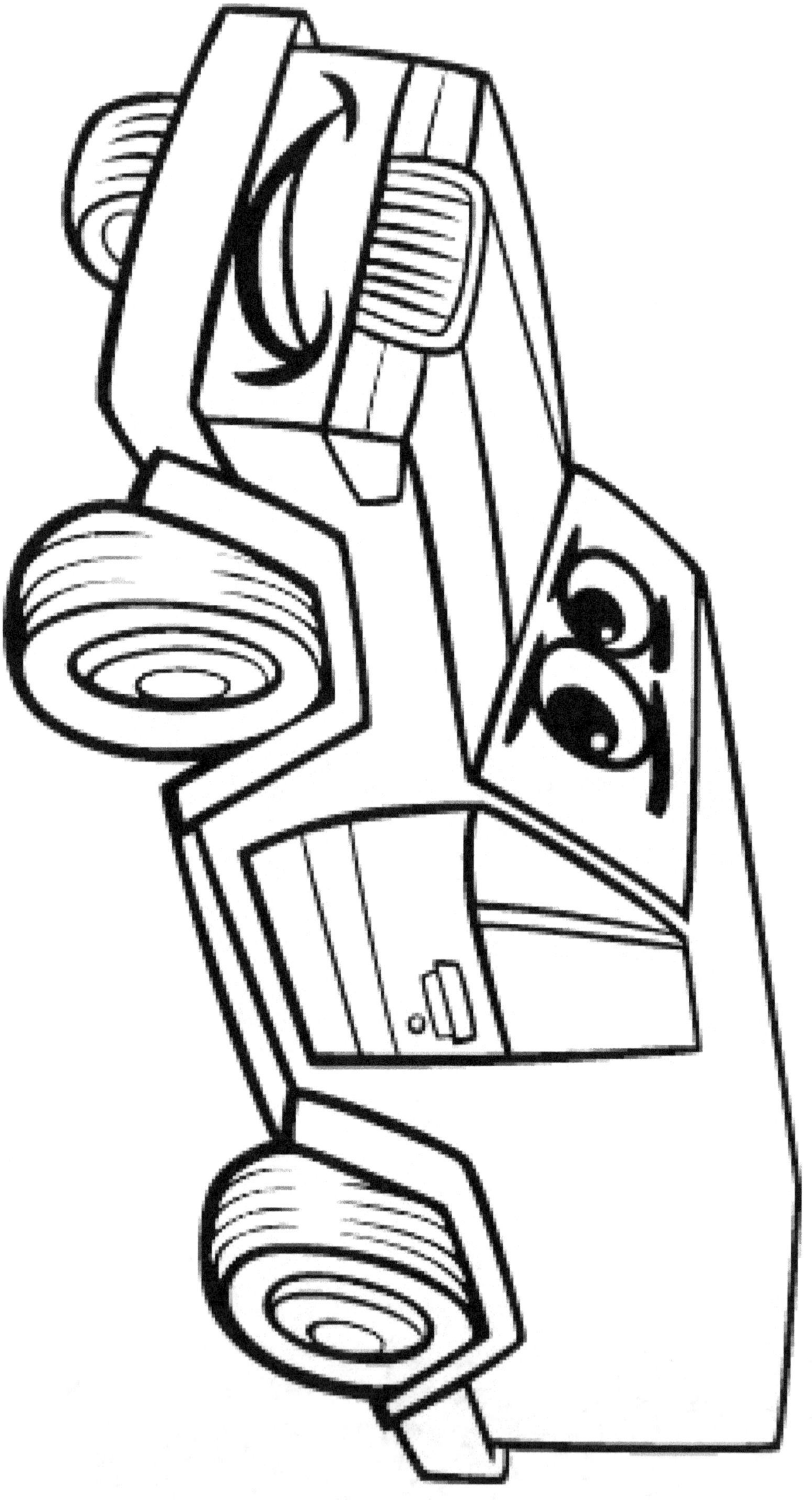

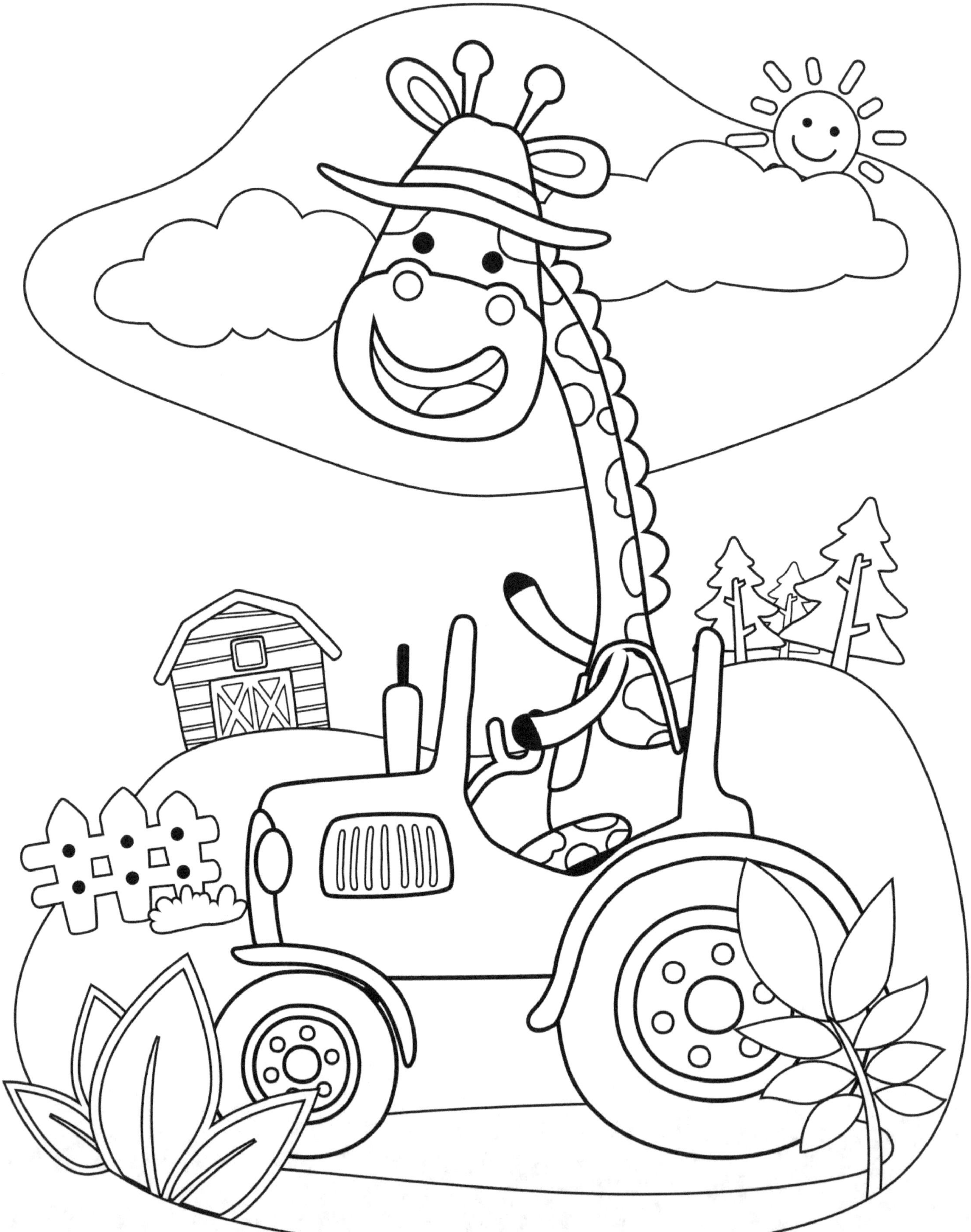

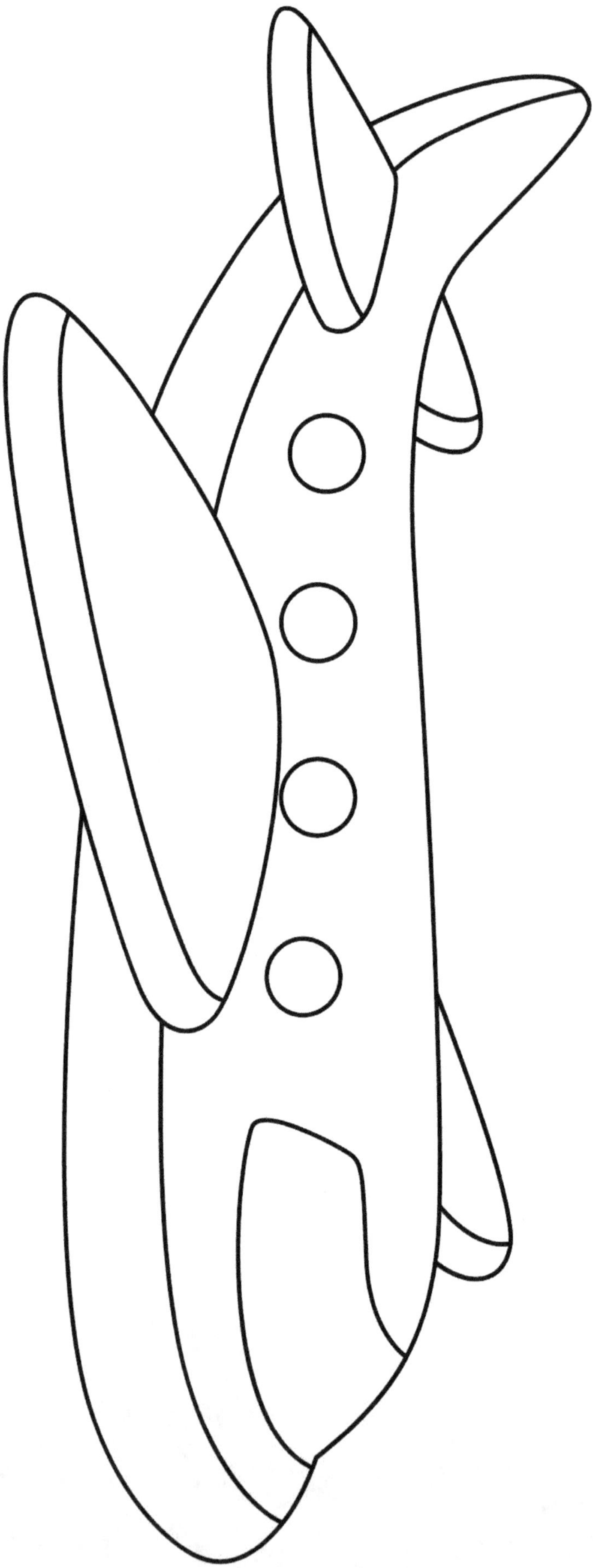

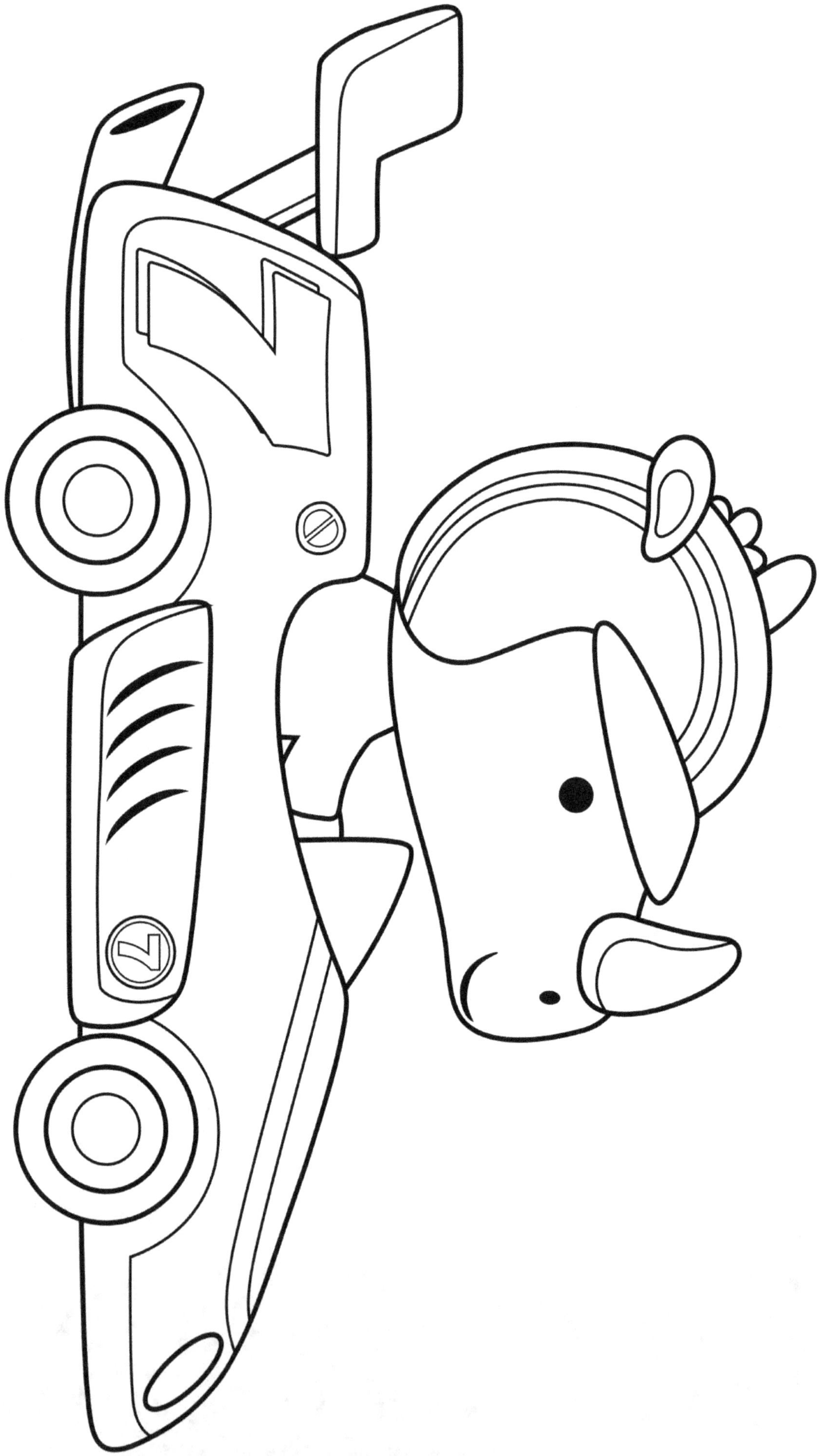
7
7

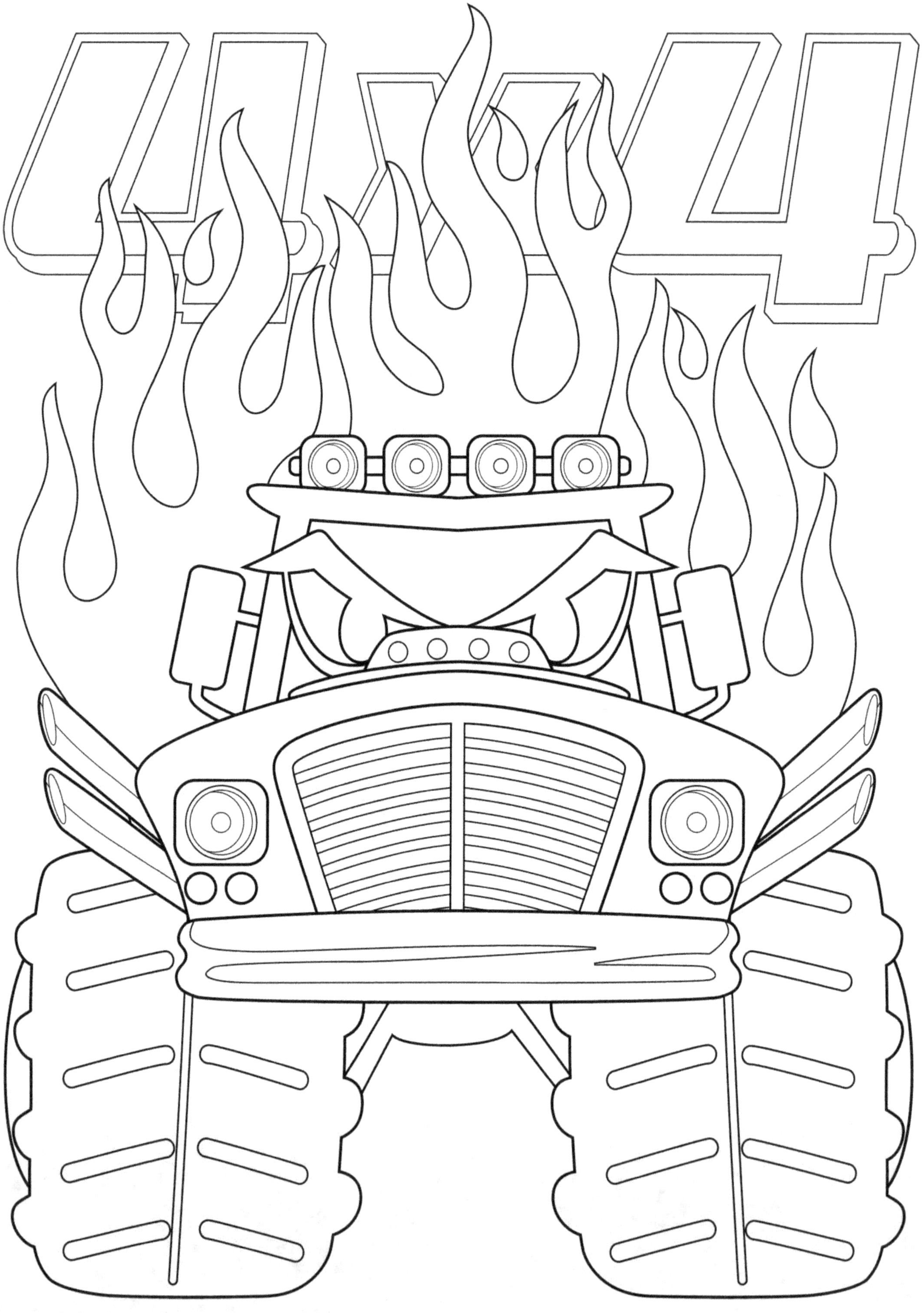
4X4

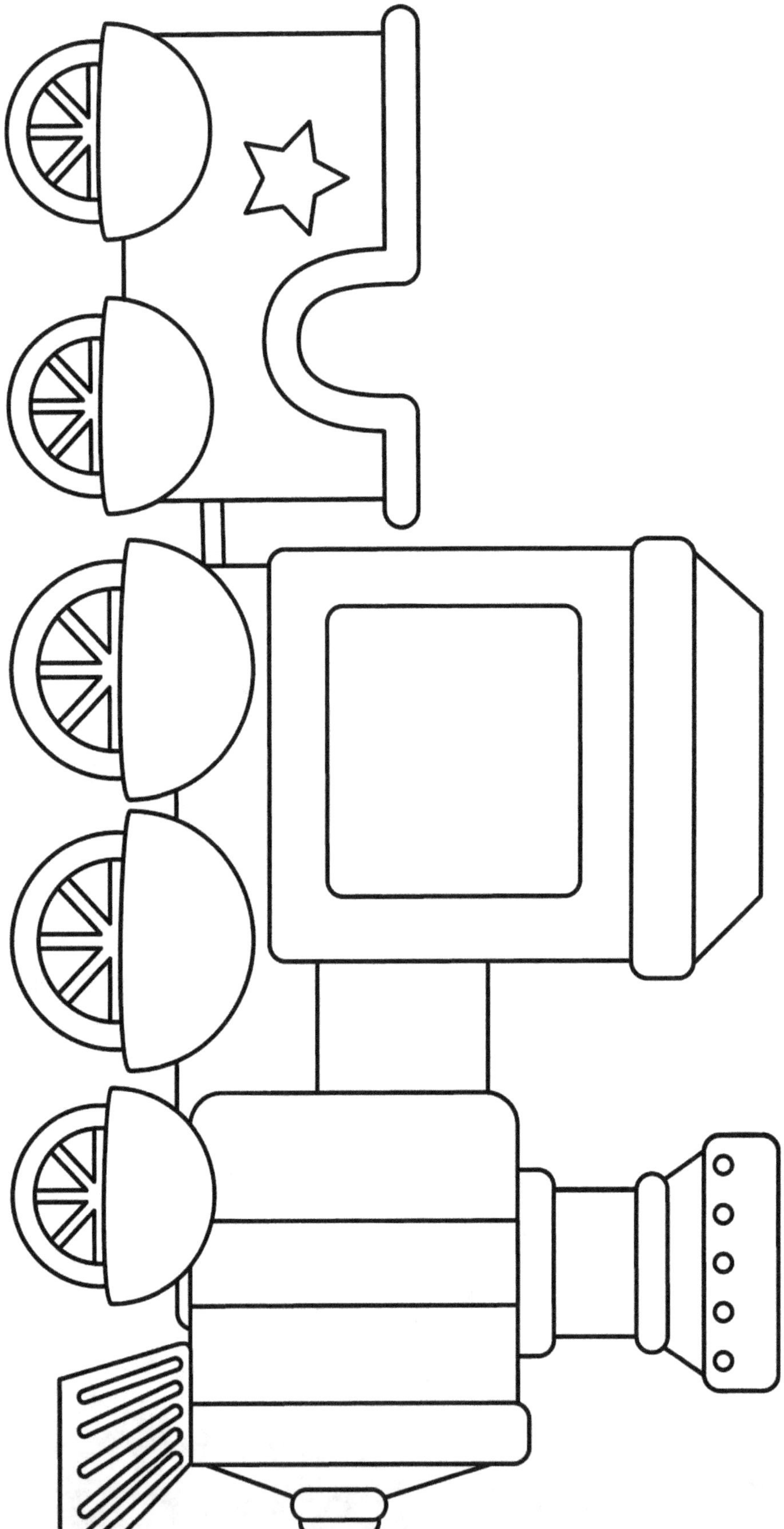

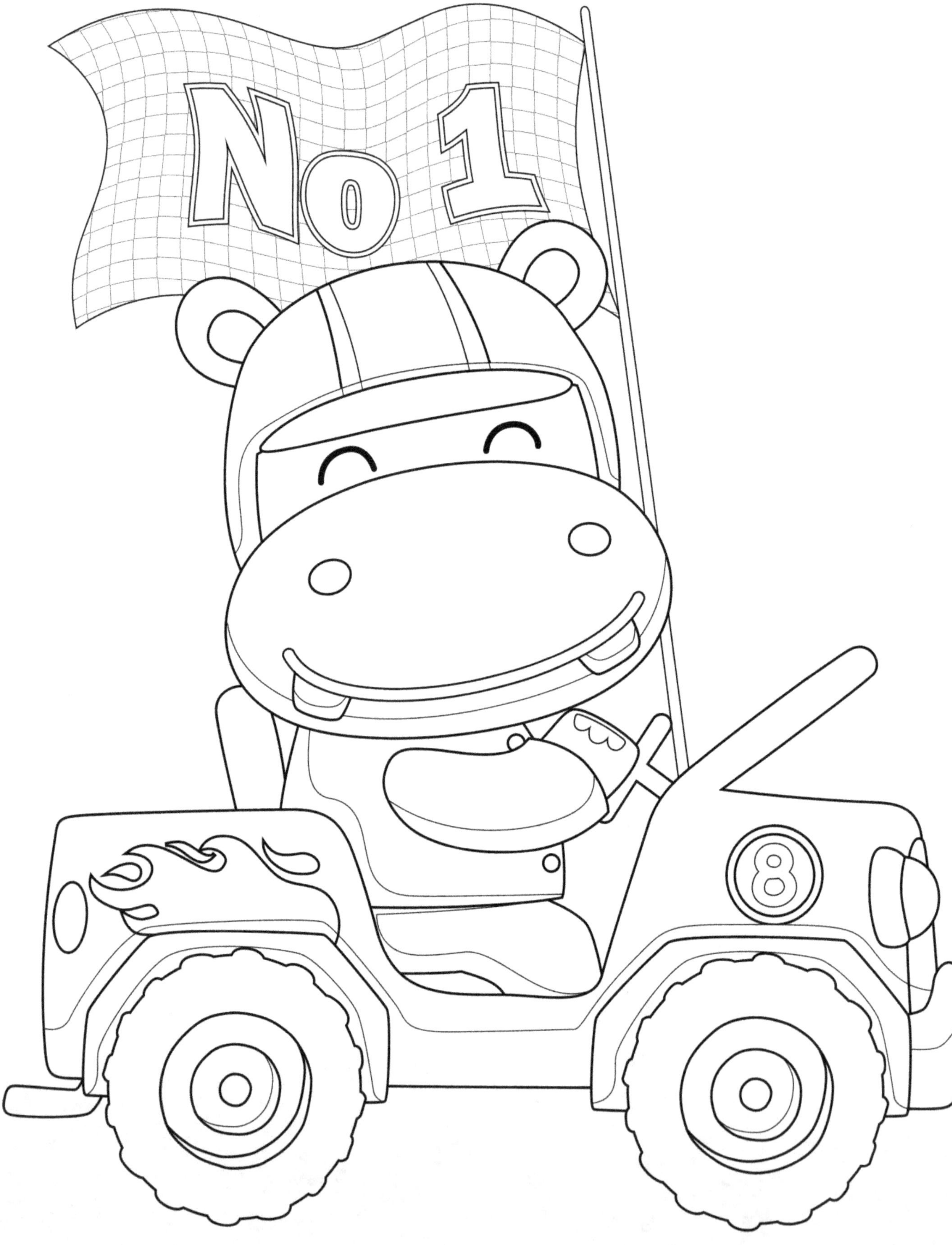
No 1
8

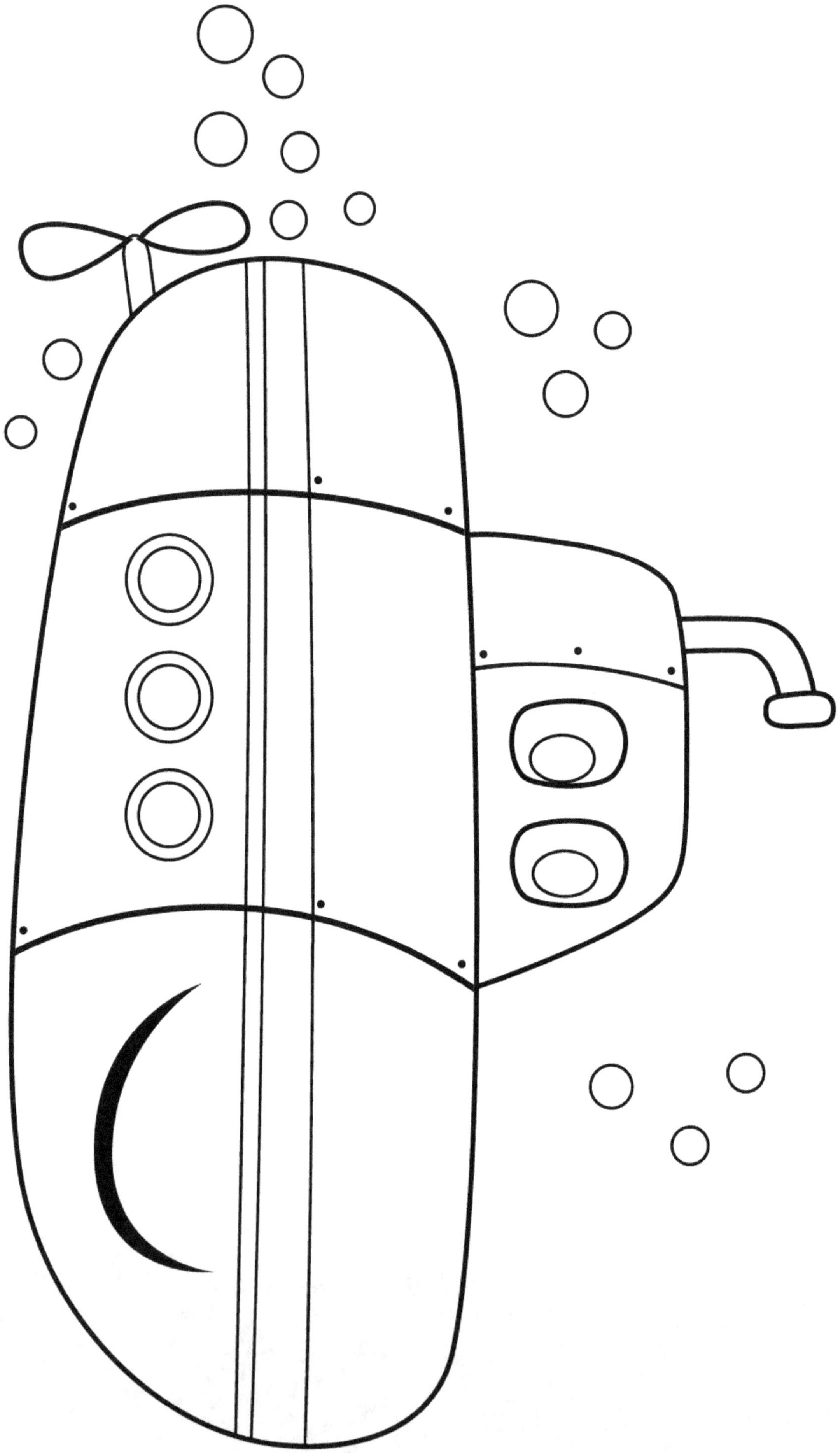

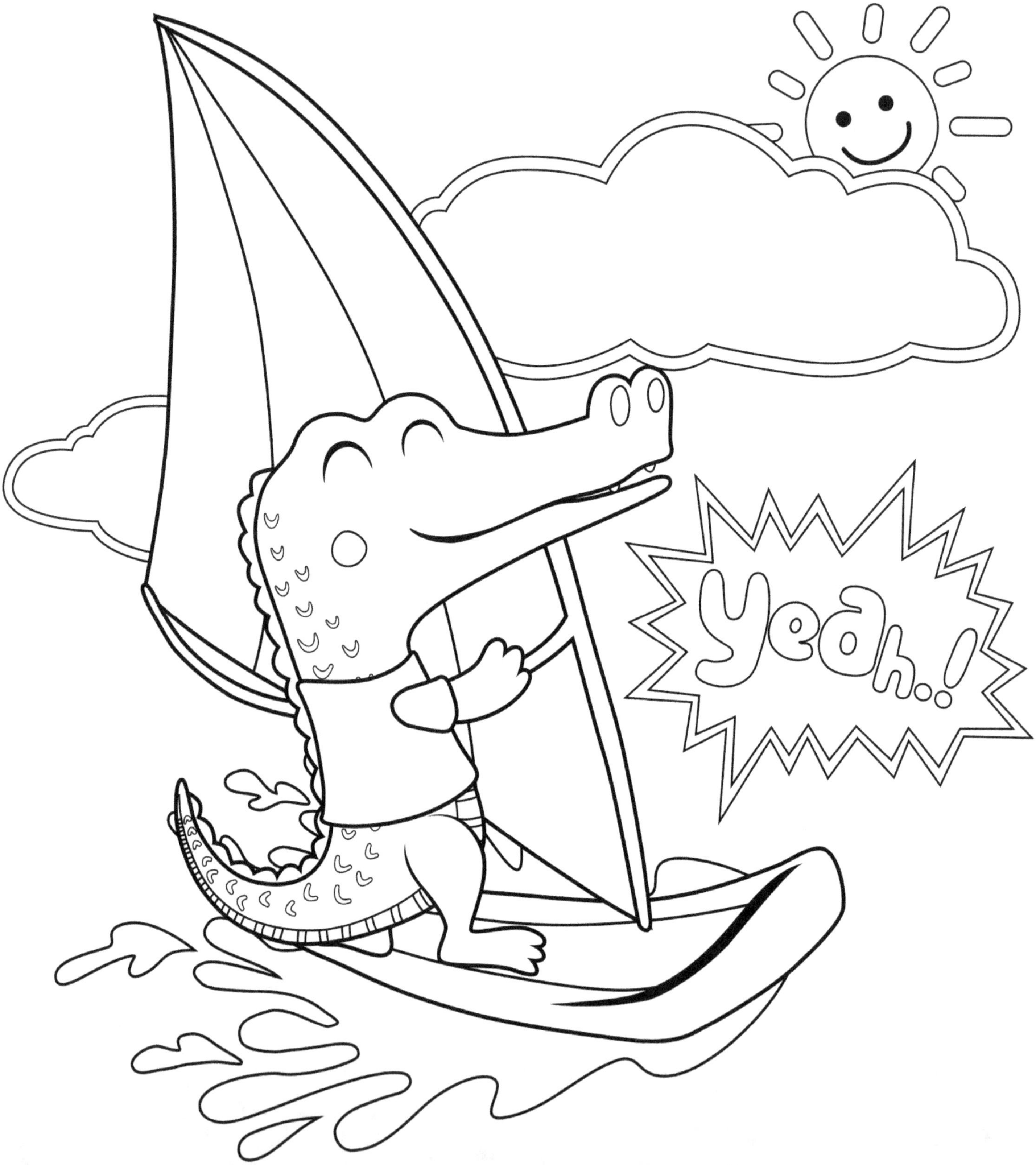
yeah..!

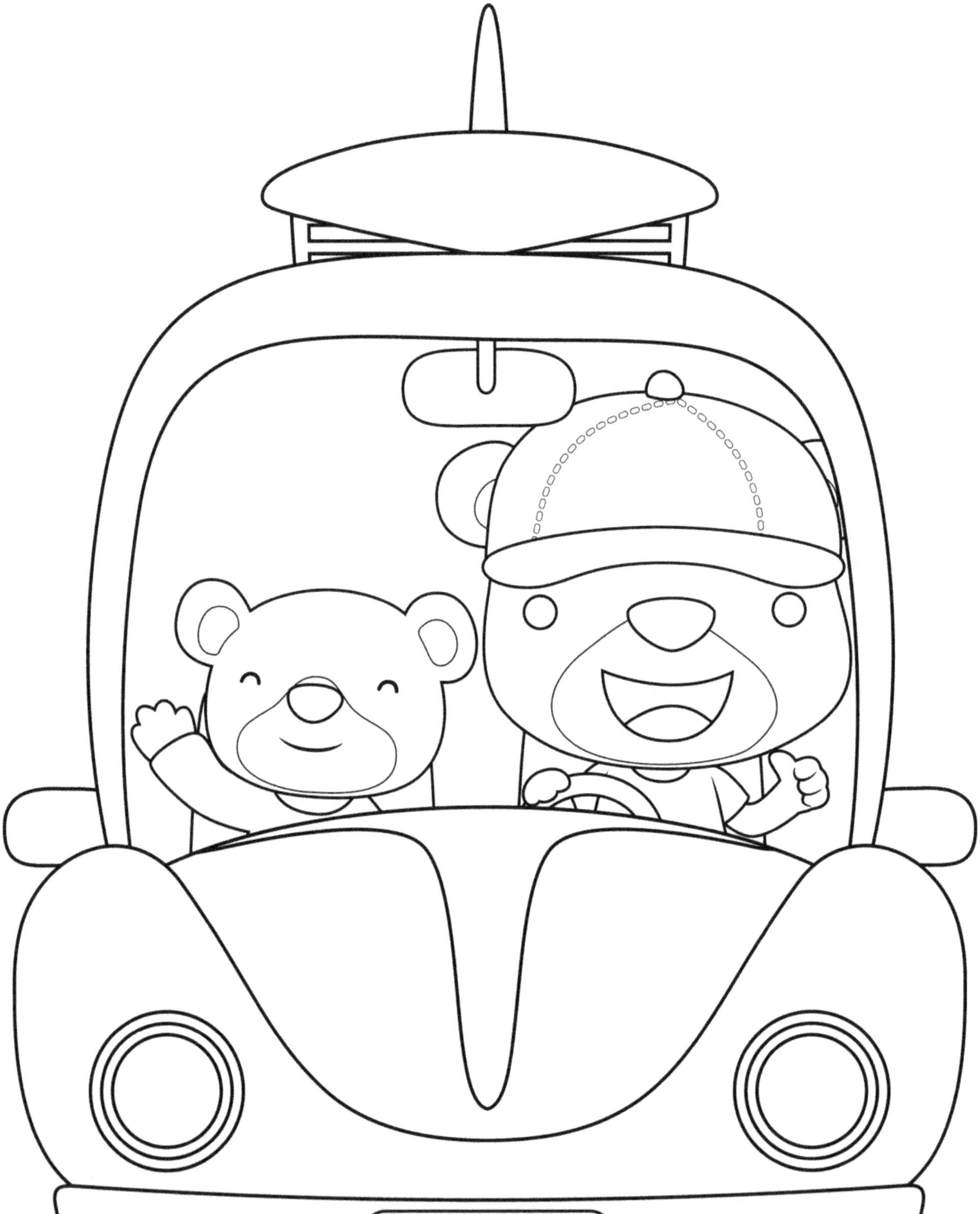
SURFER

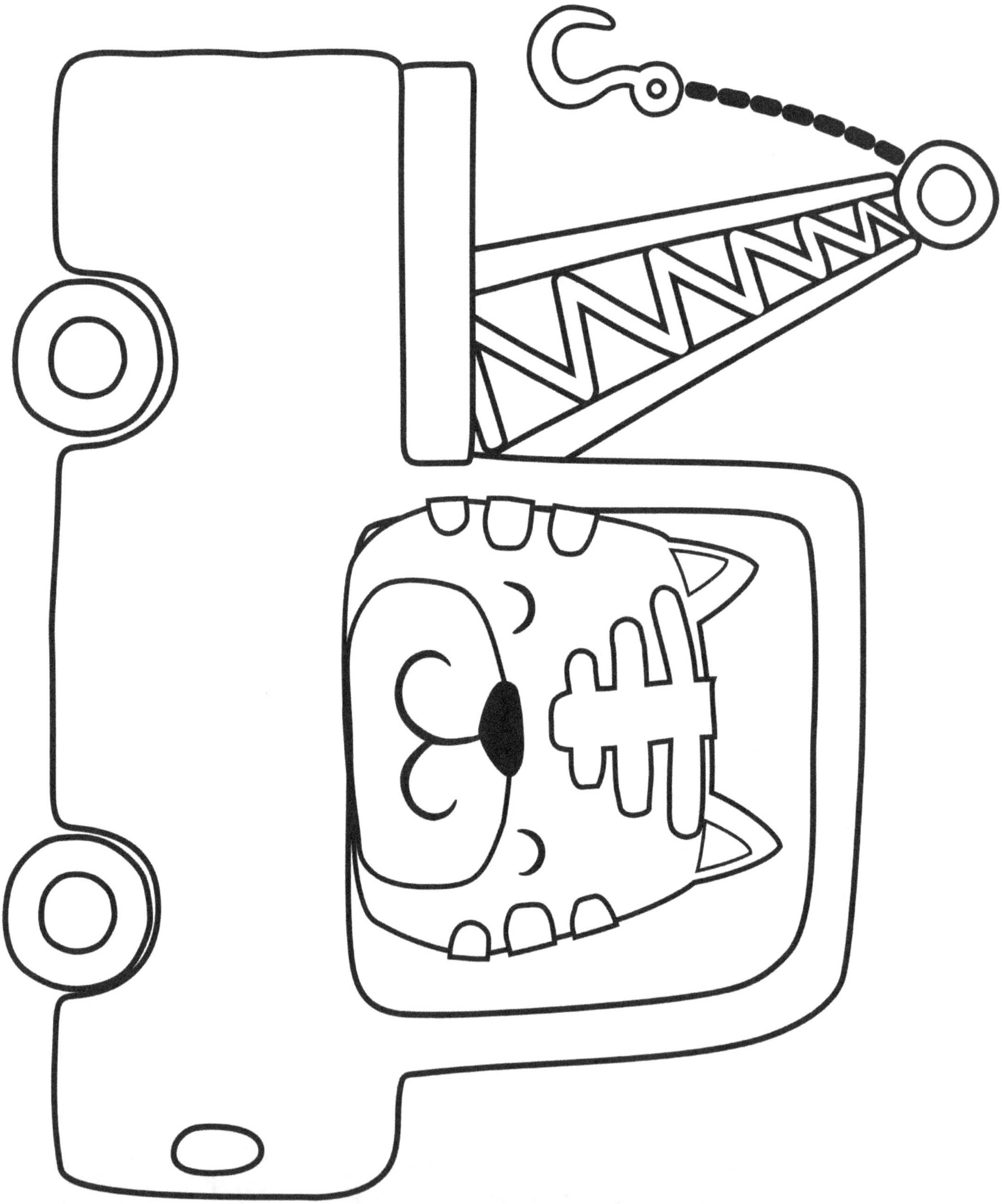

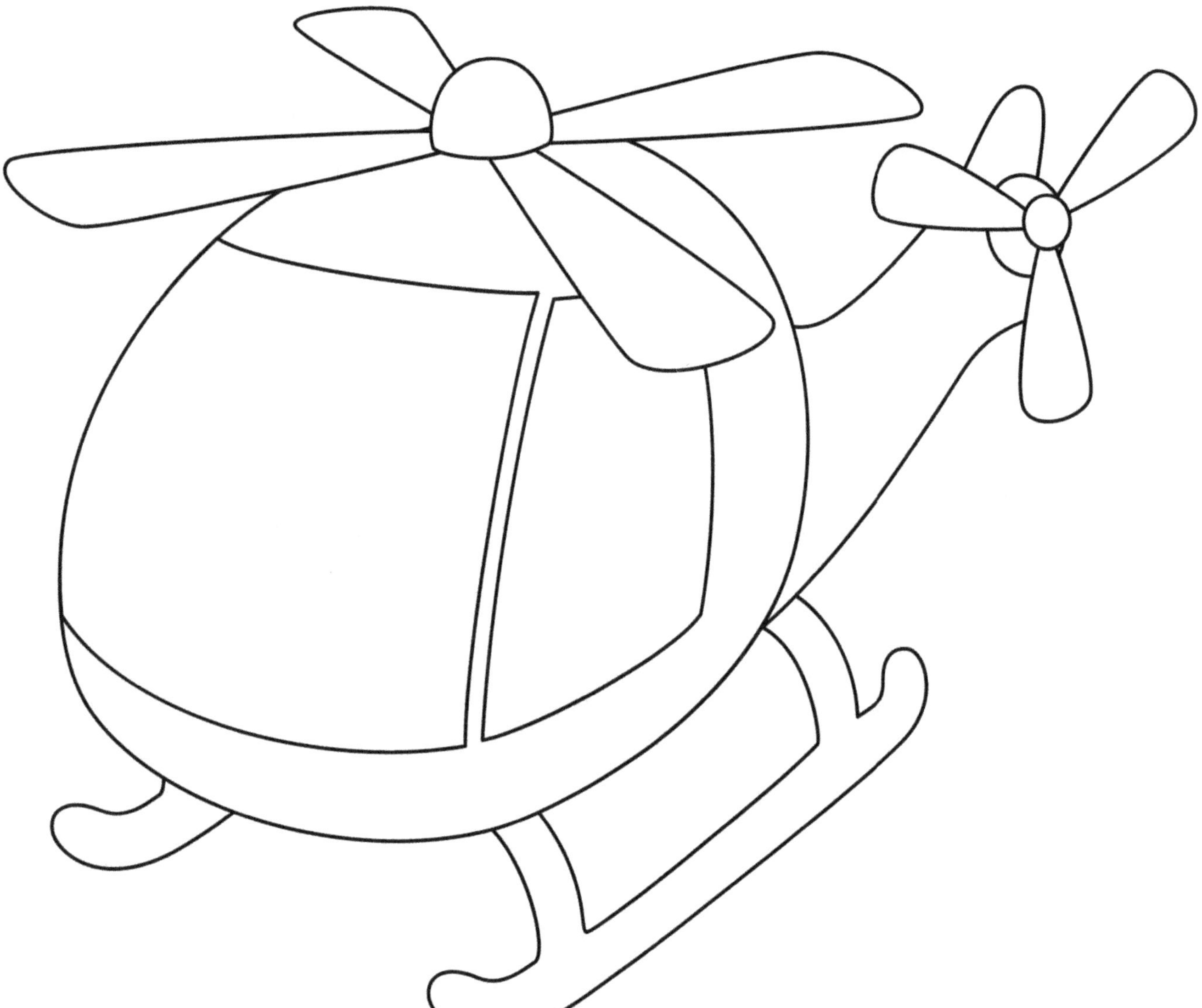

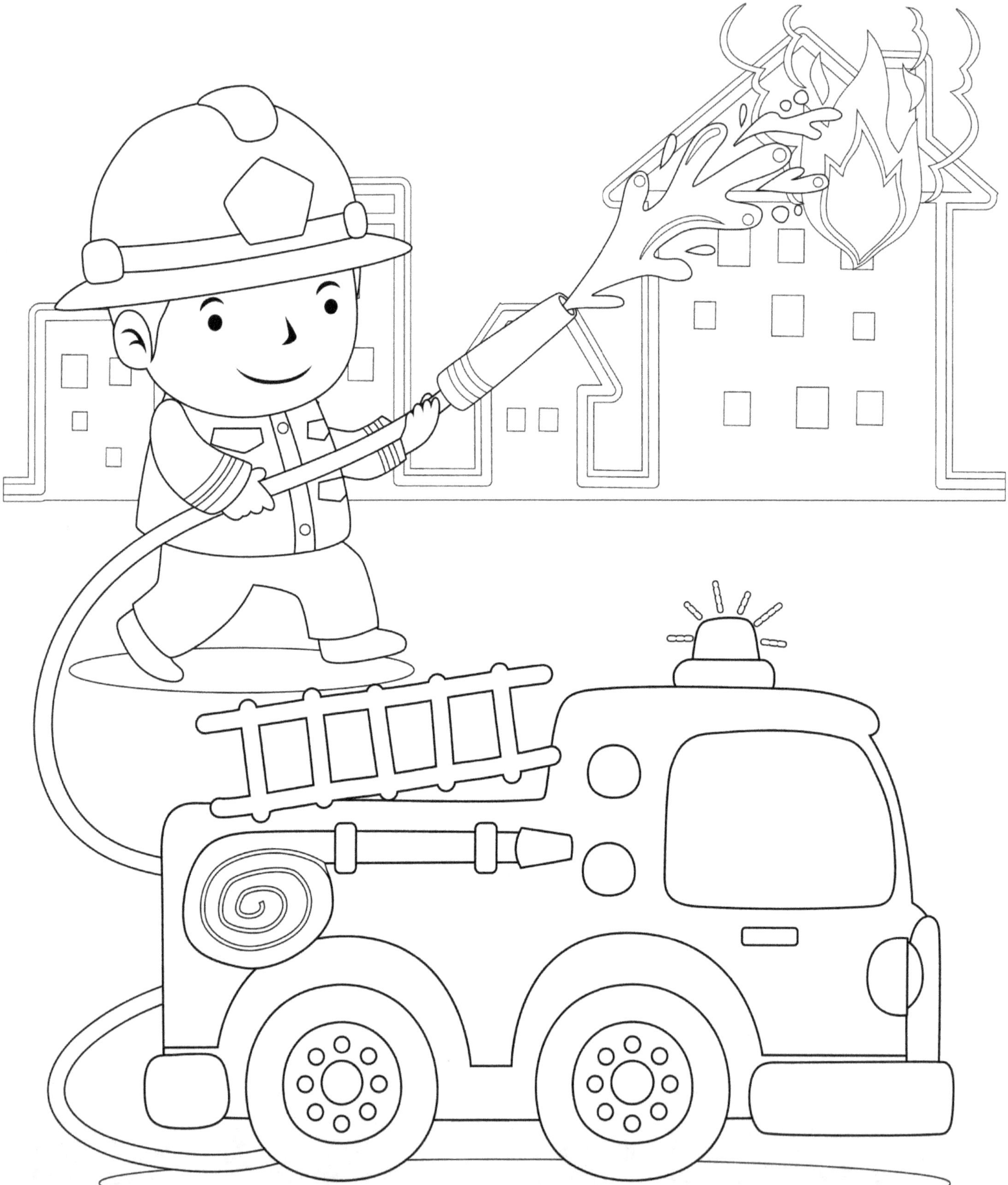

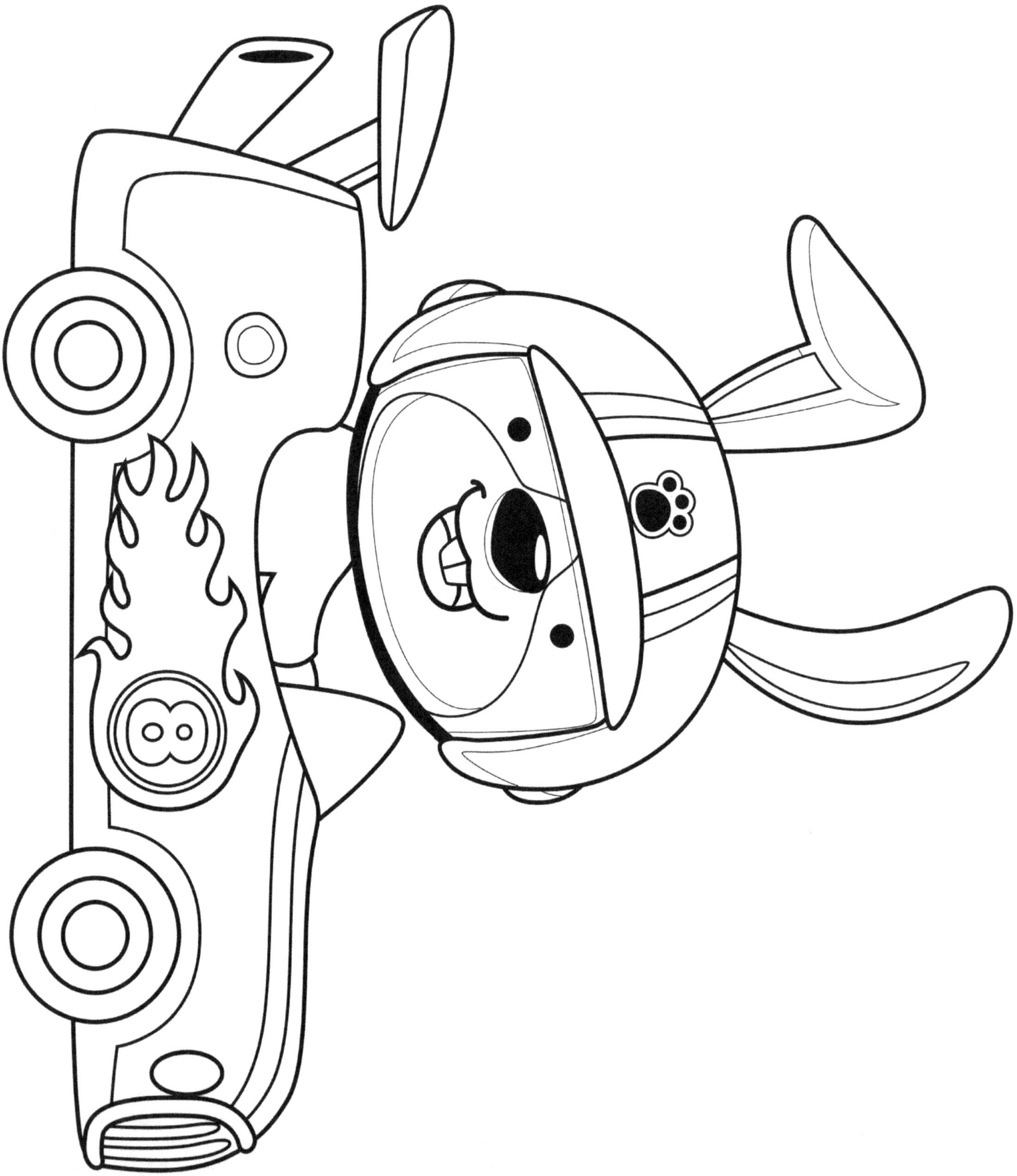
8

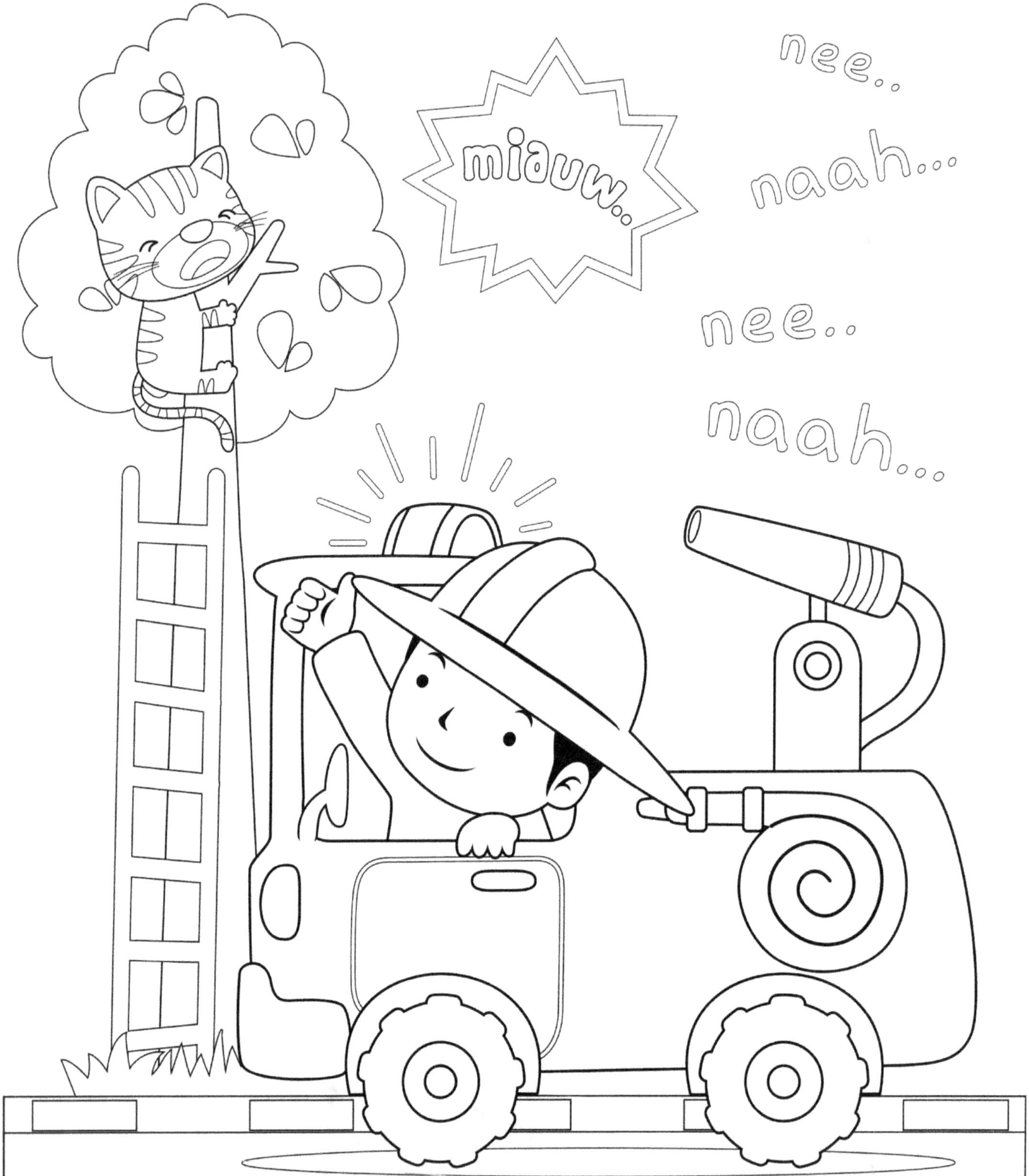
miauw..
nee..
naah...
nee..
naah...

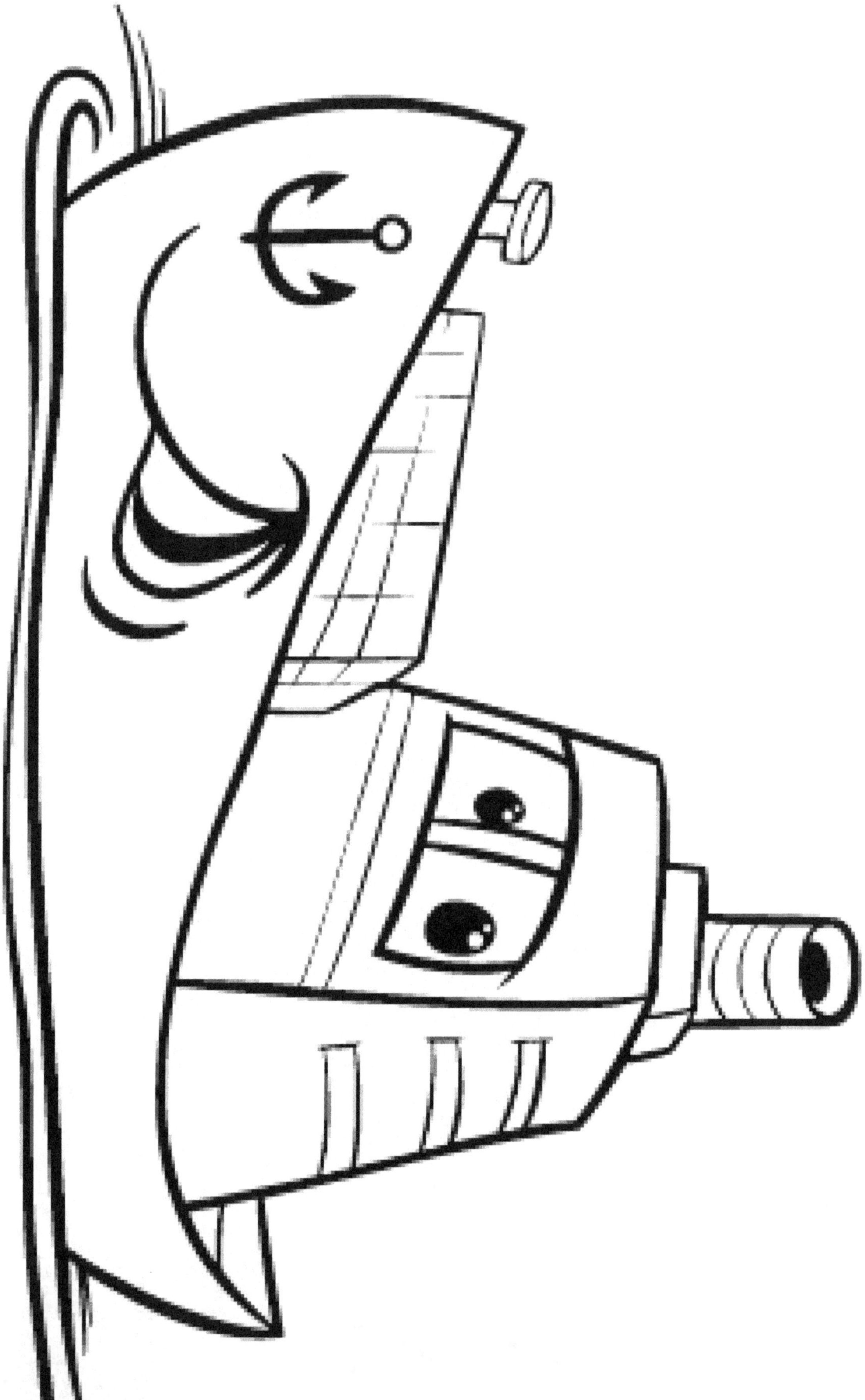

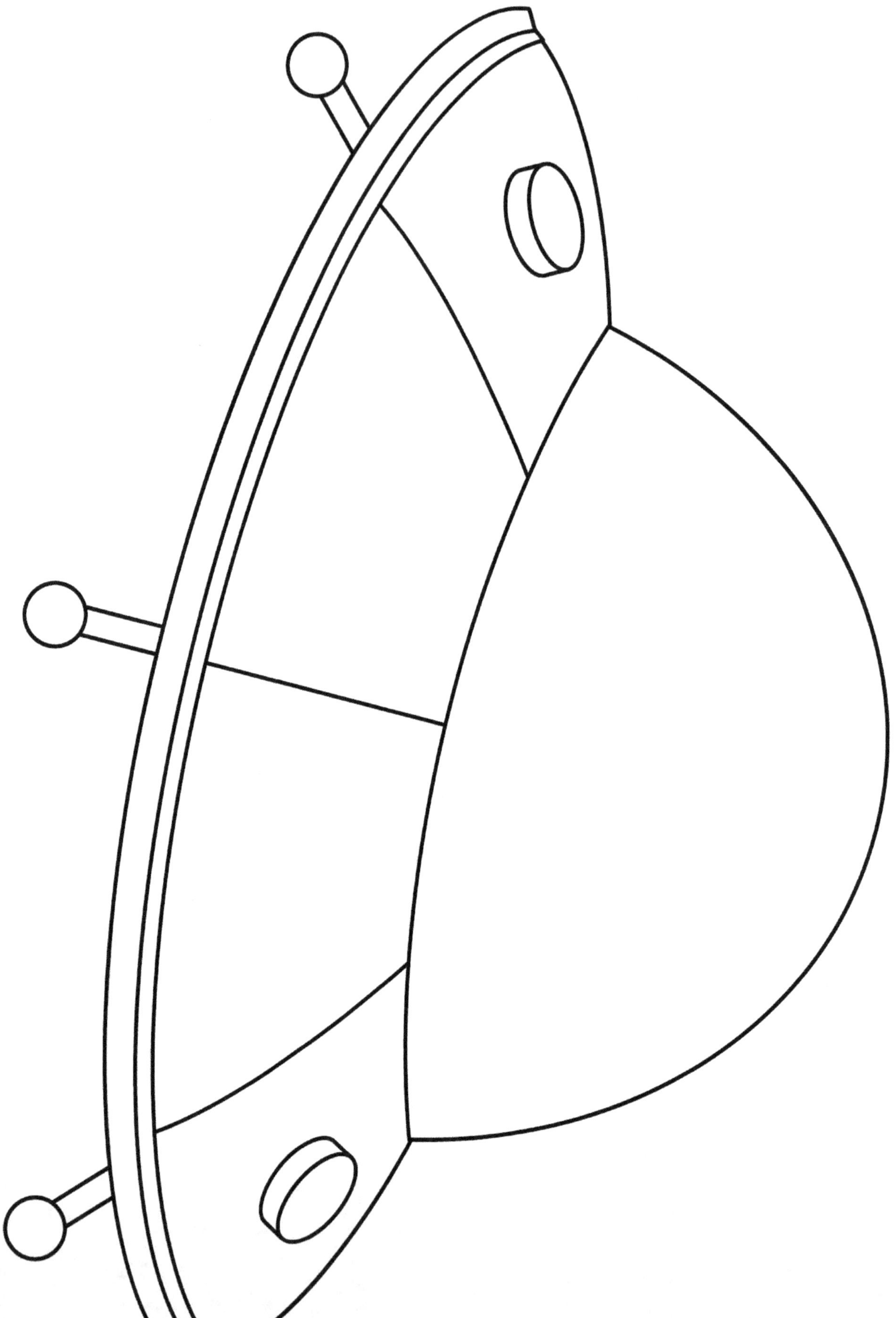

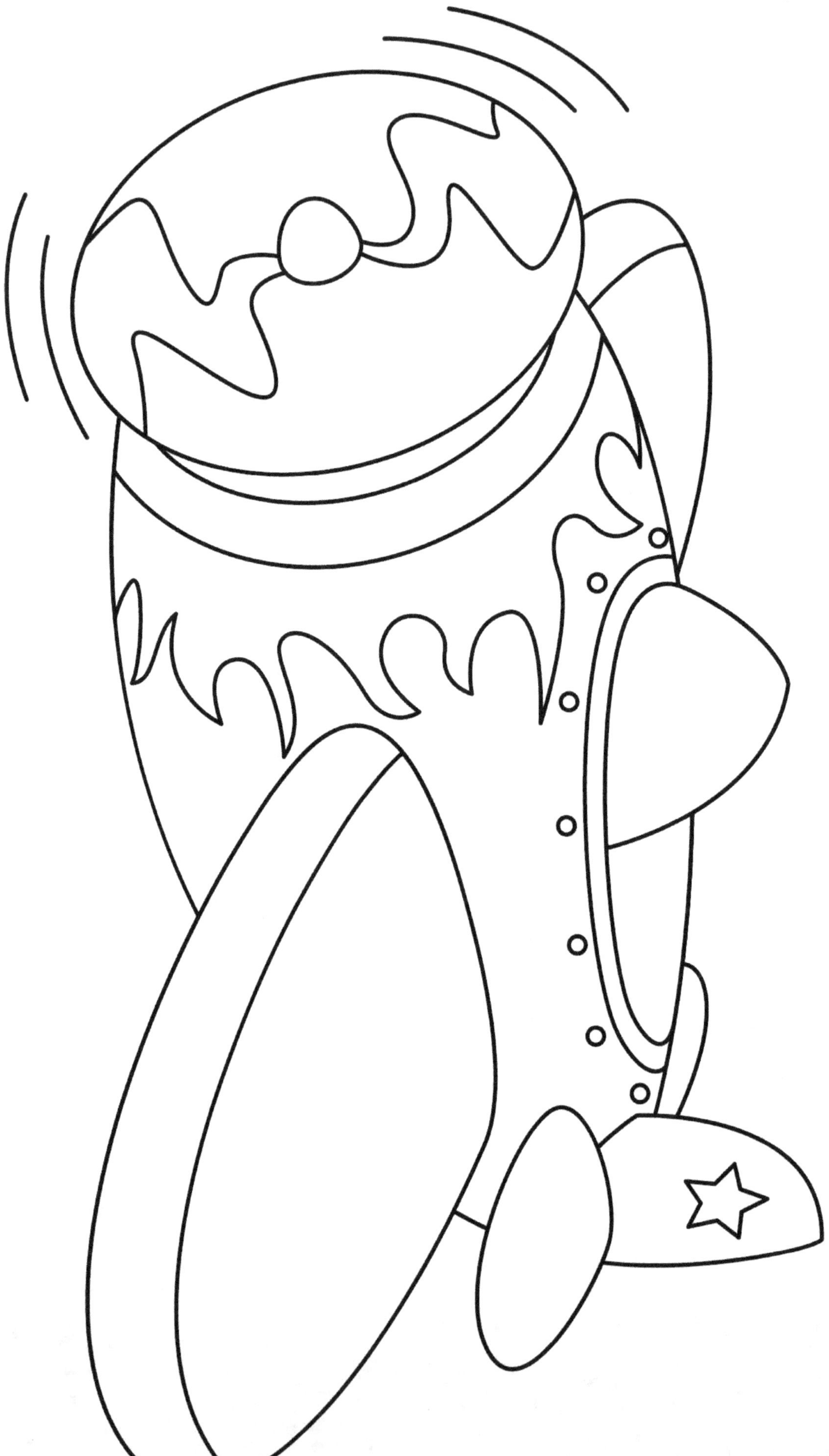

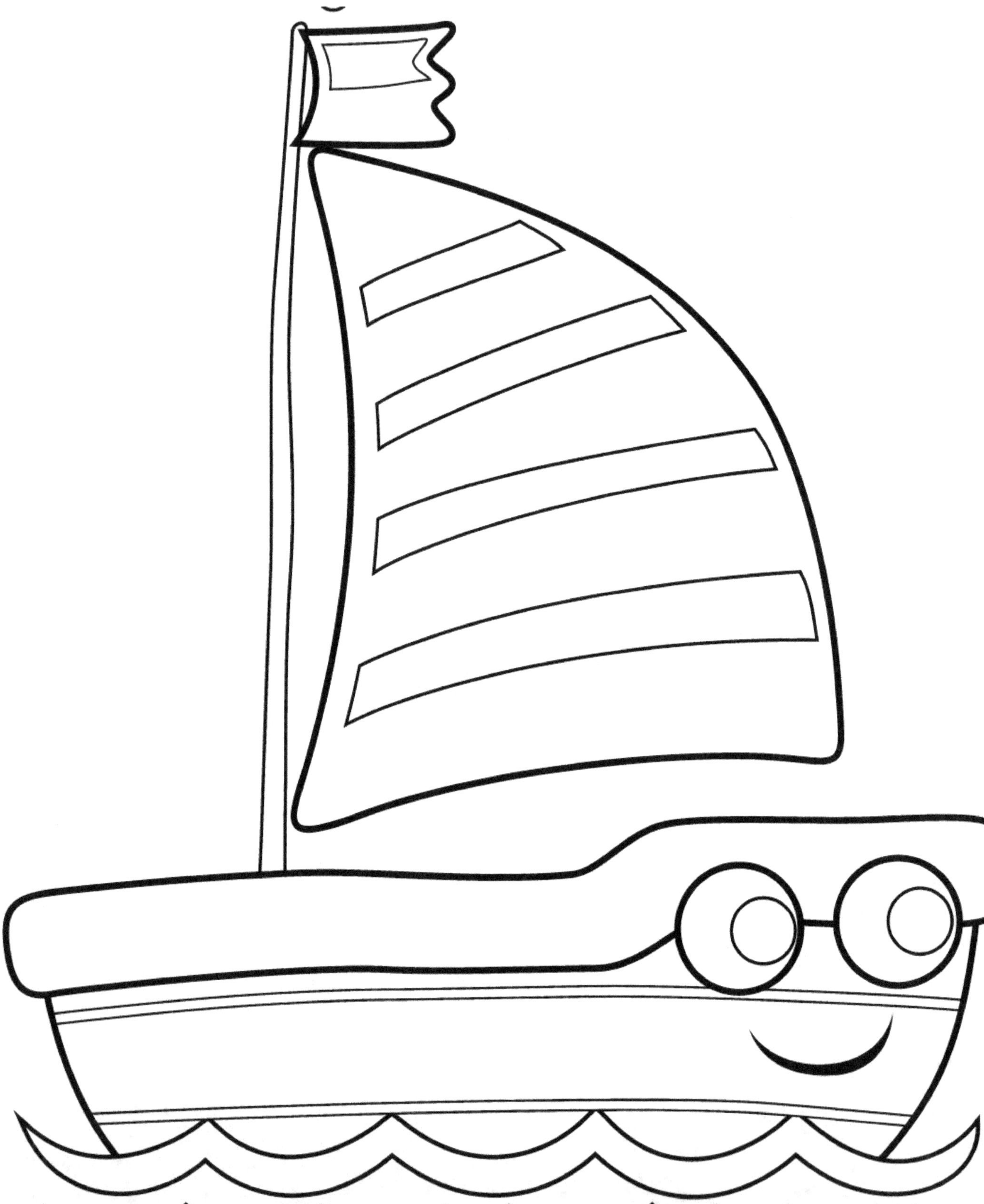

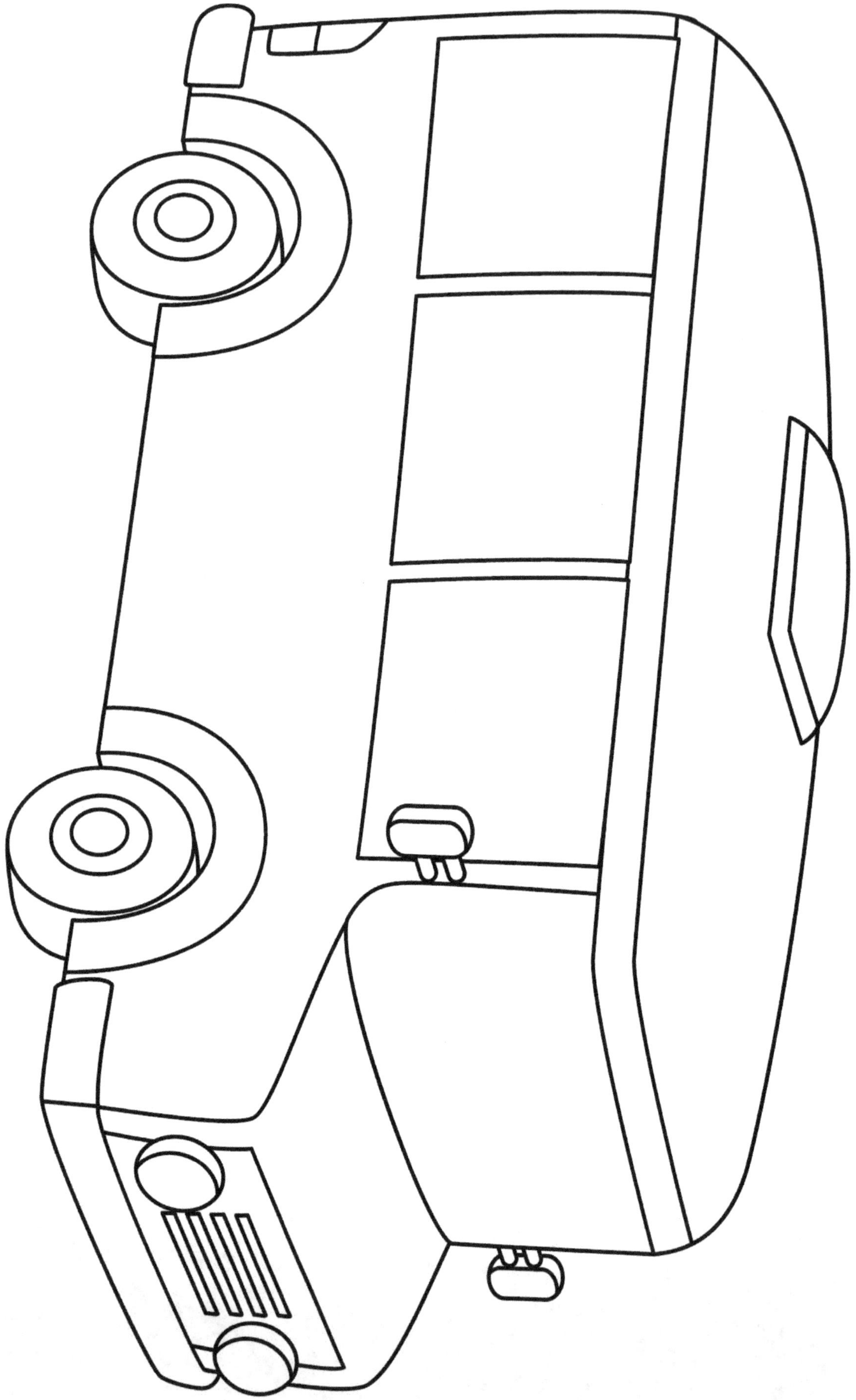

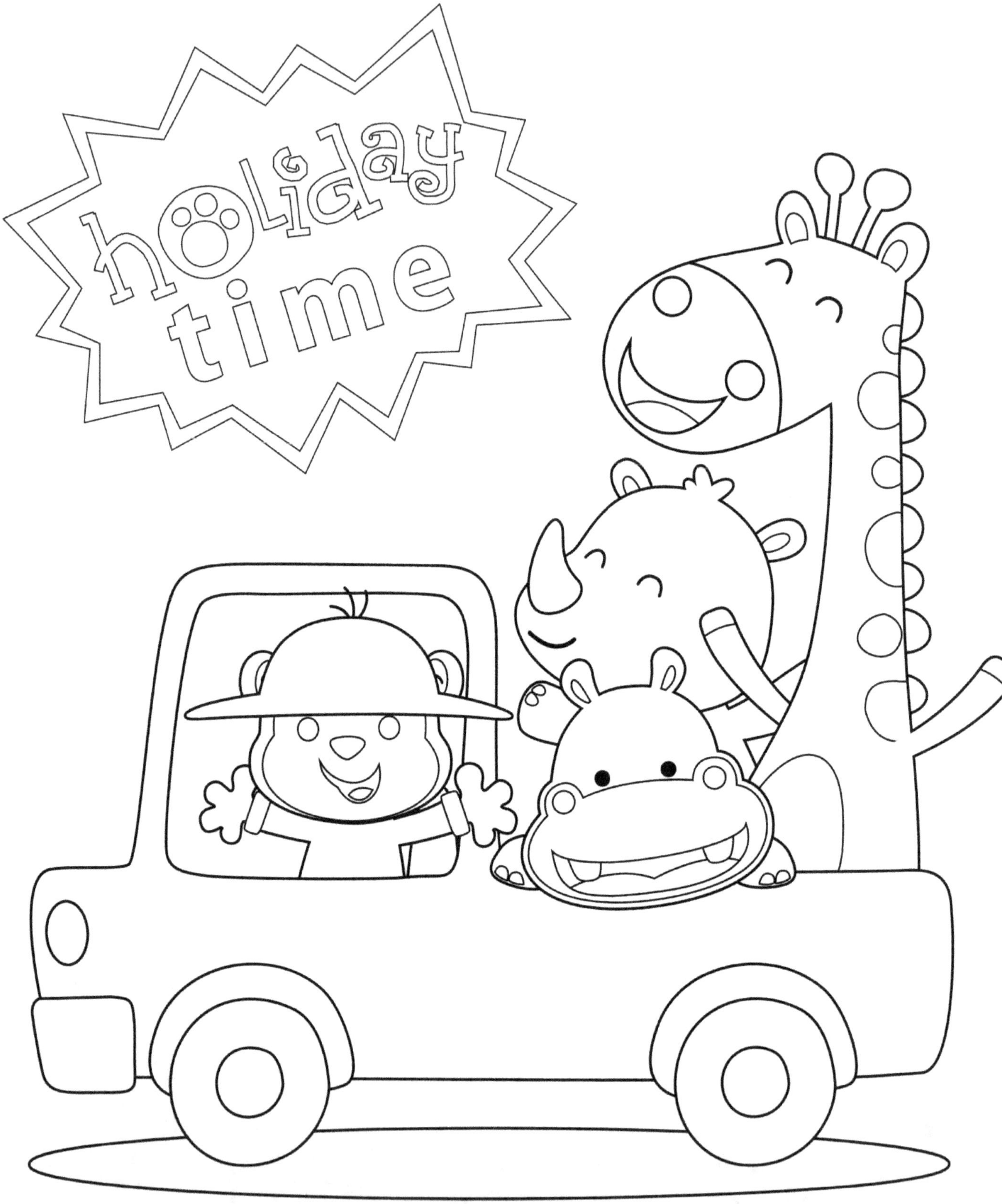
holiday
time

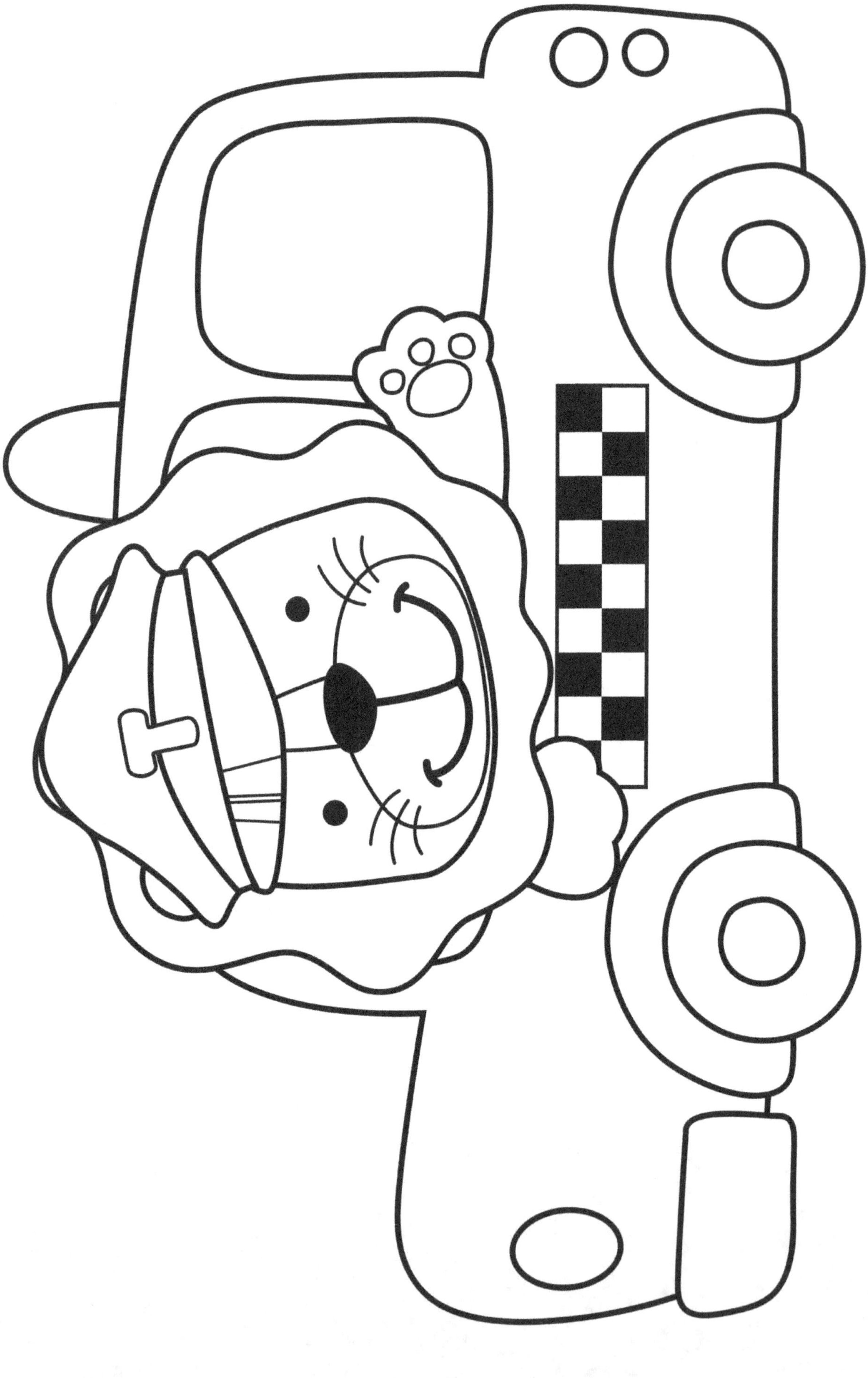

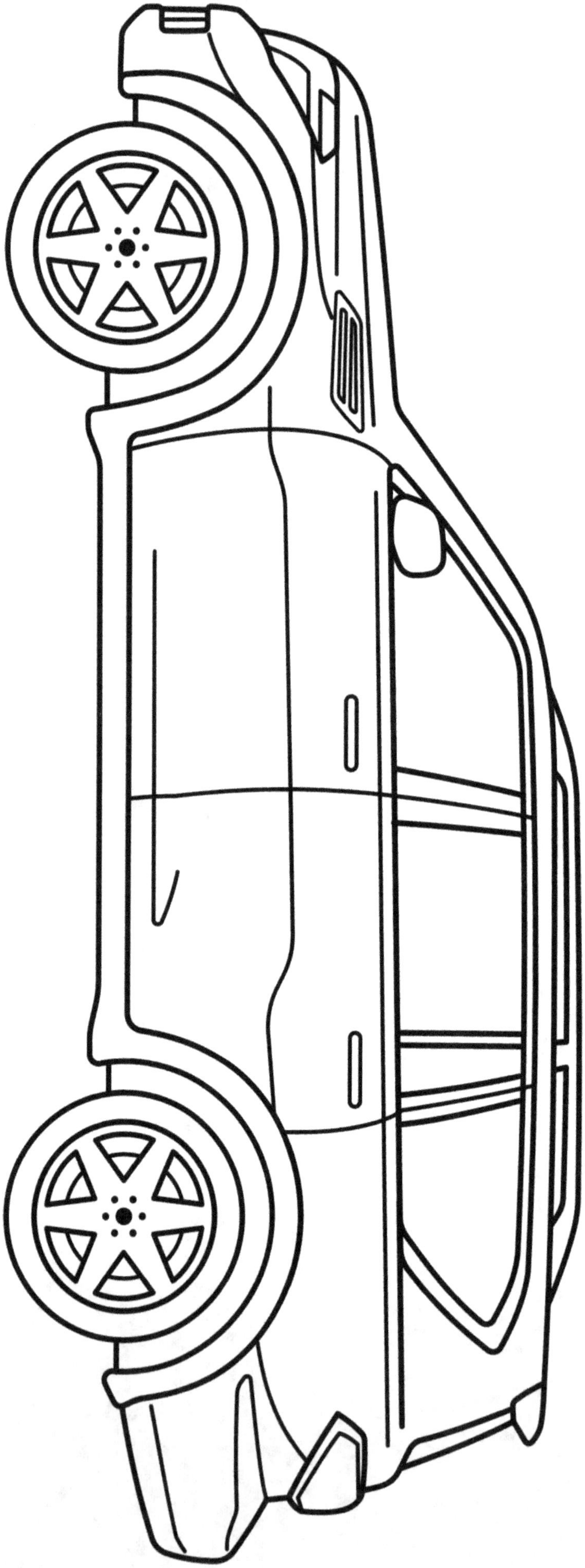

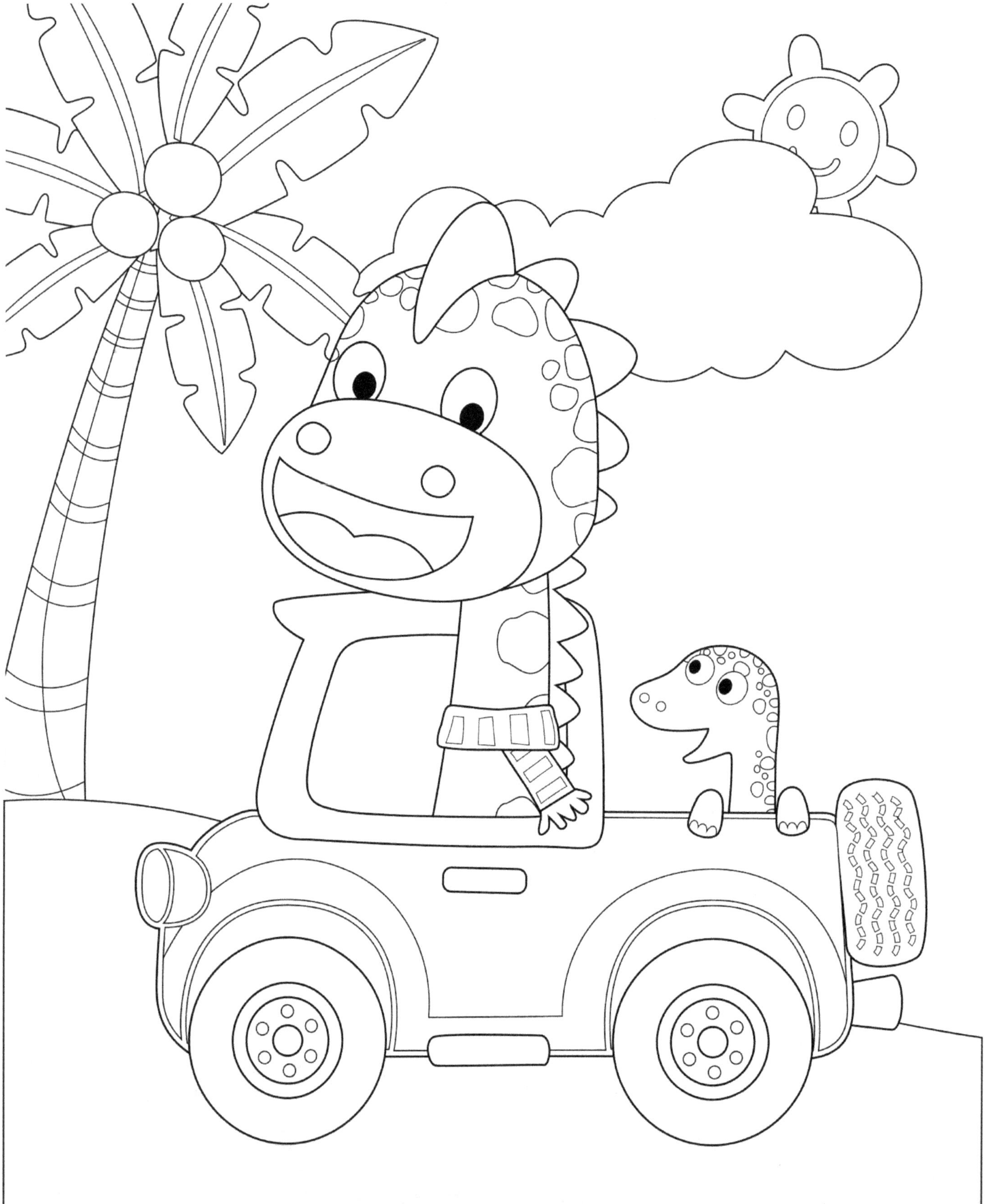

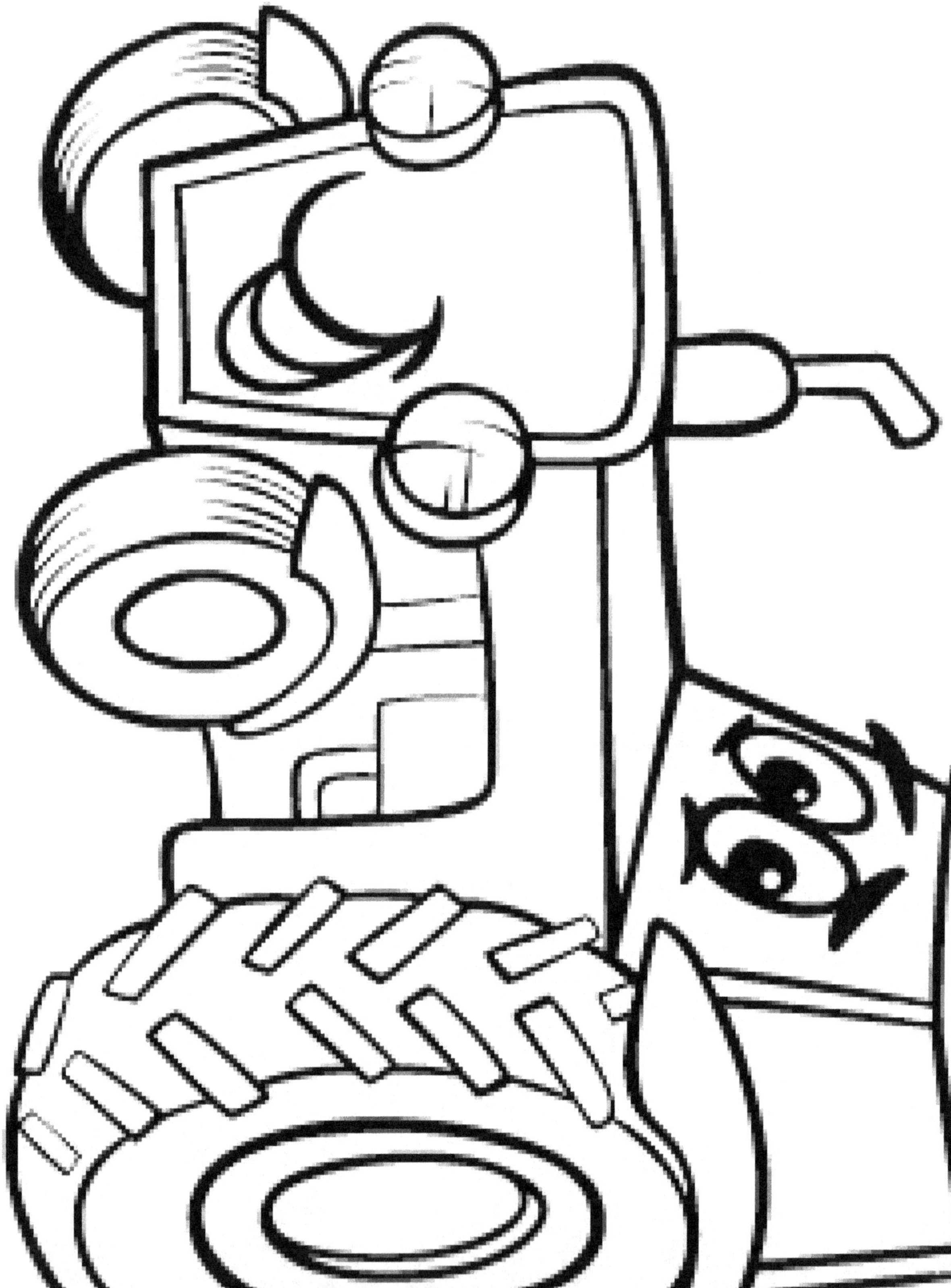

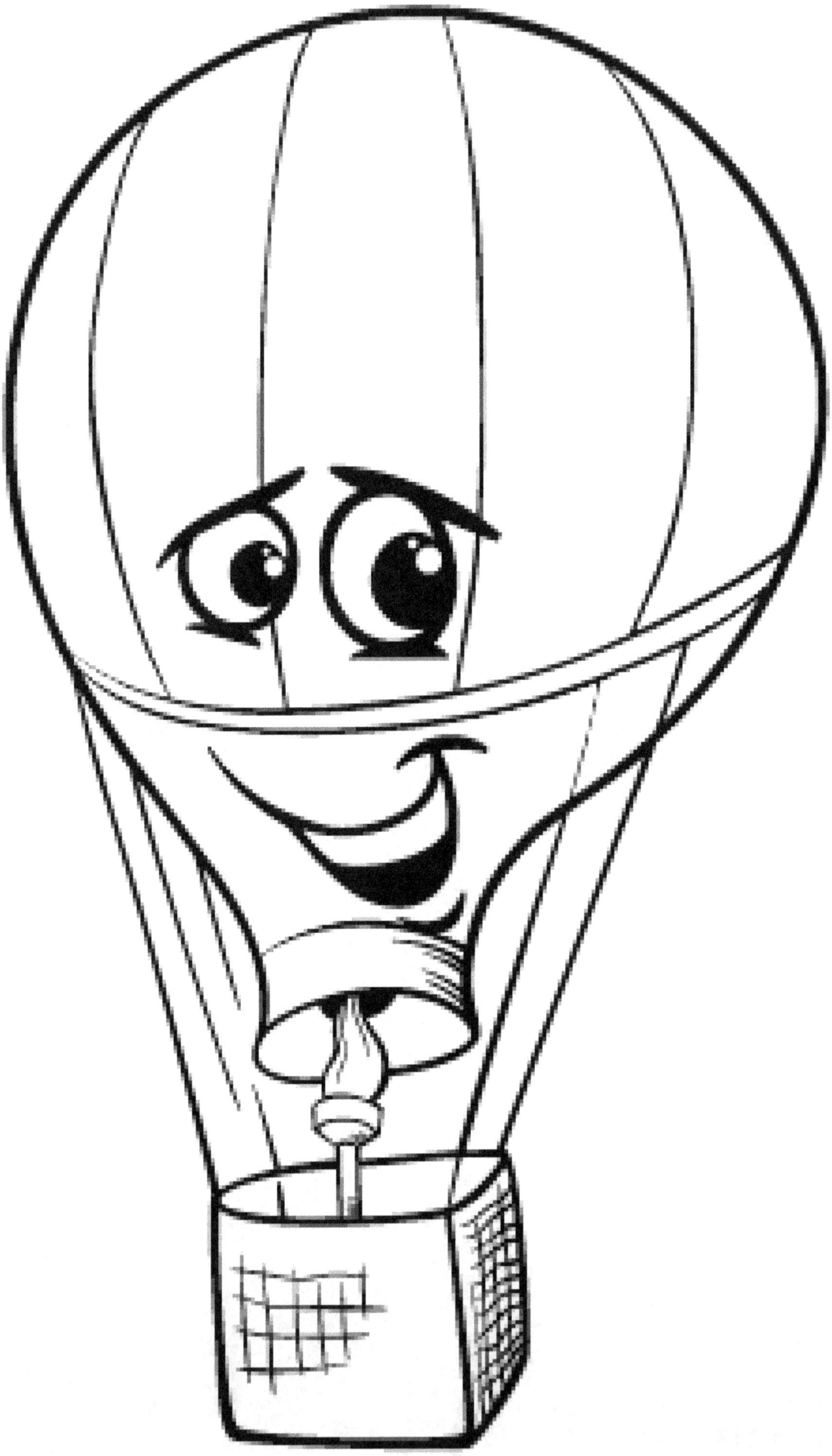

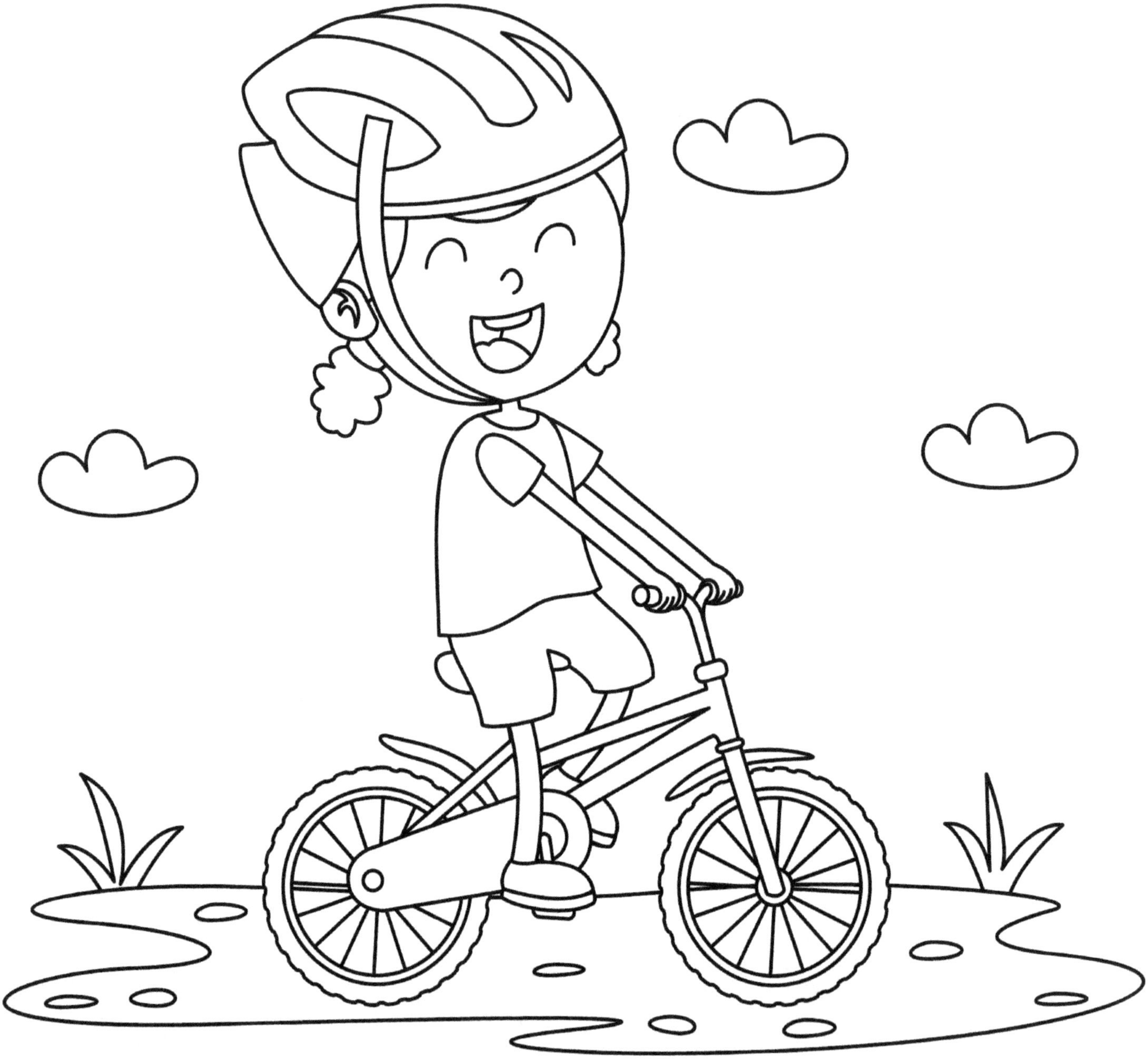

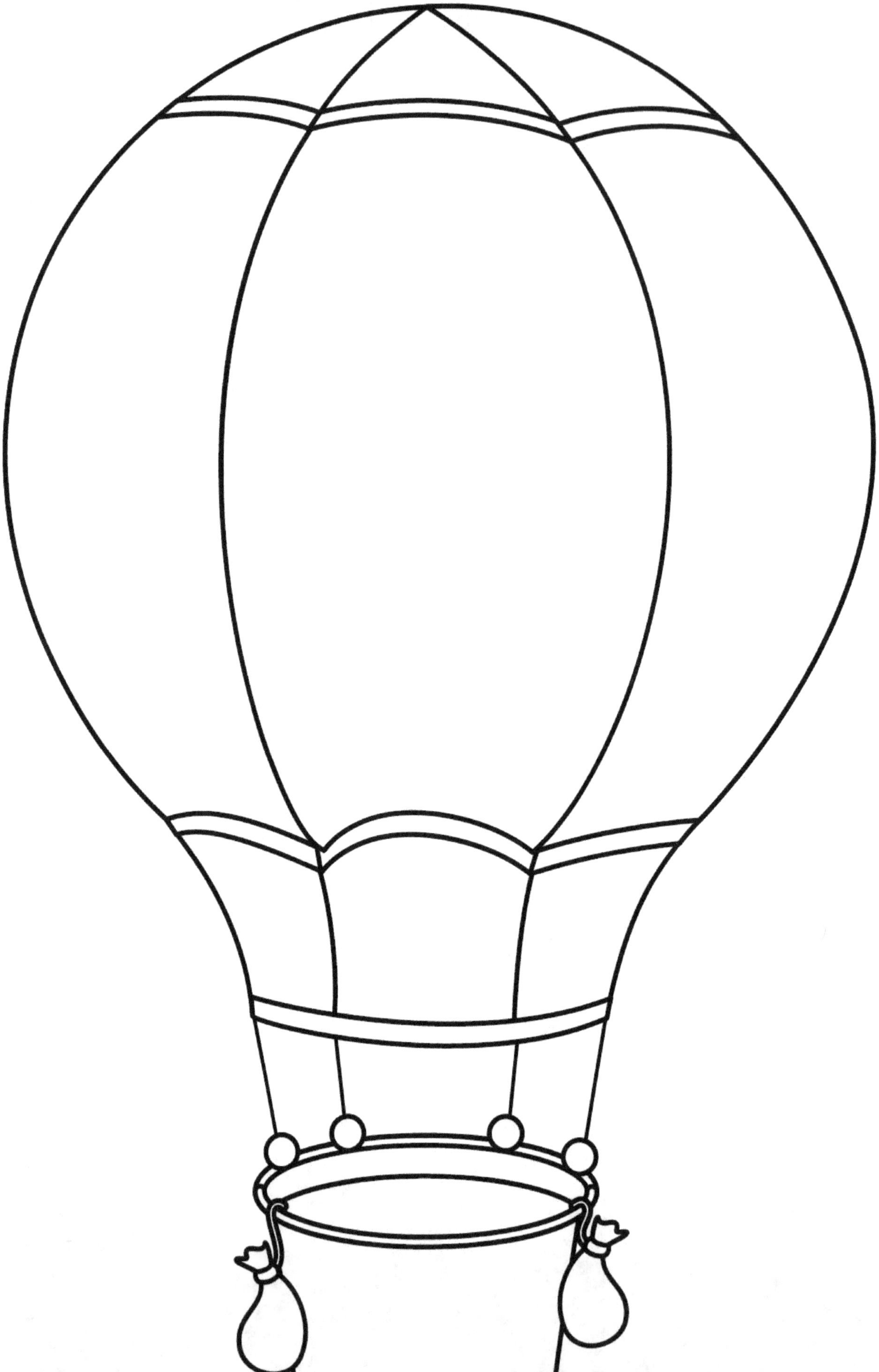

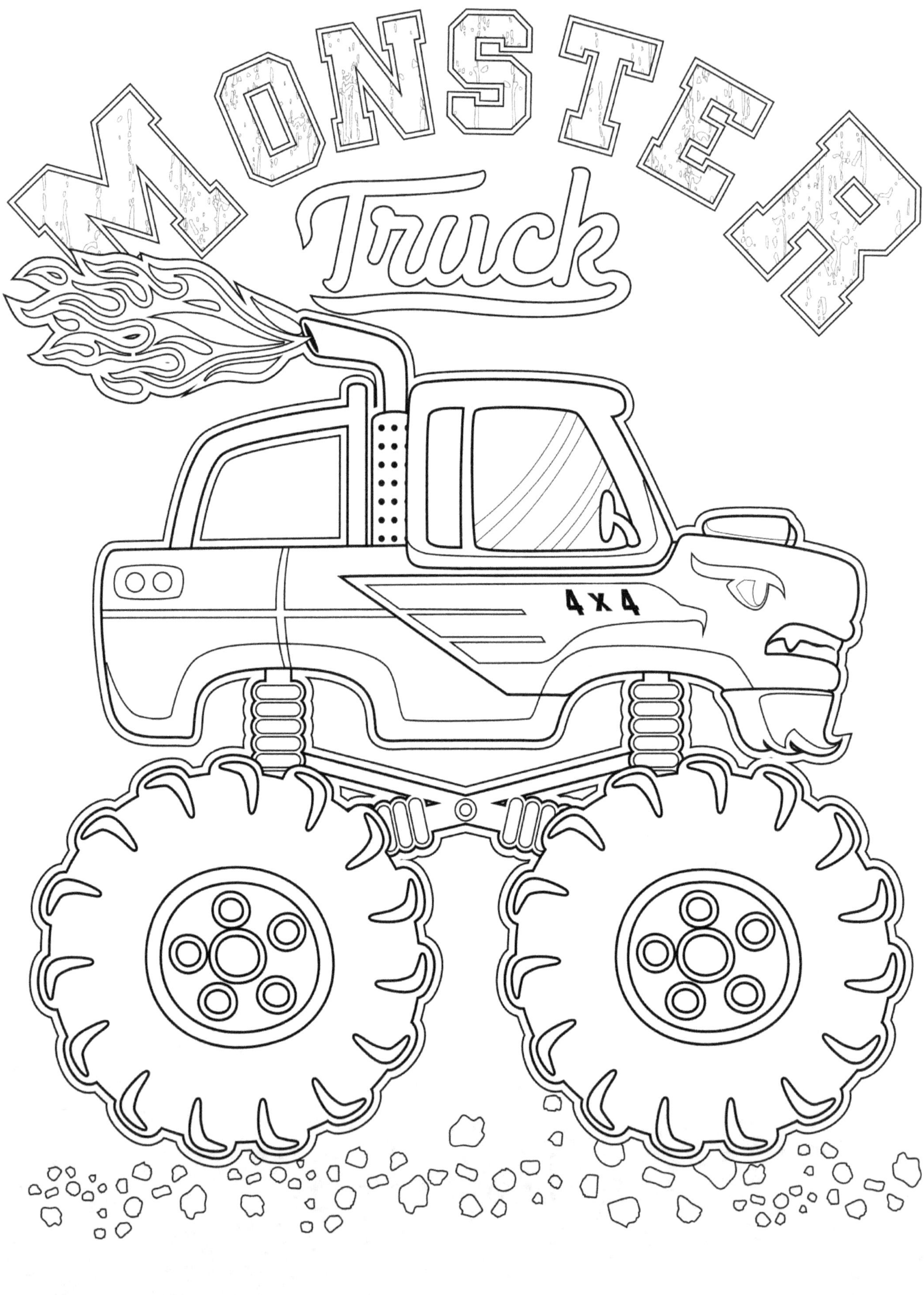
MONSTER
Truck
4 x 4

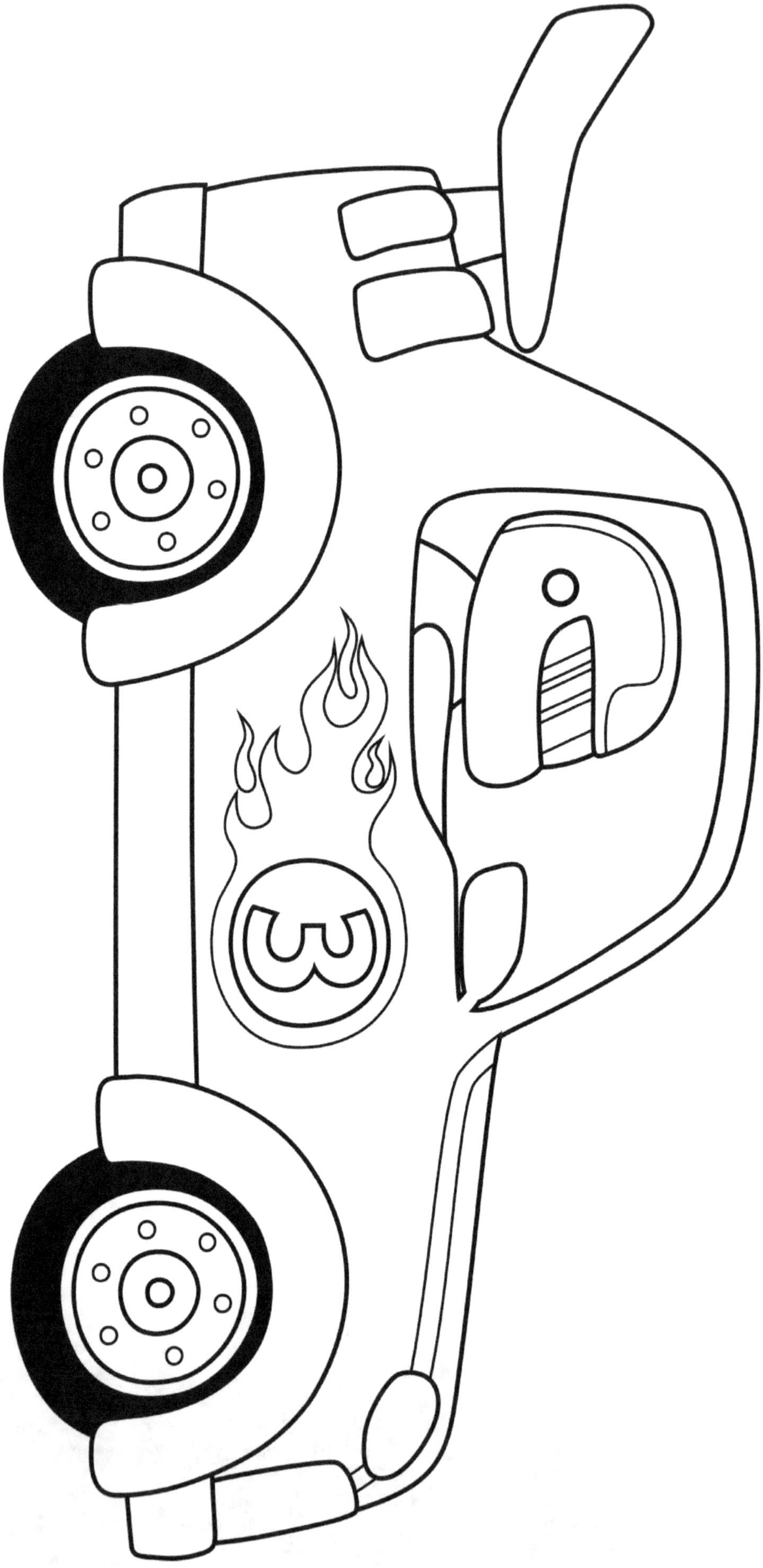
3

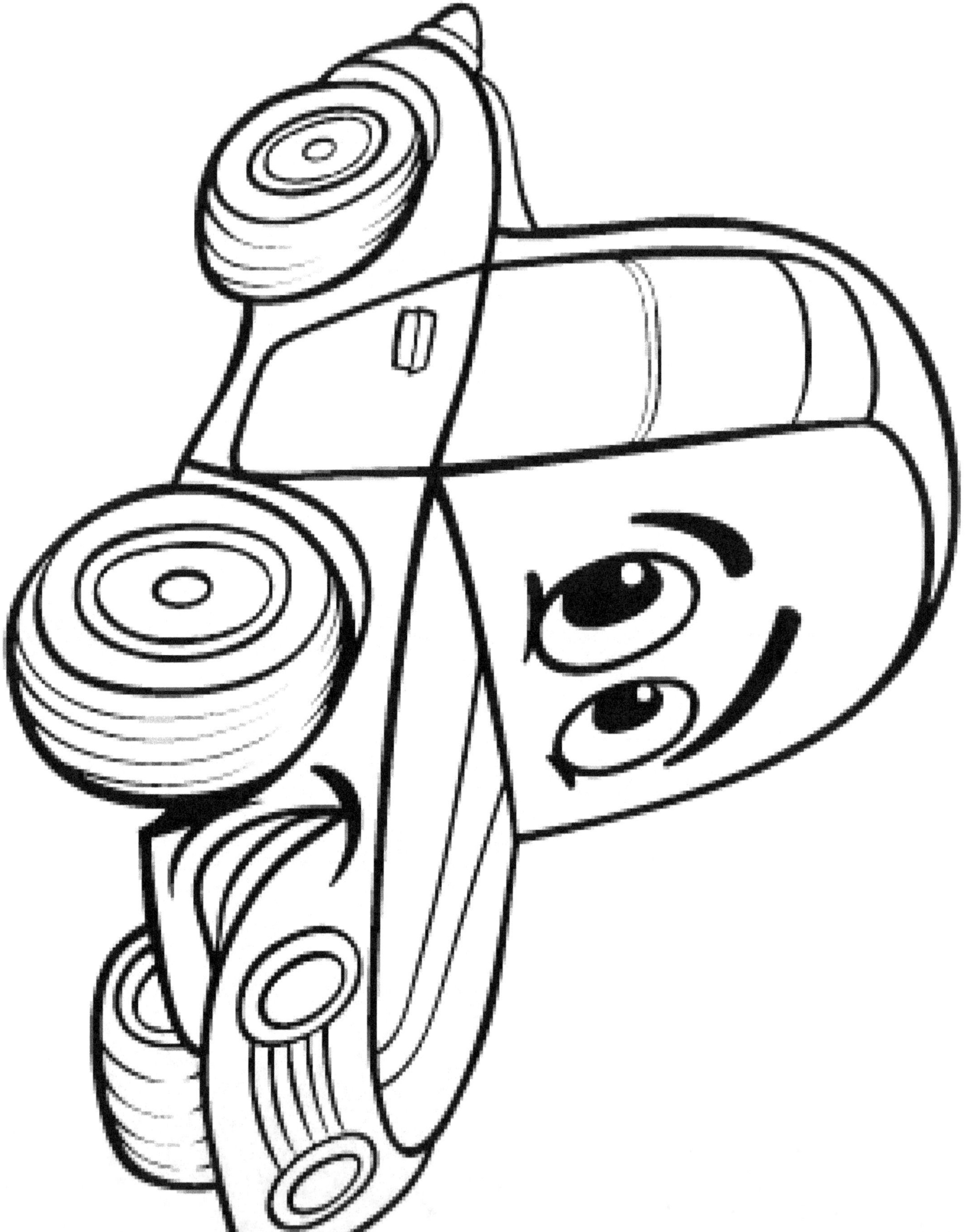

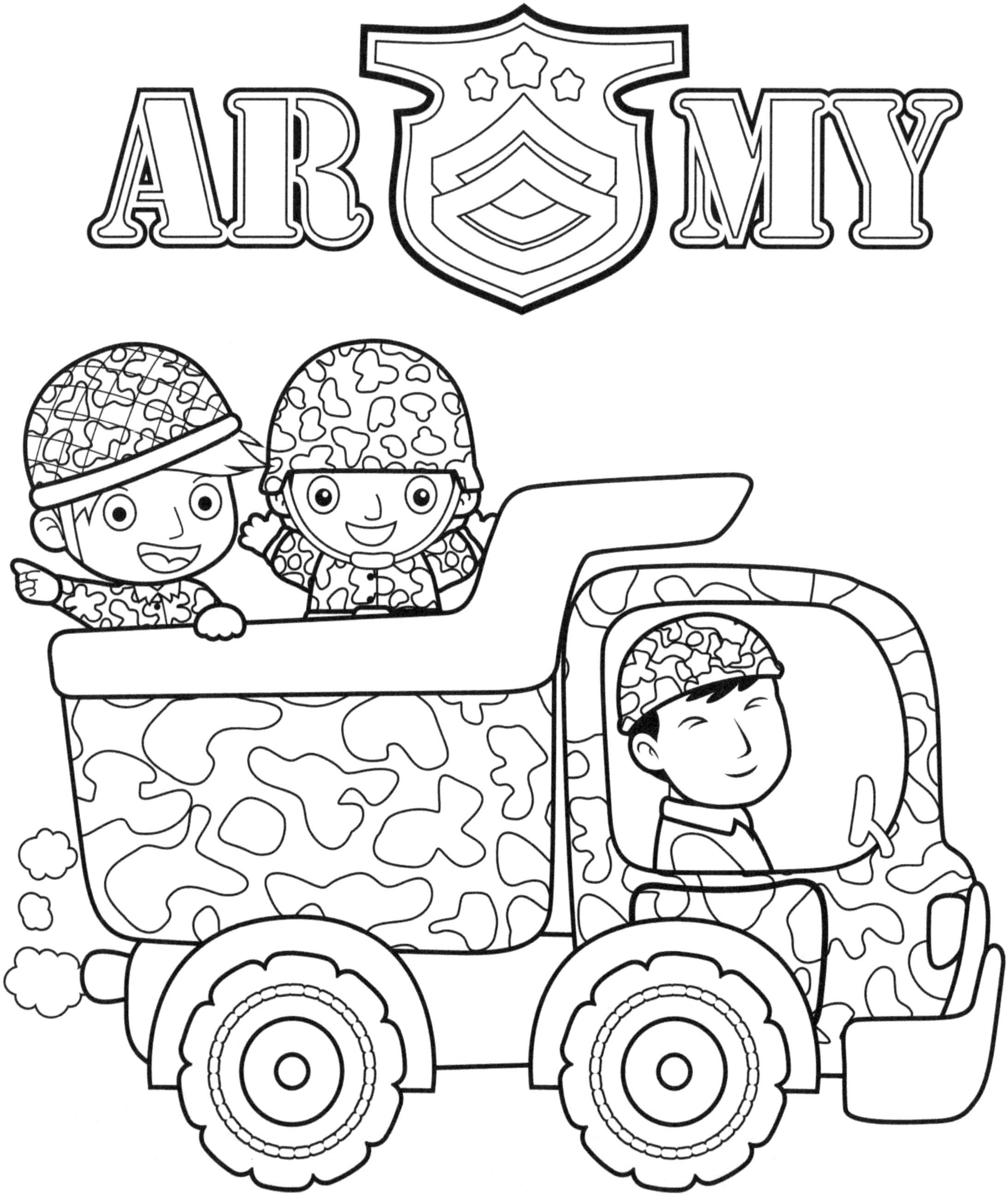
ARMY

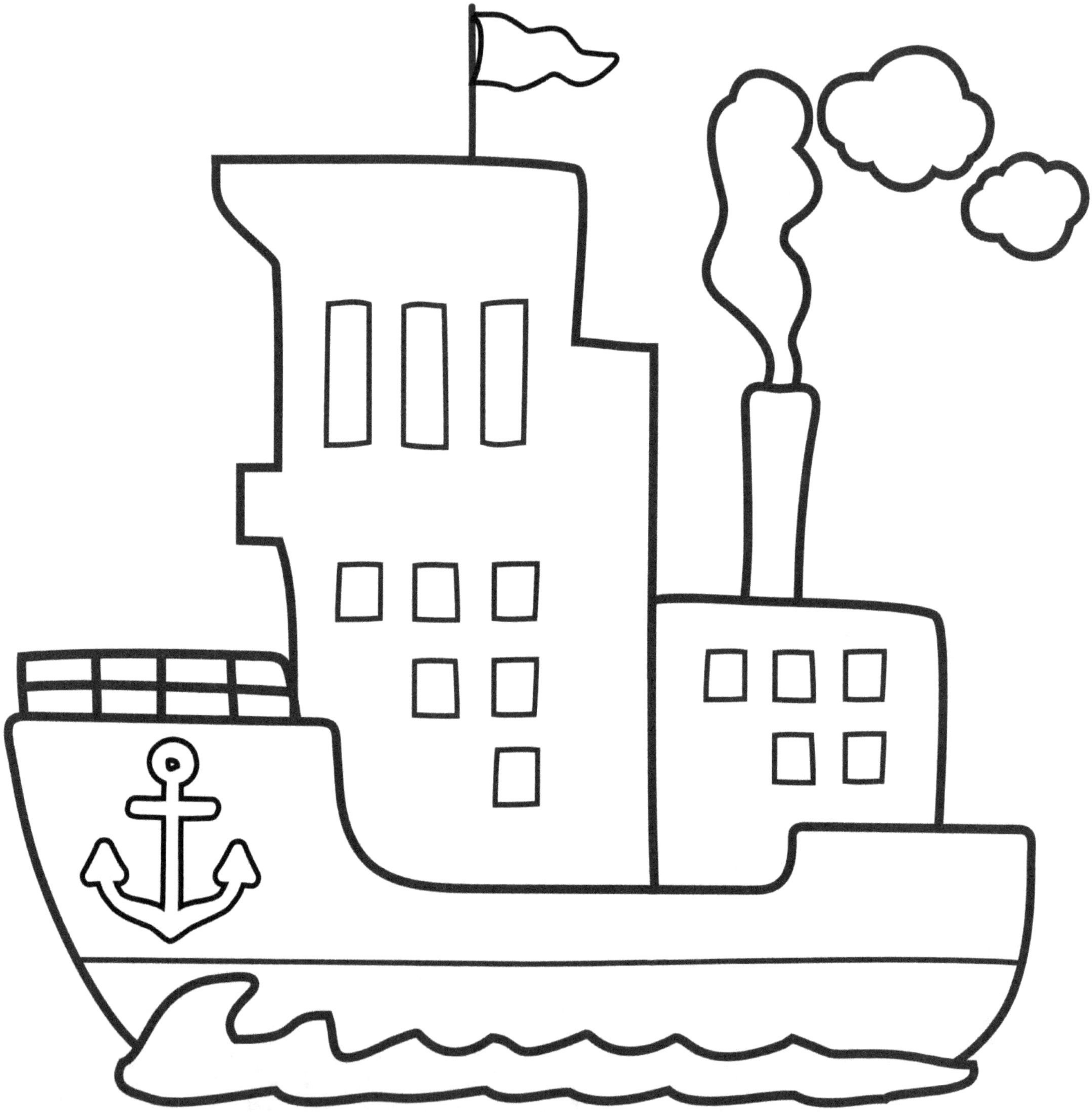

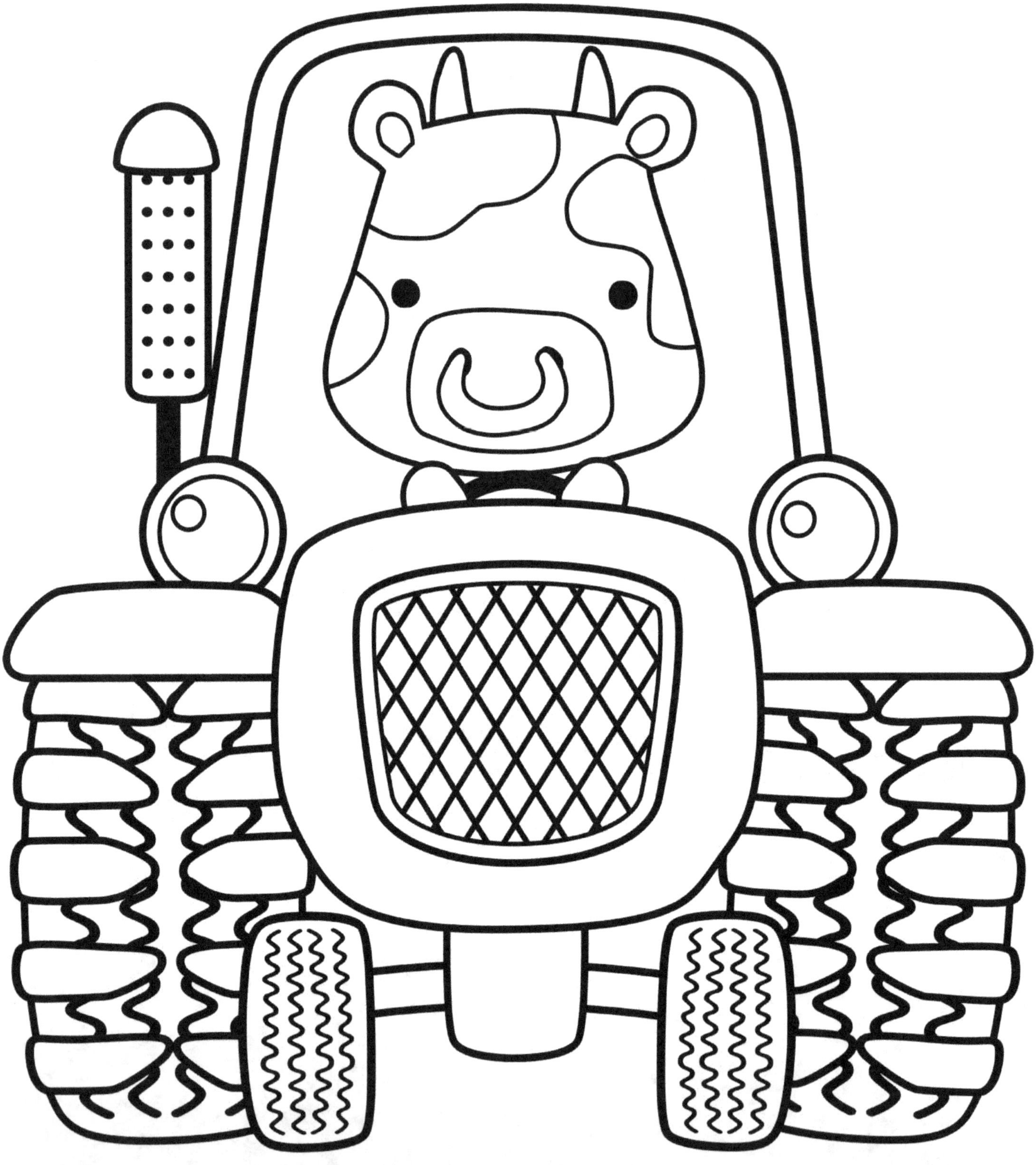

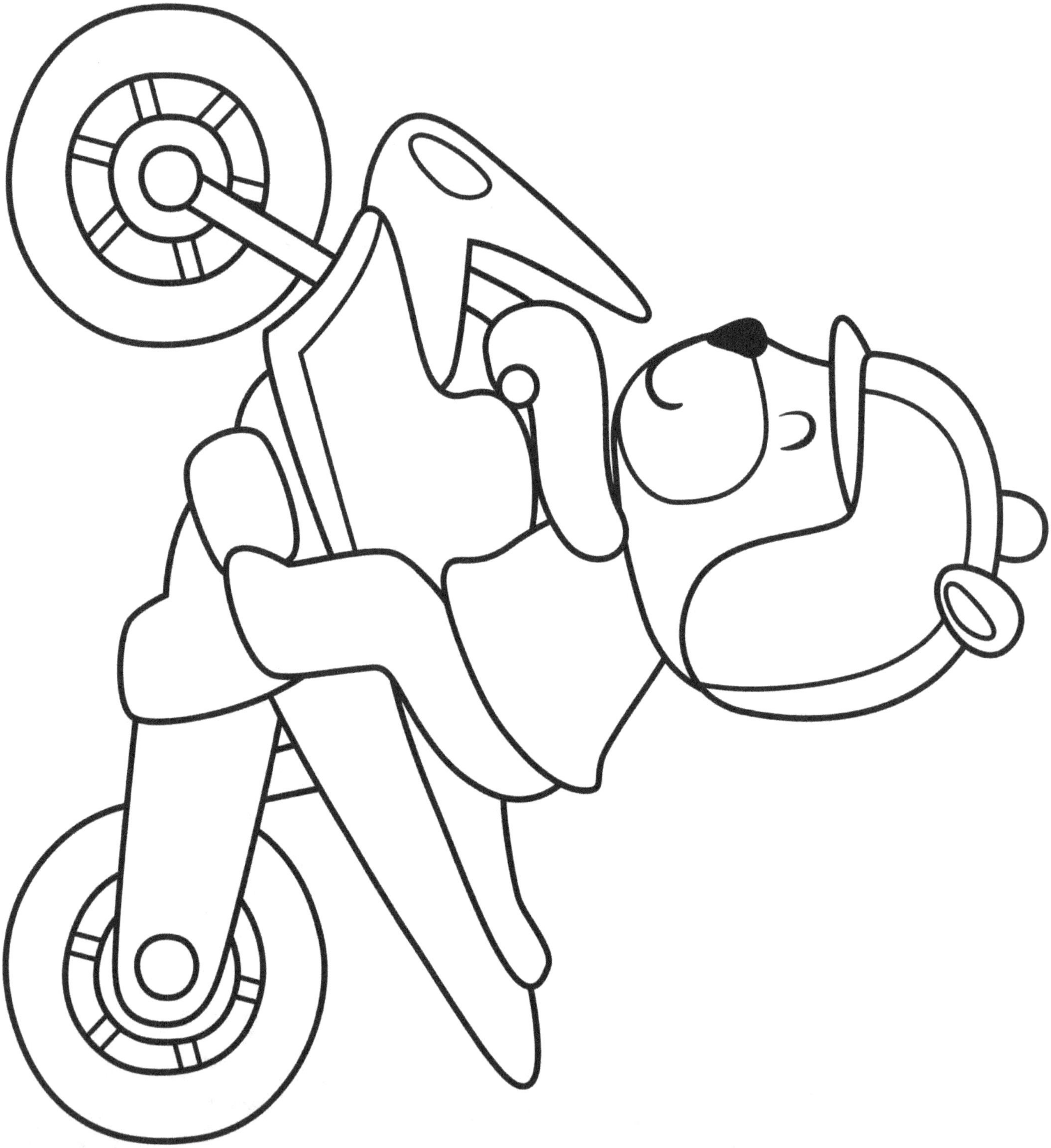

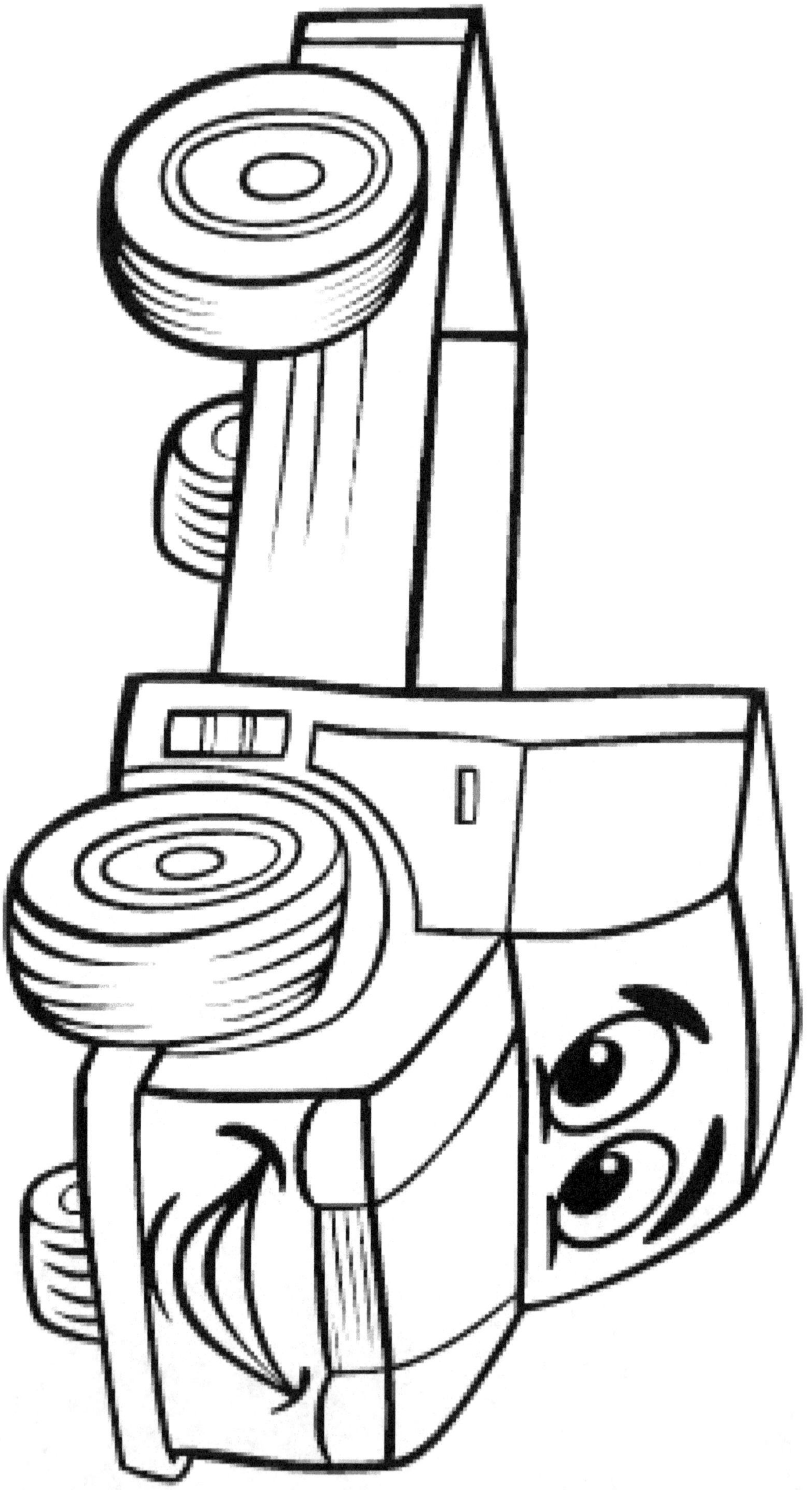

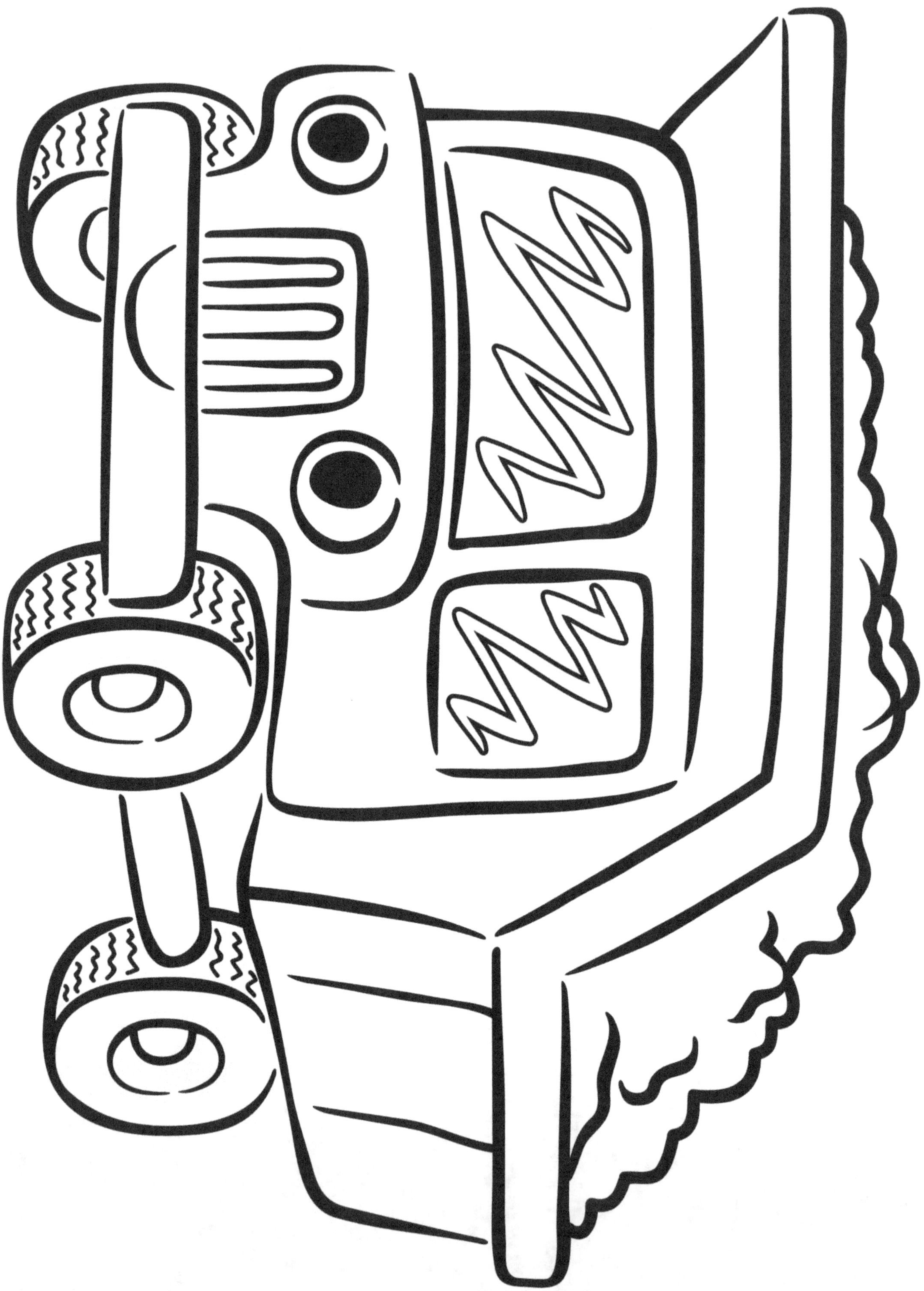

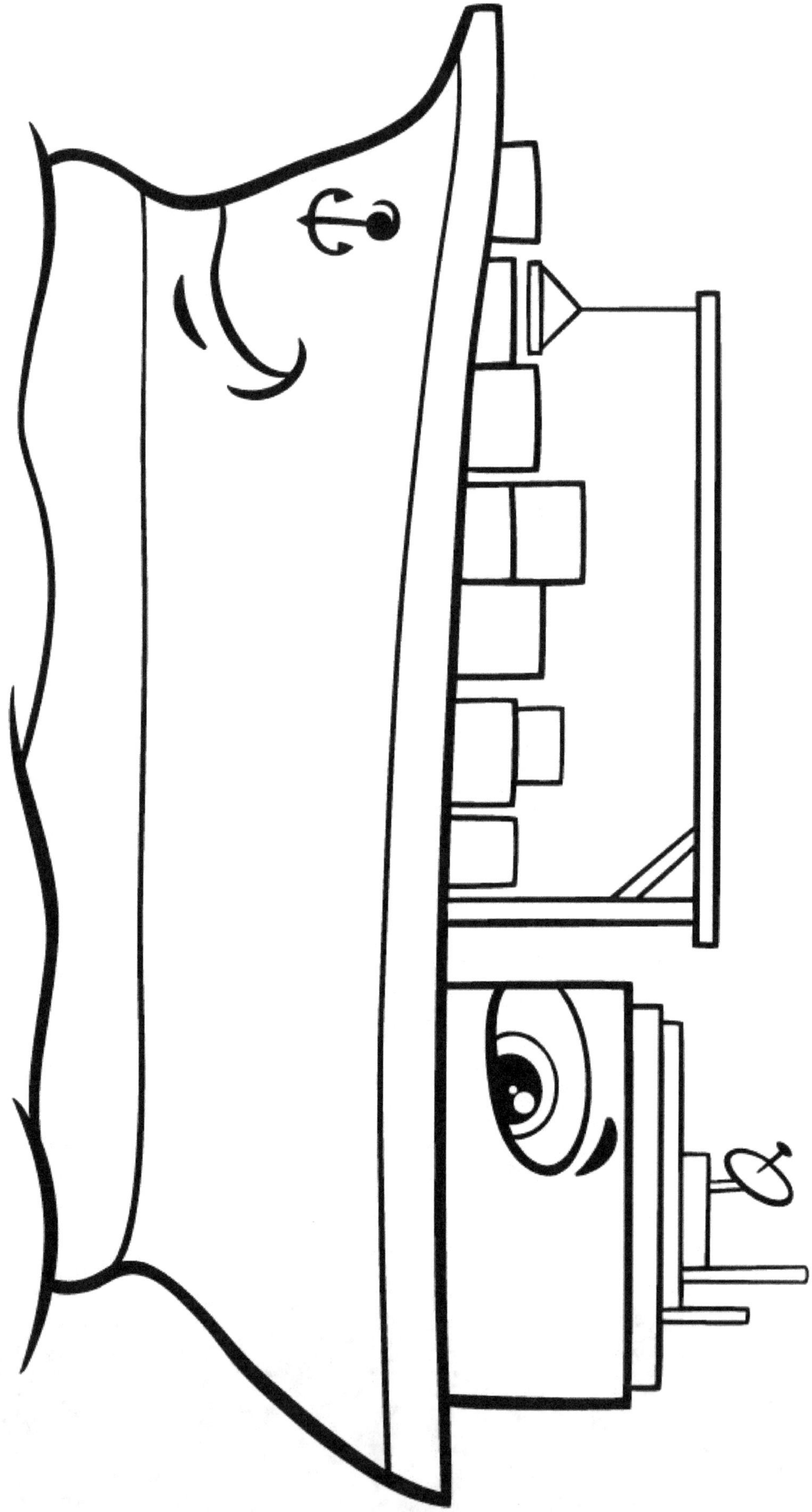

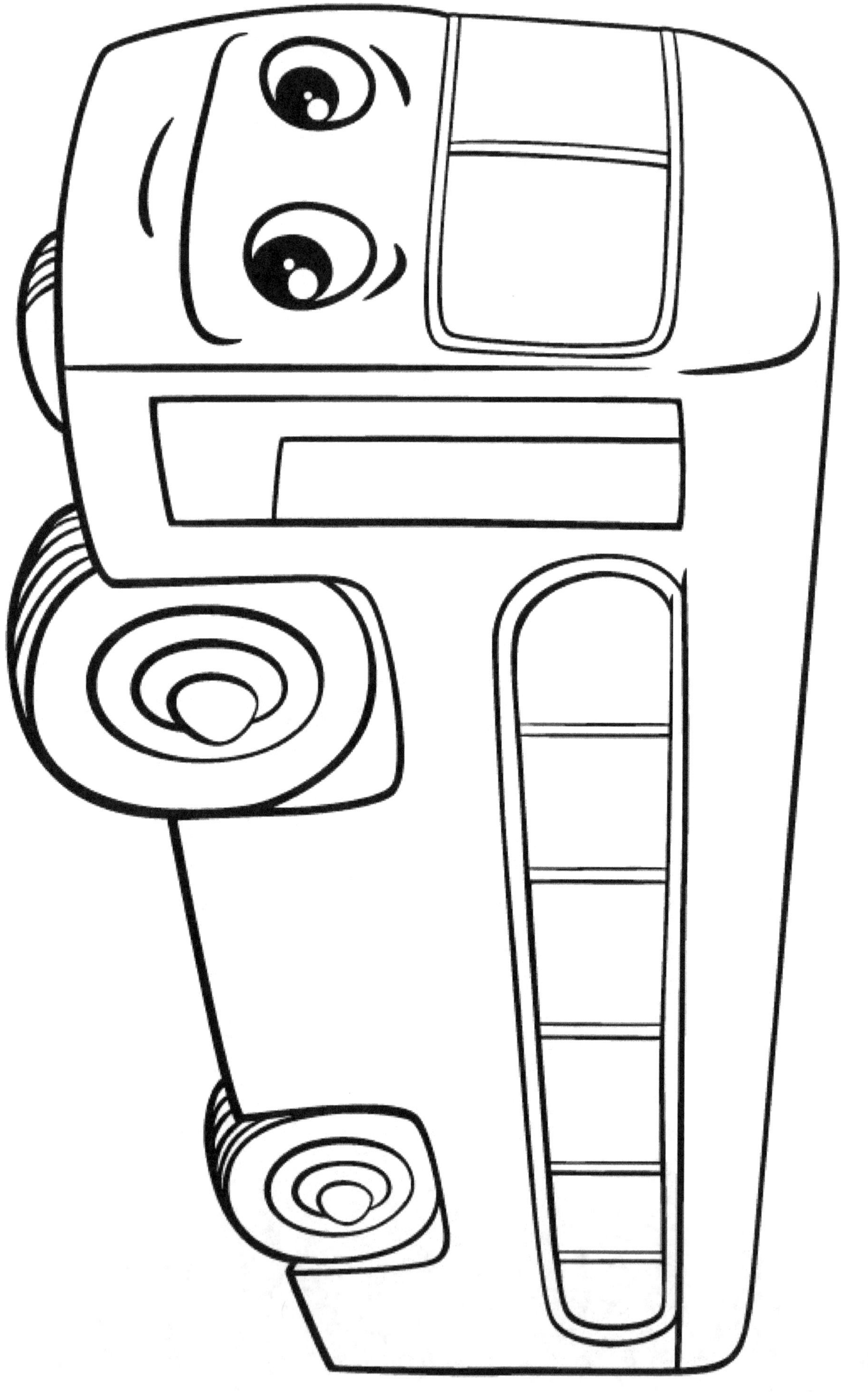

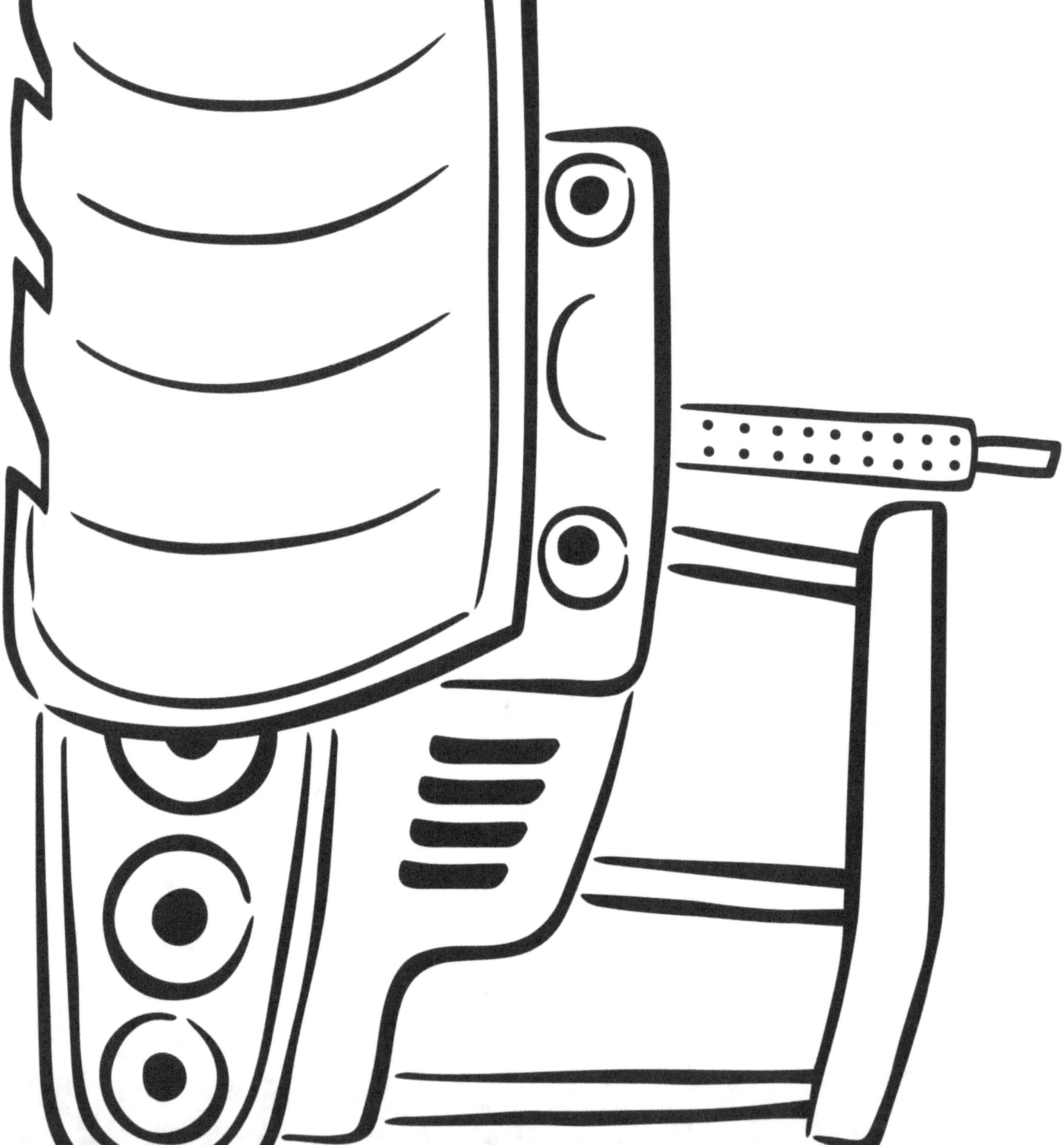

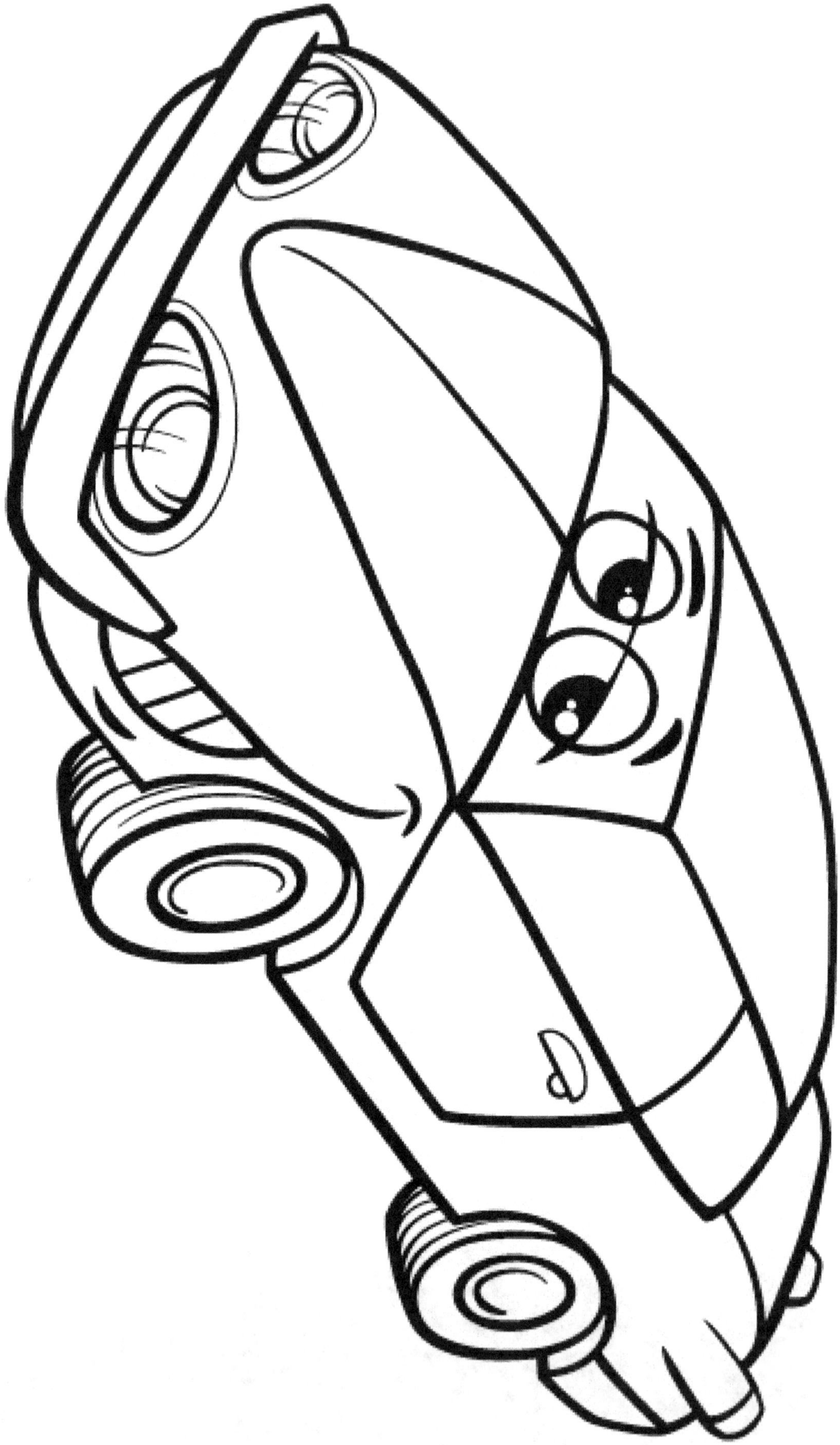

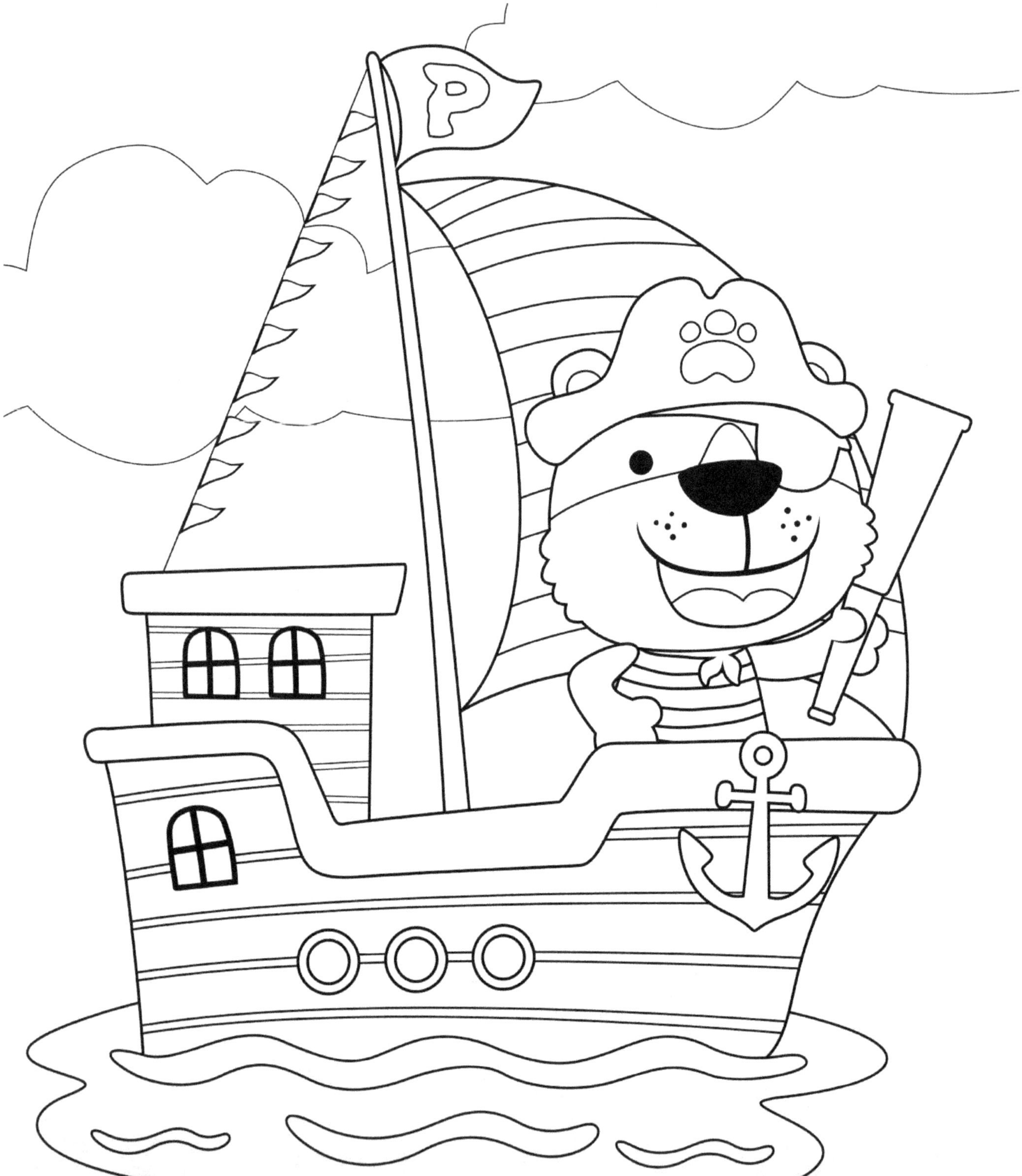
P

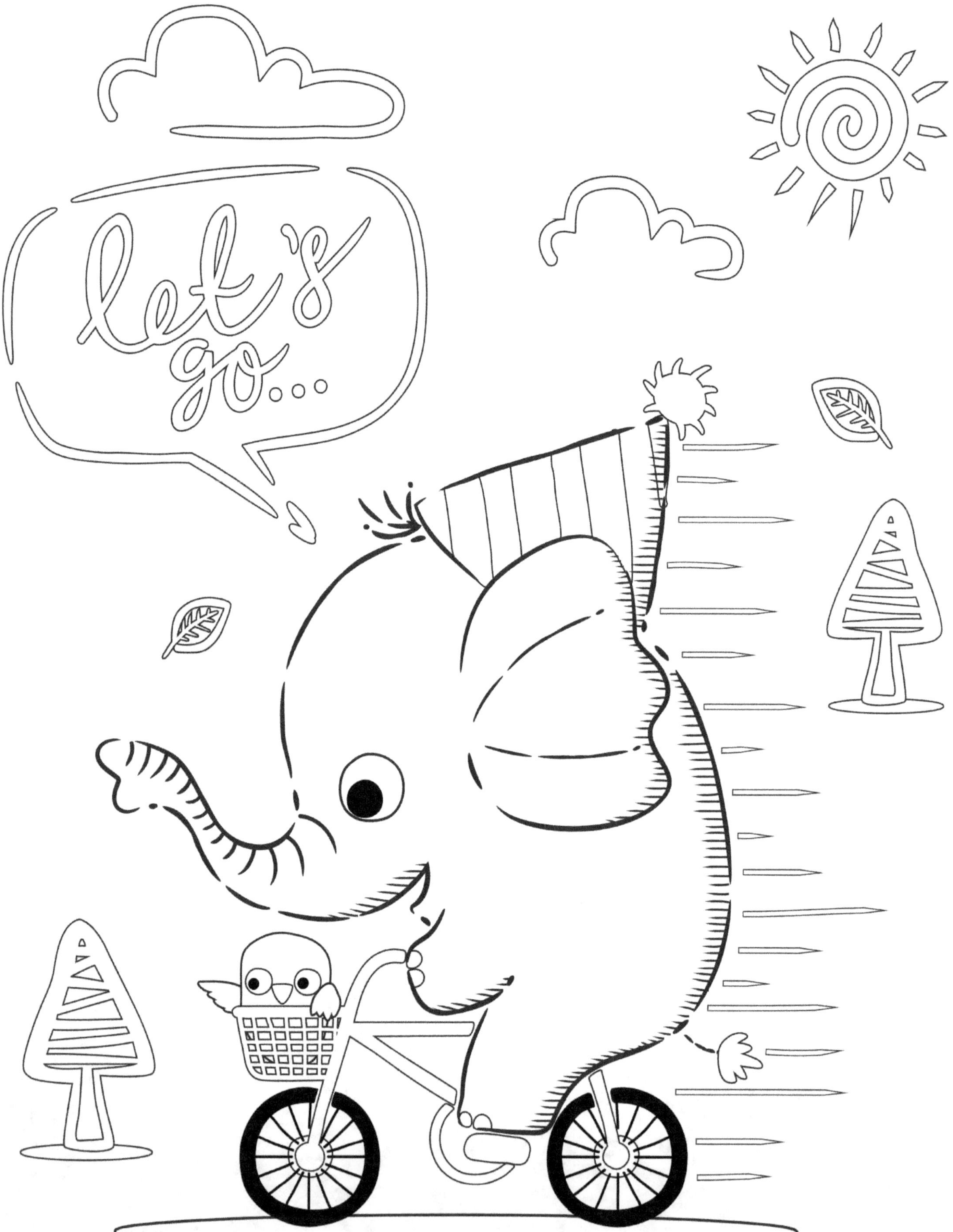
let's go...

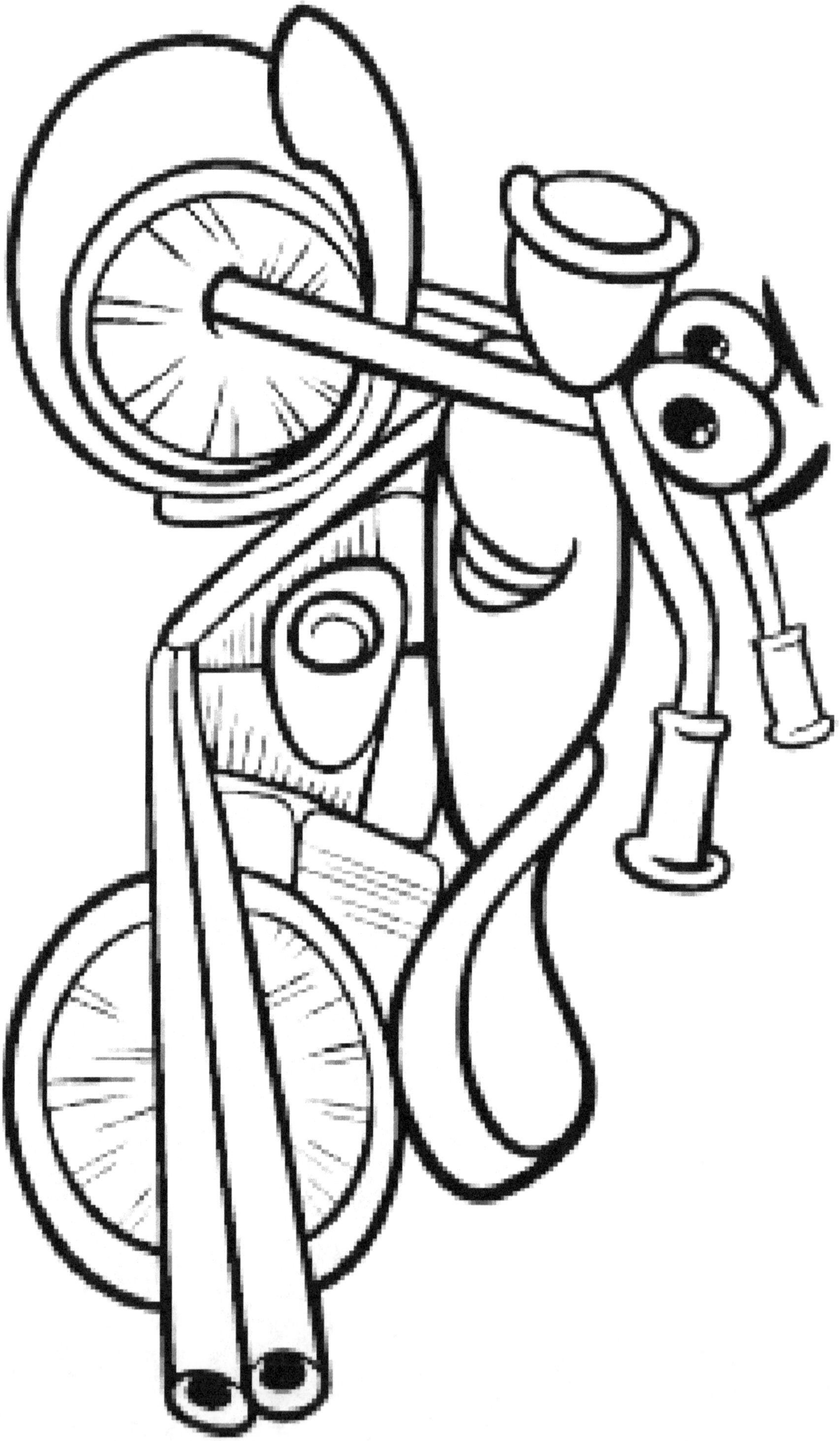

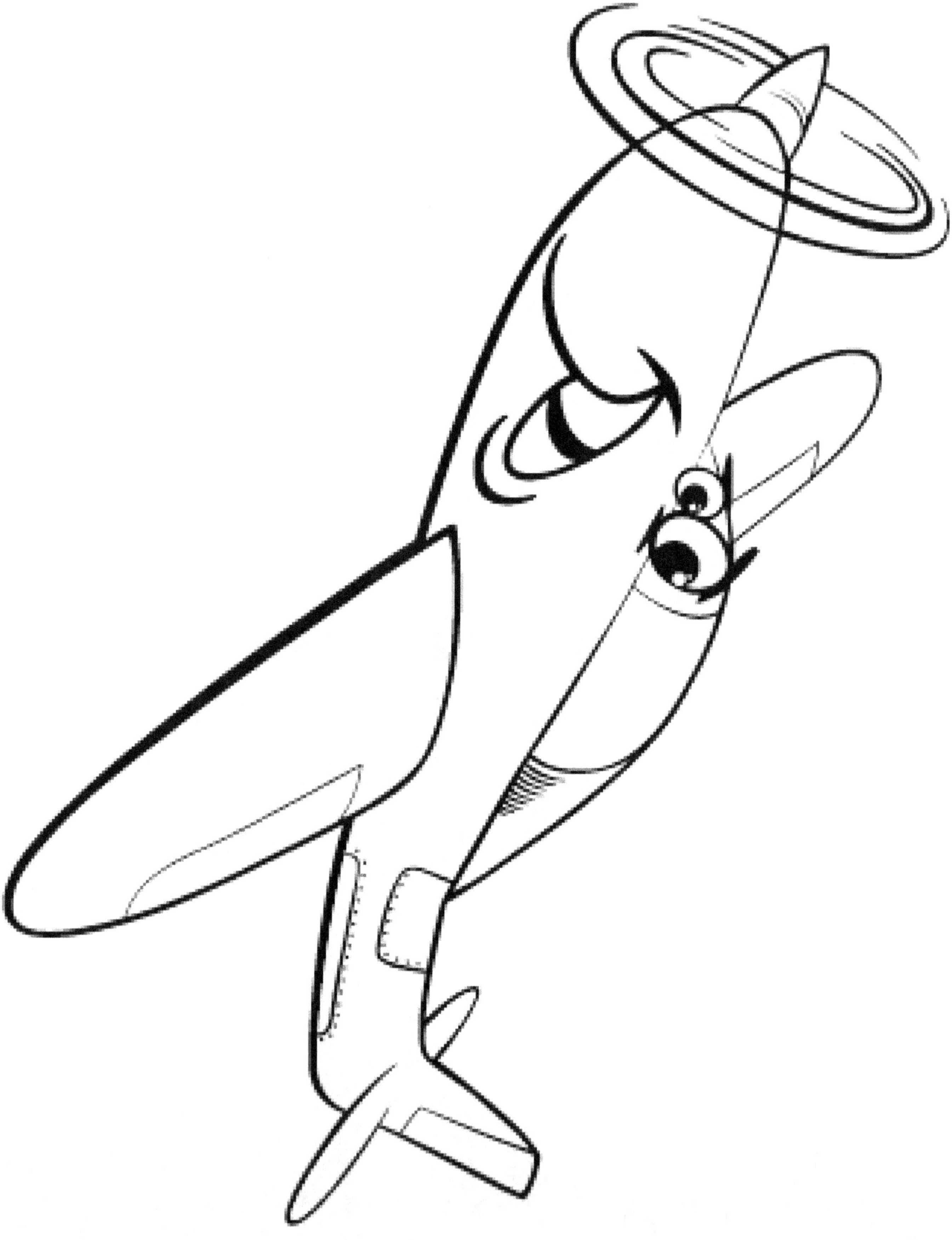

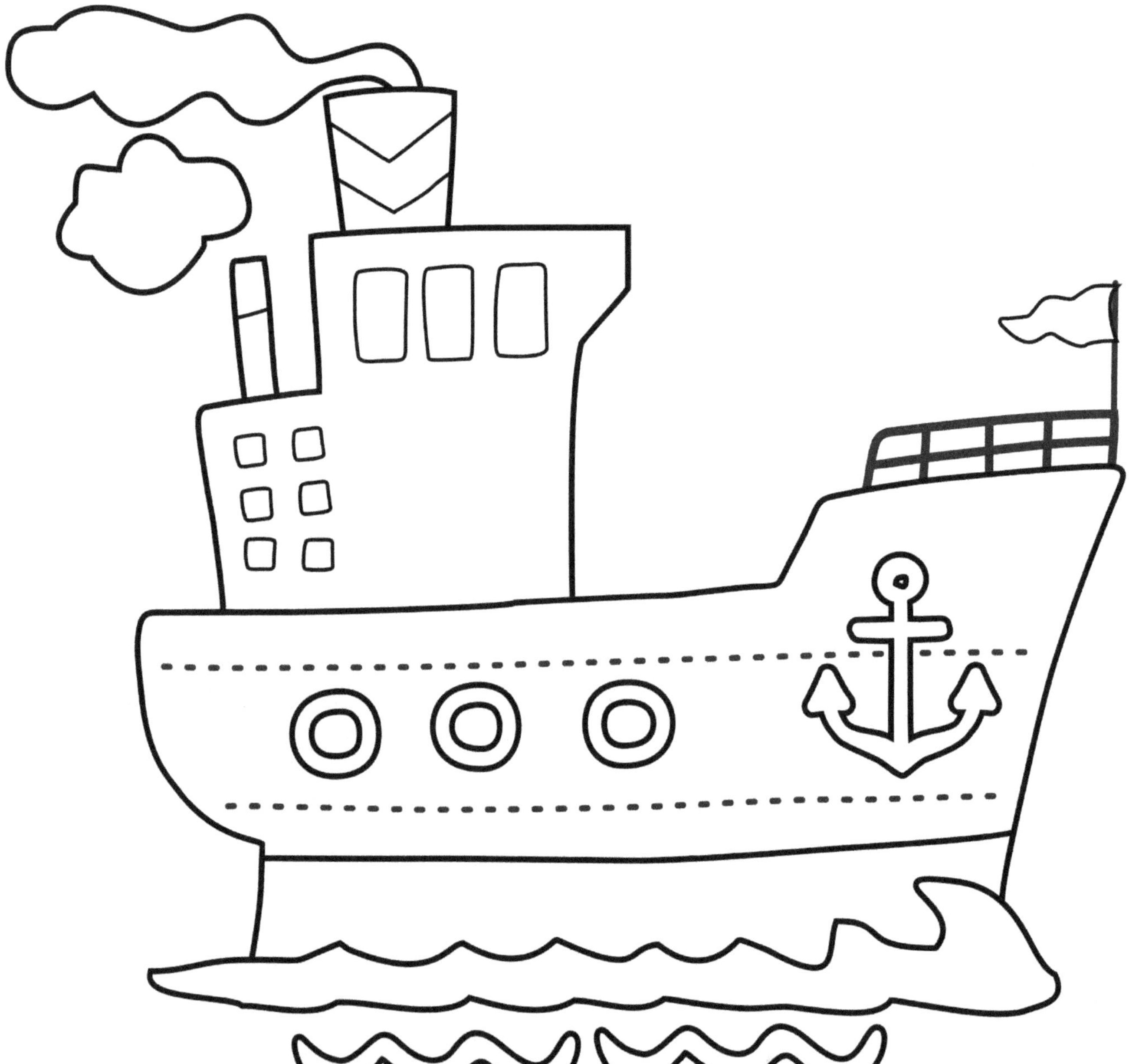

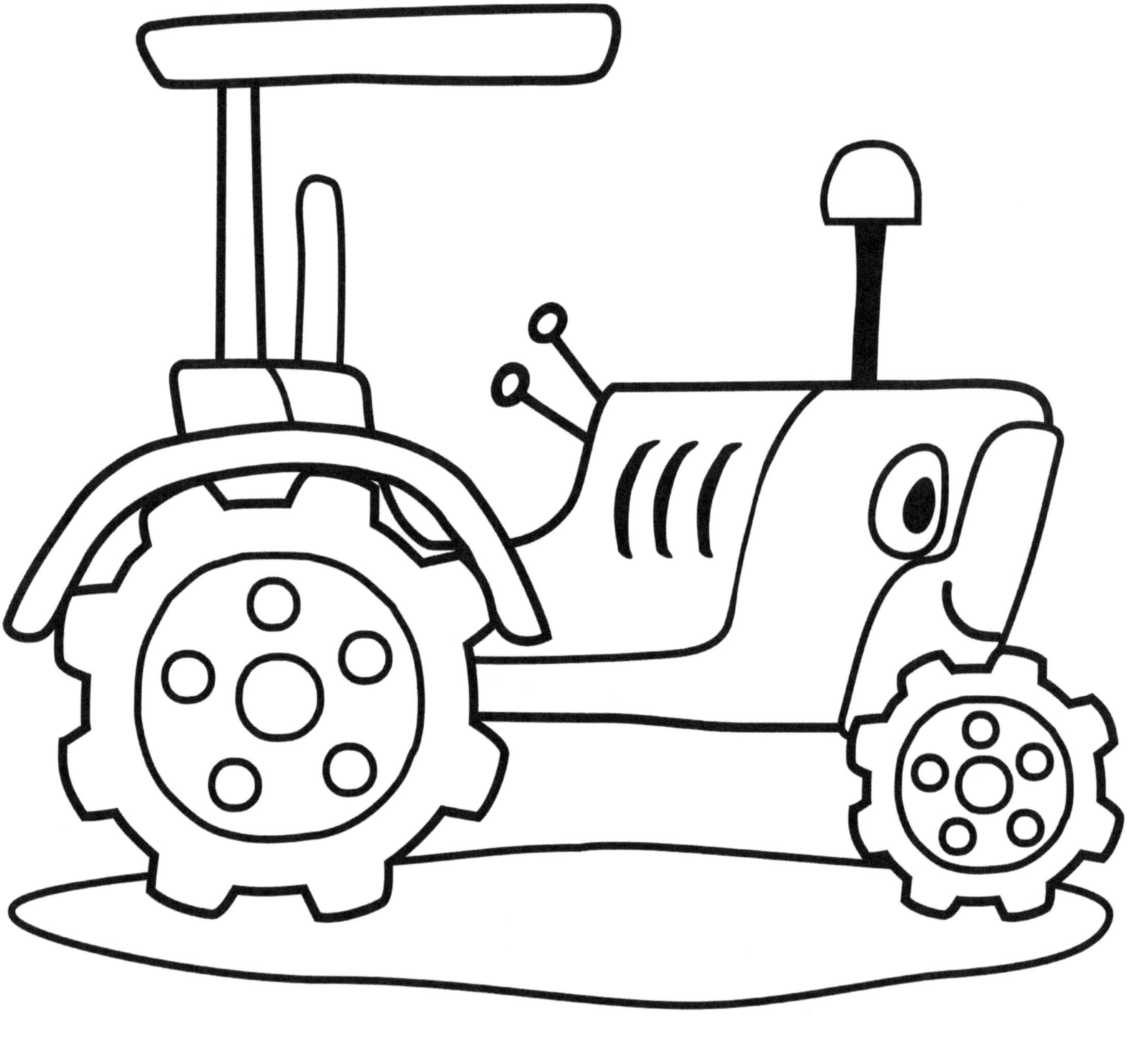

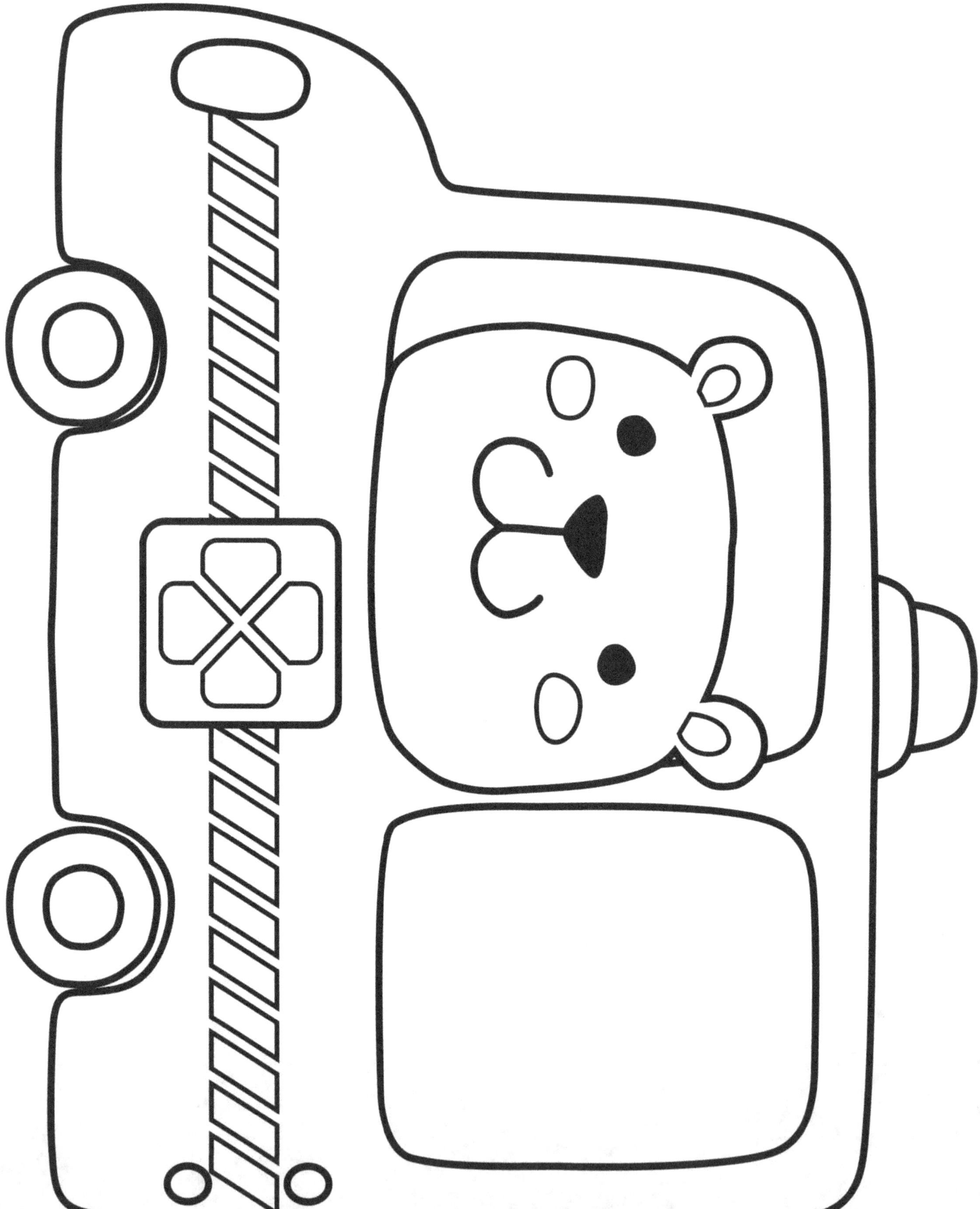

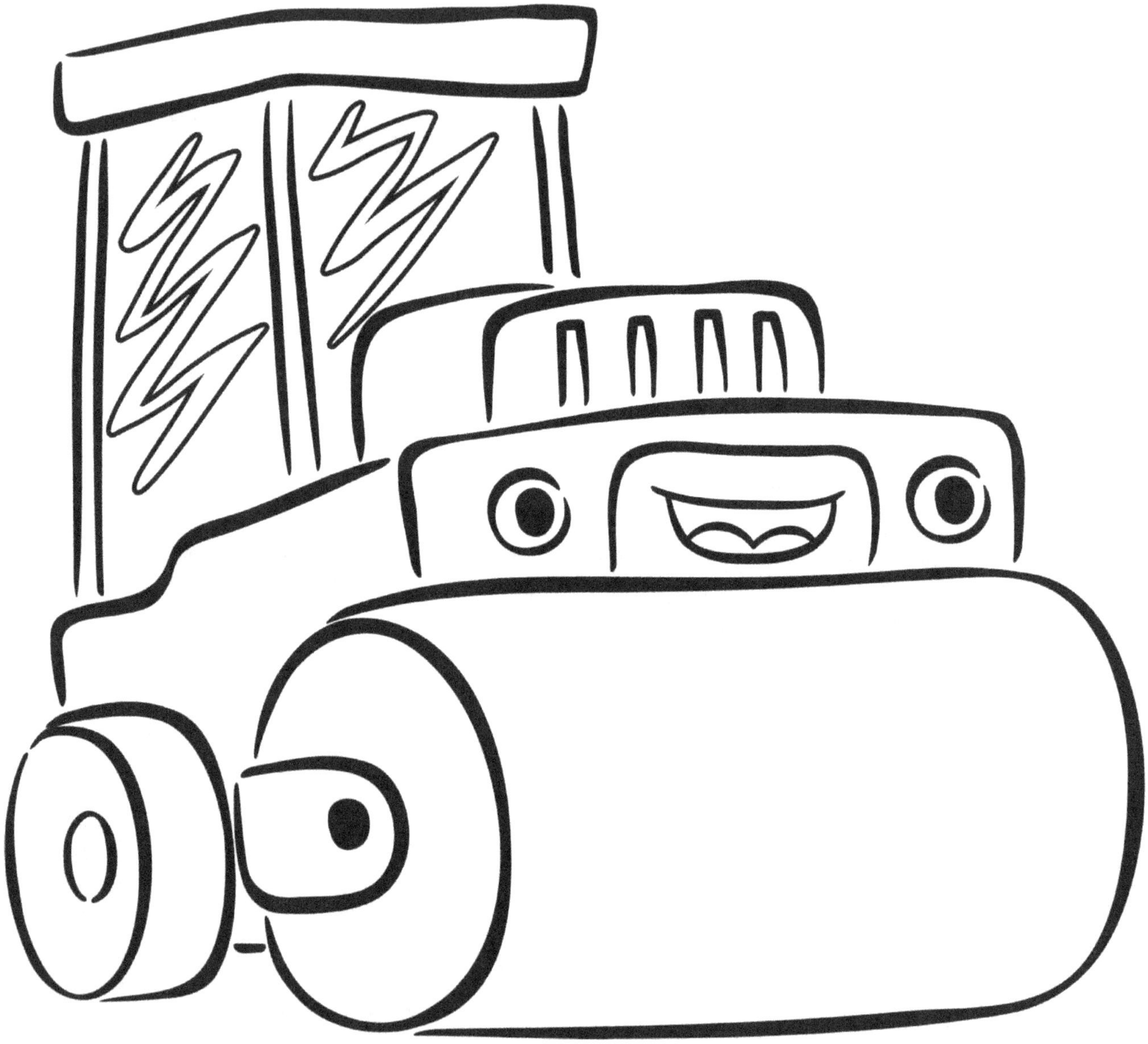

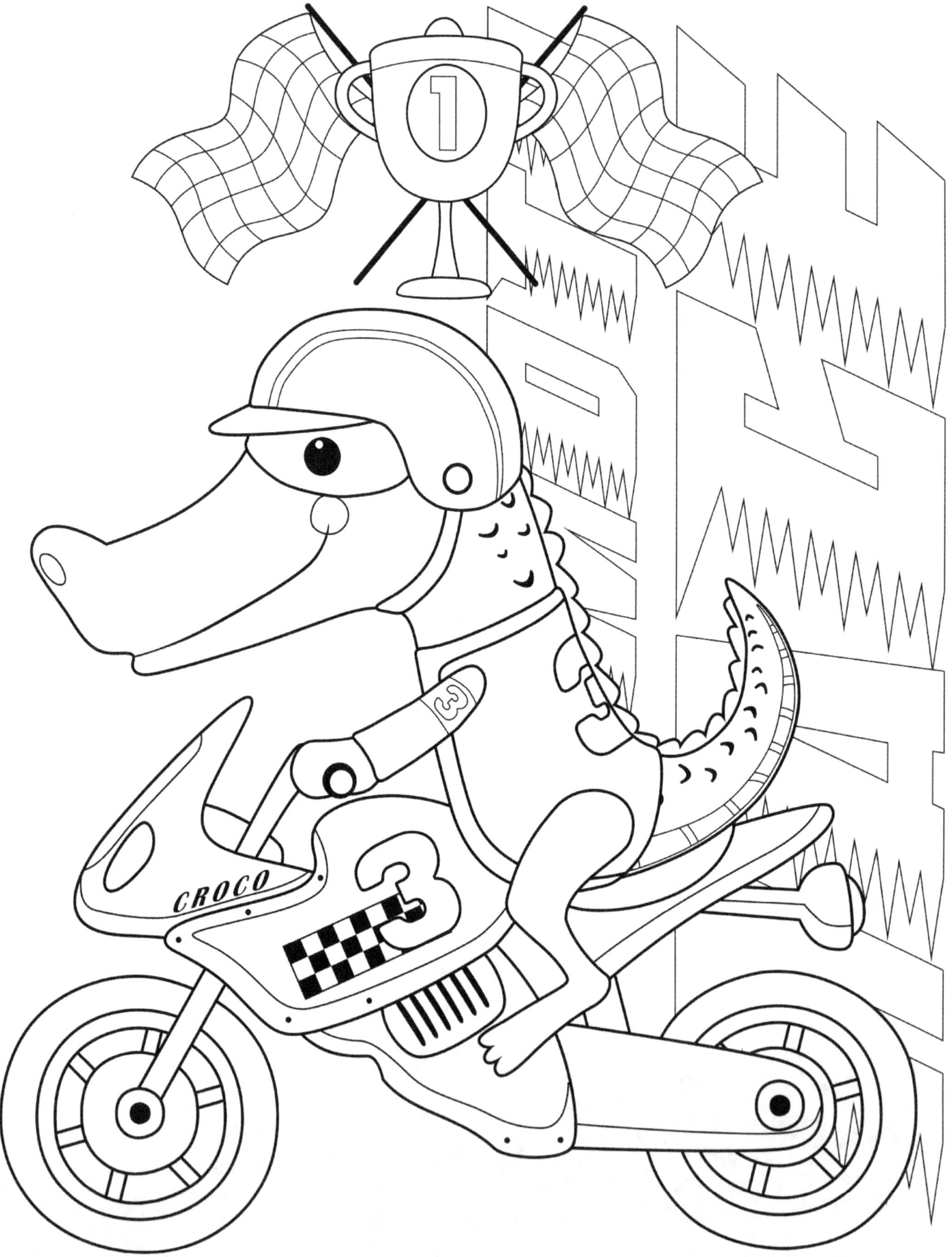
1
CROCO
3

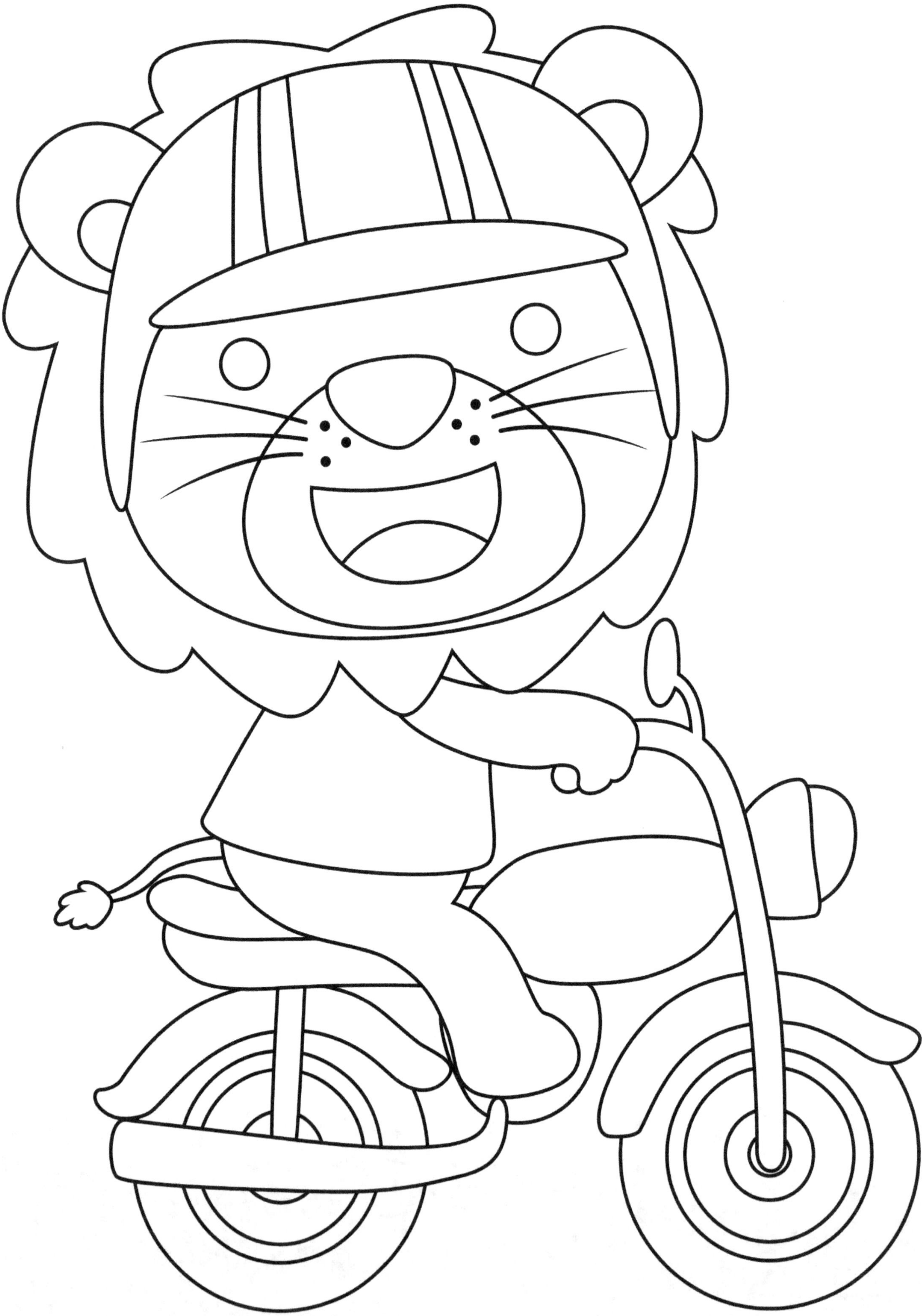

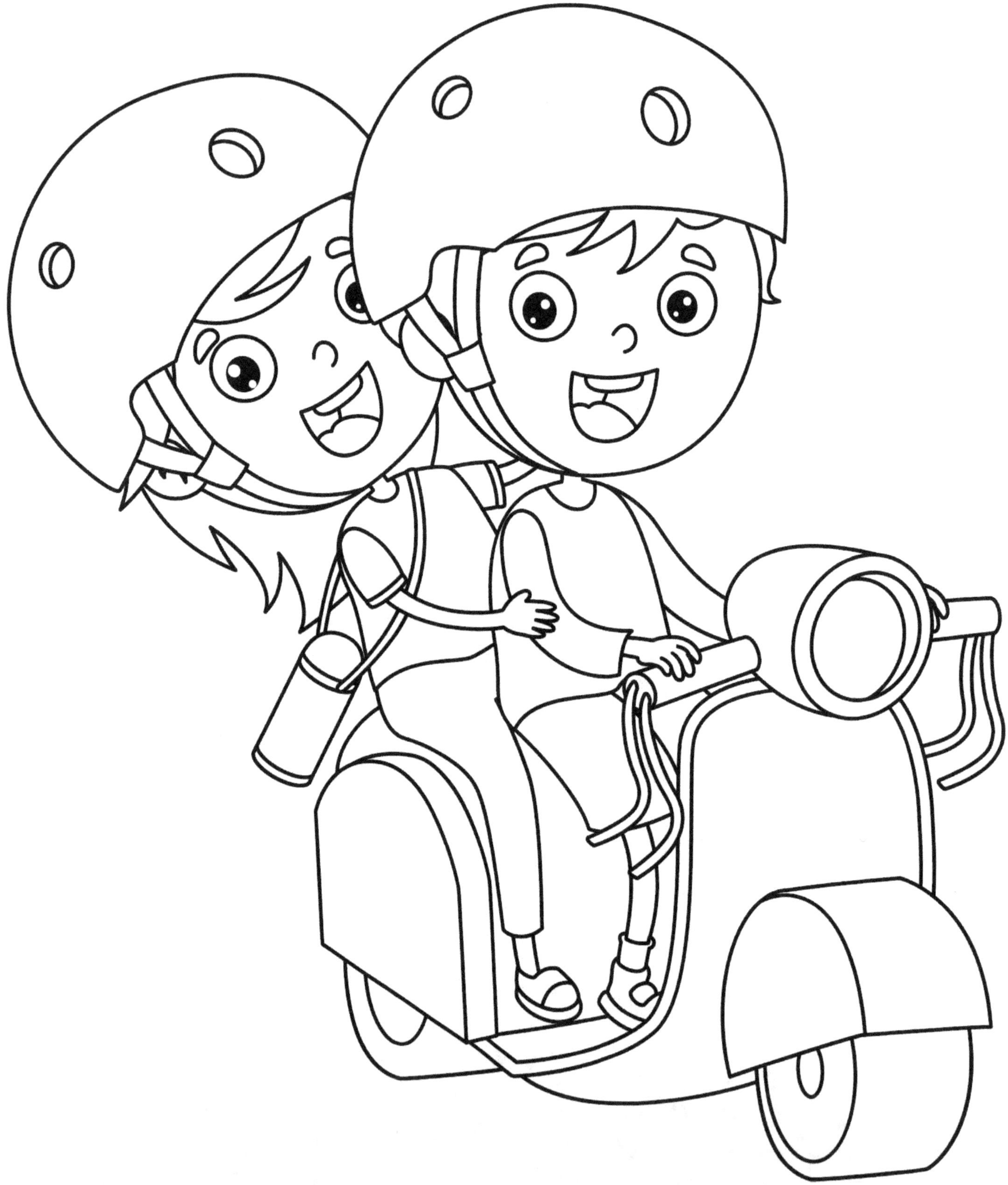

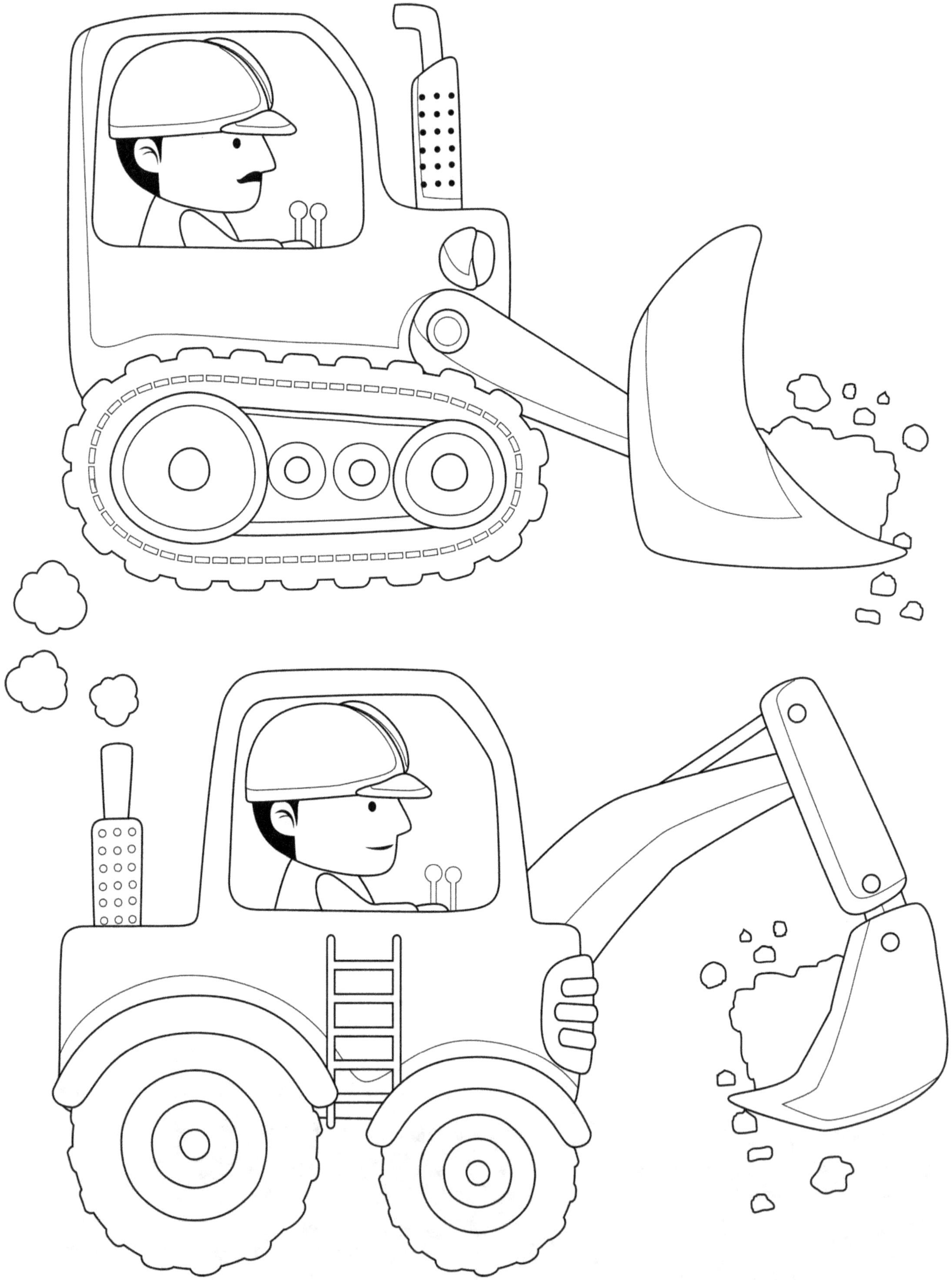

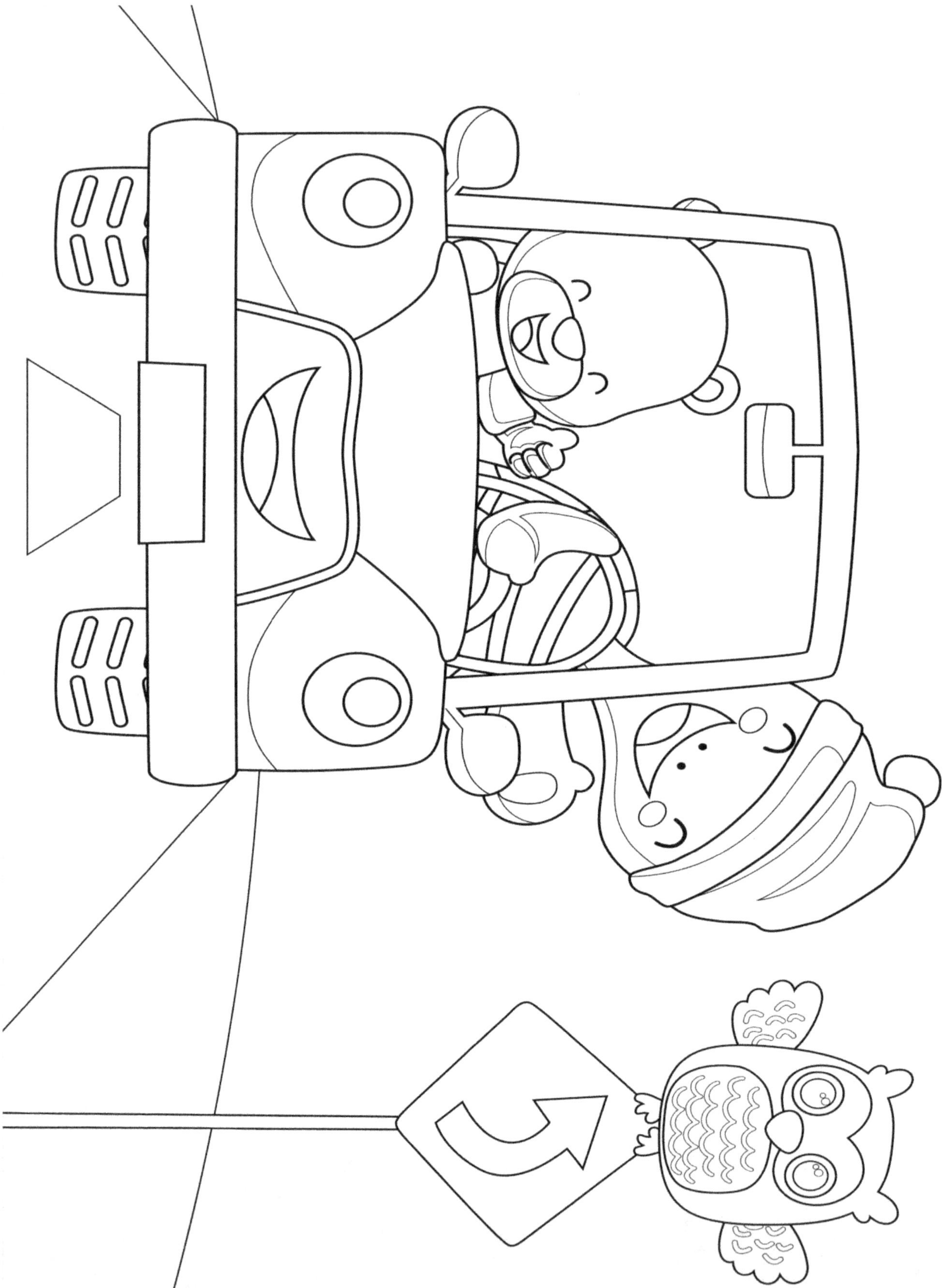

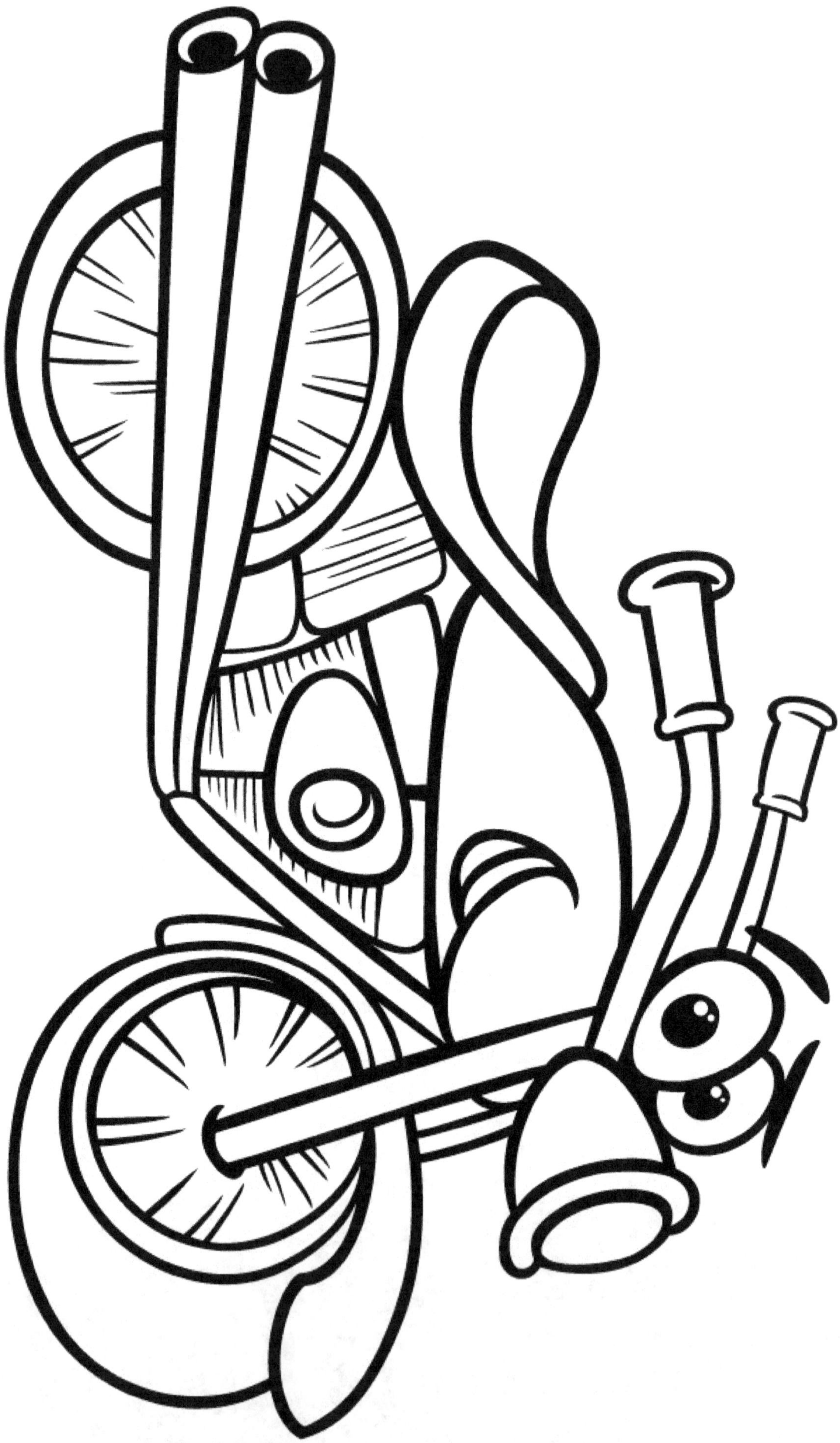

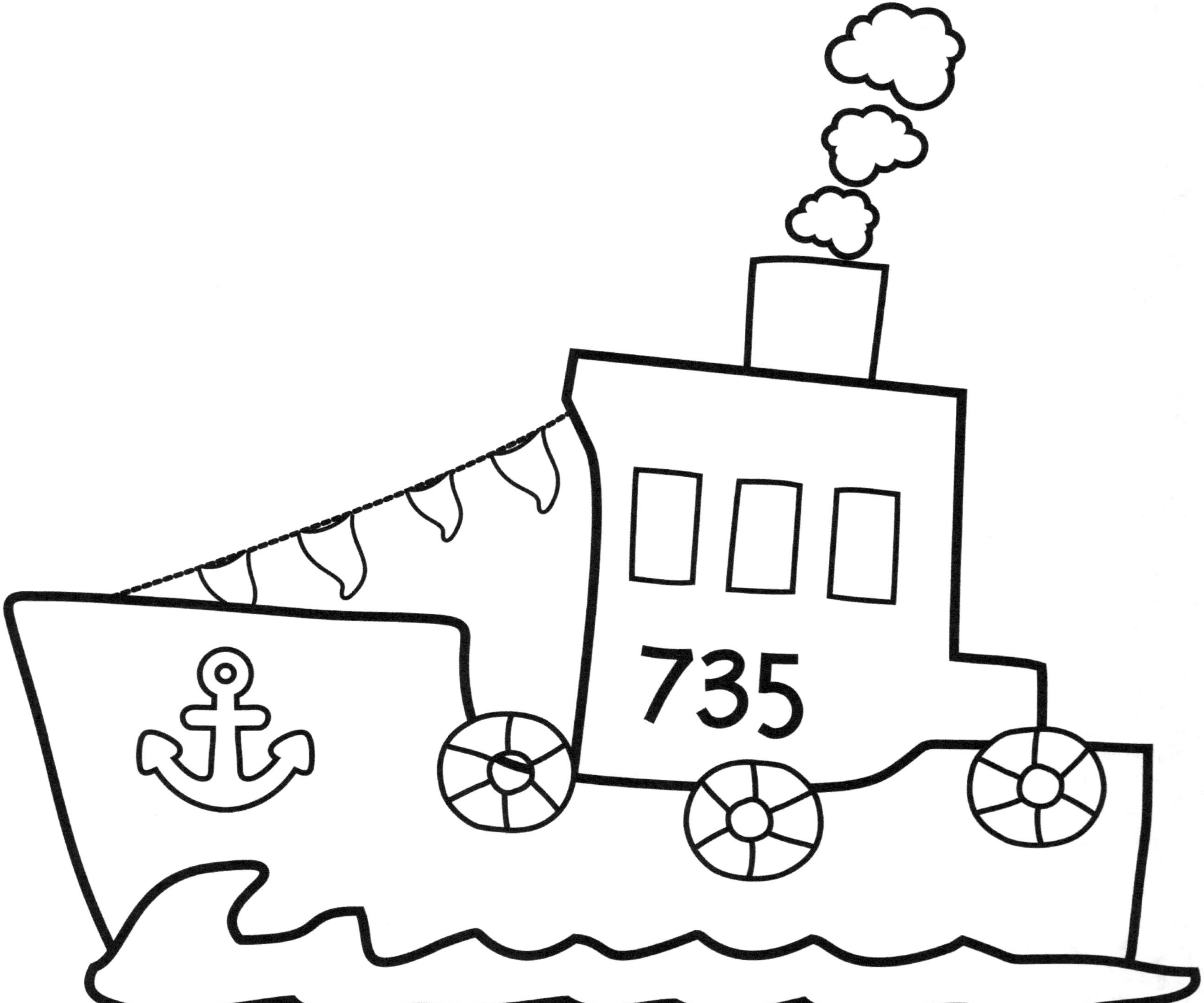
735

T is for

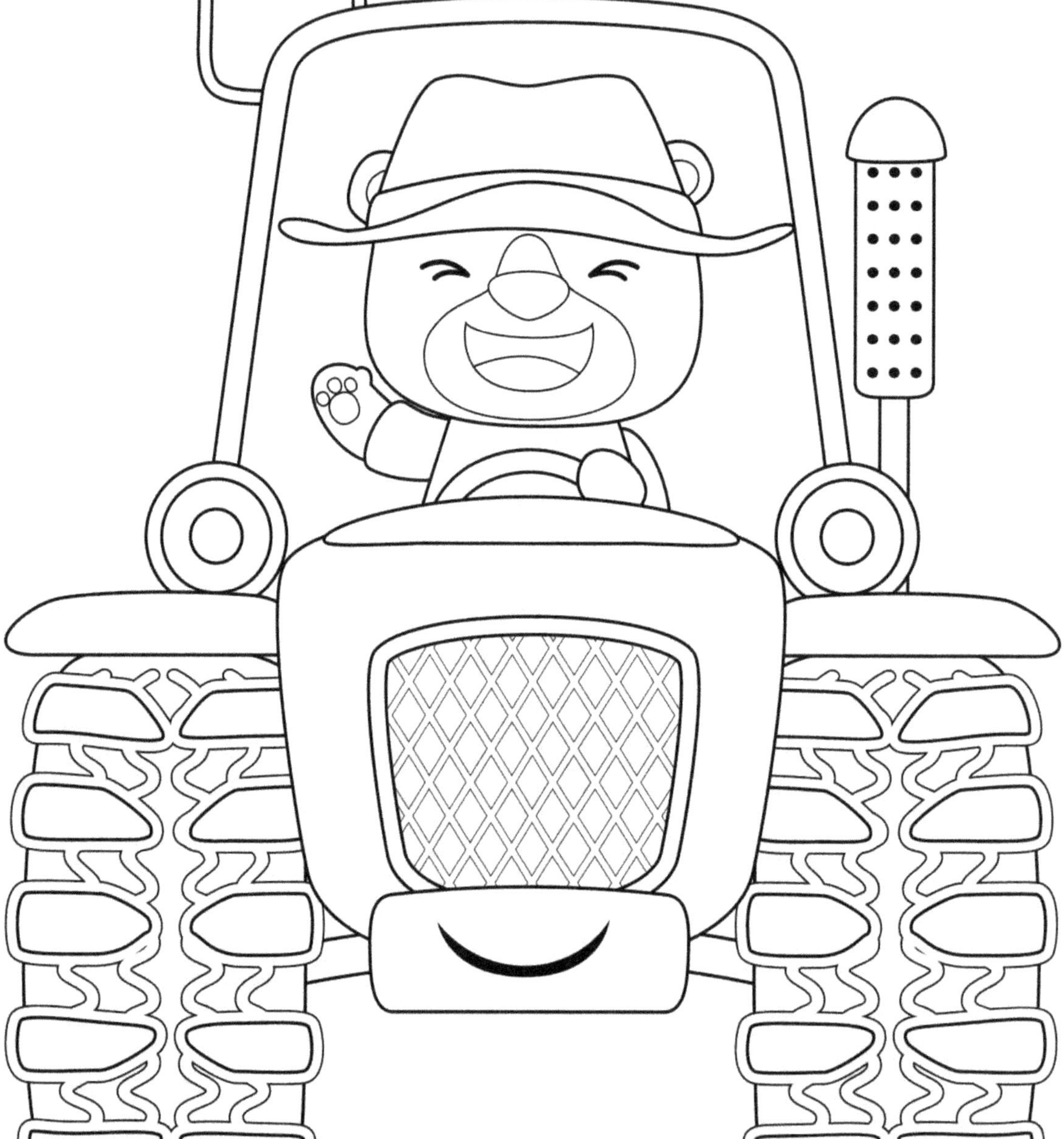

tractor

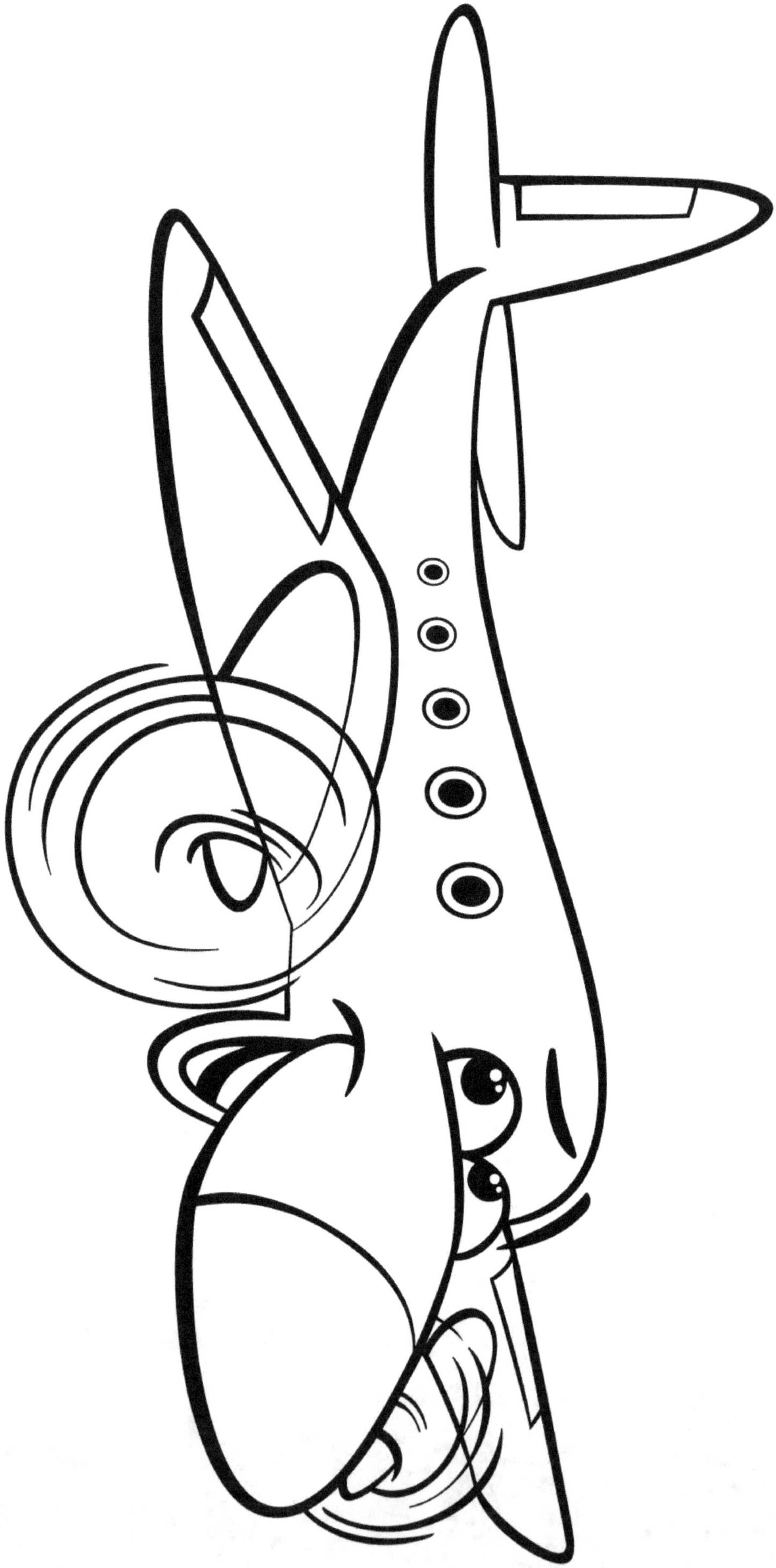

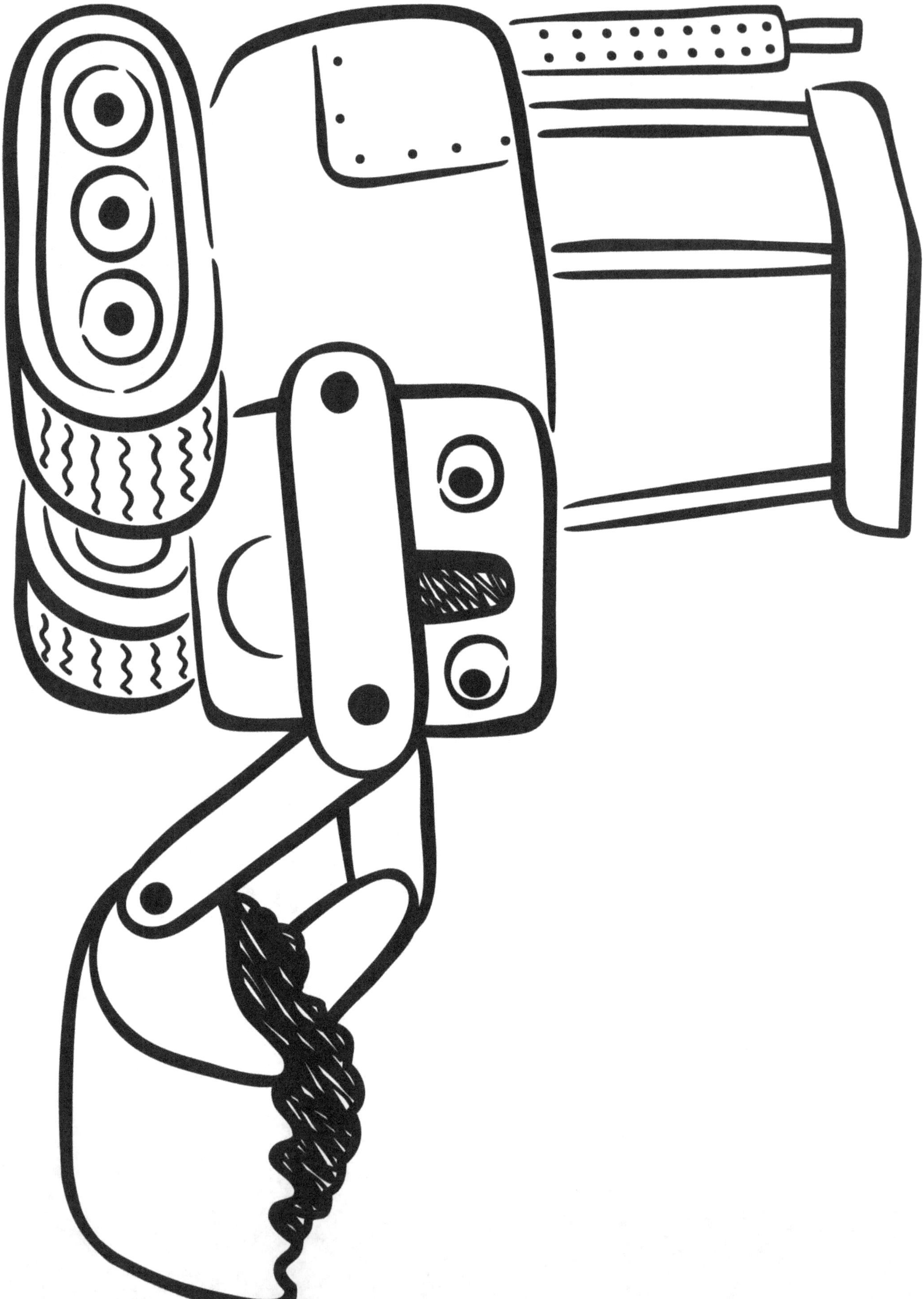

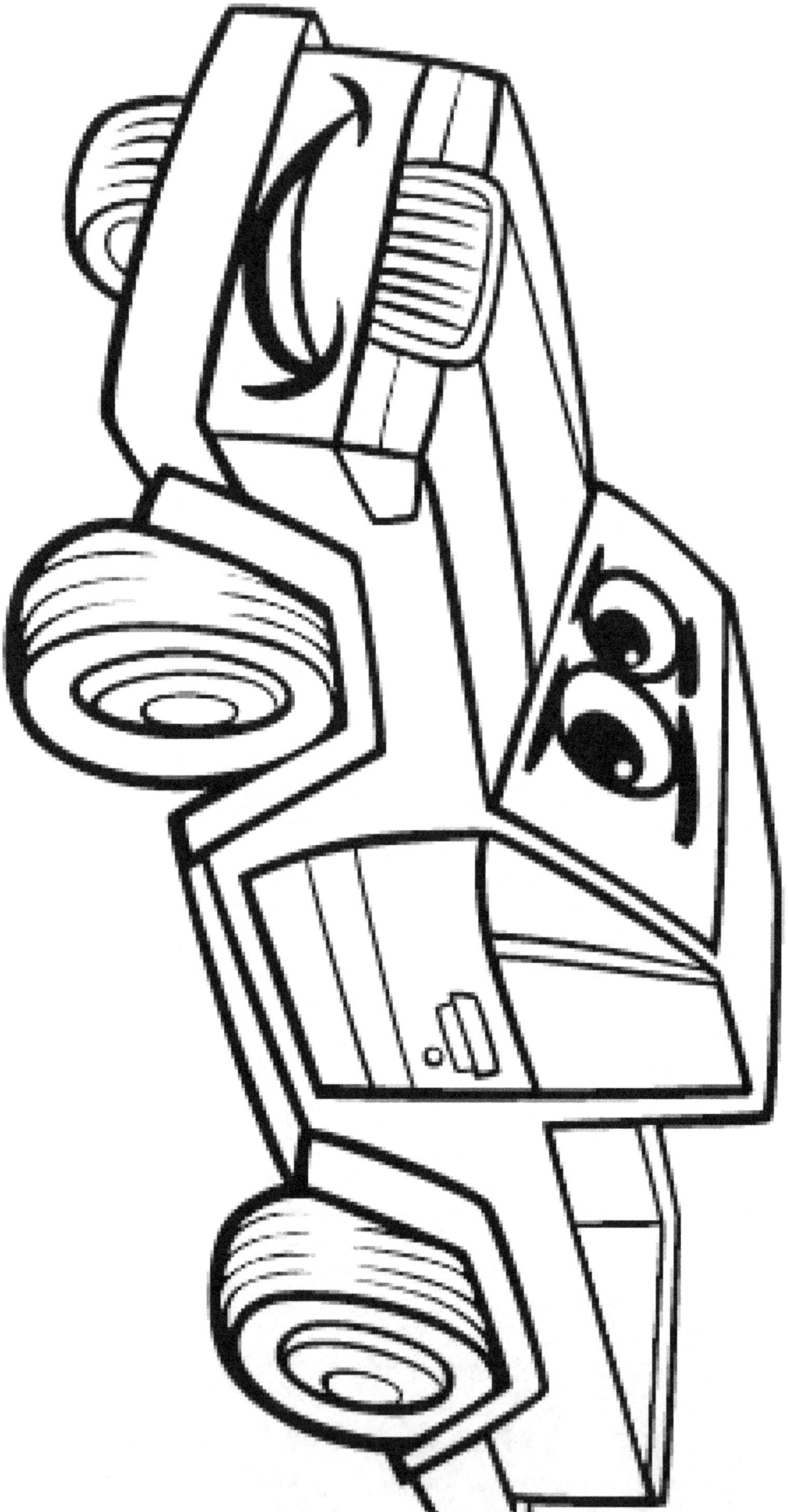

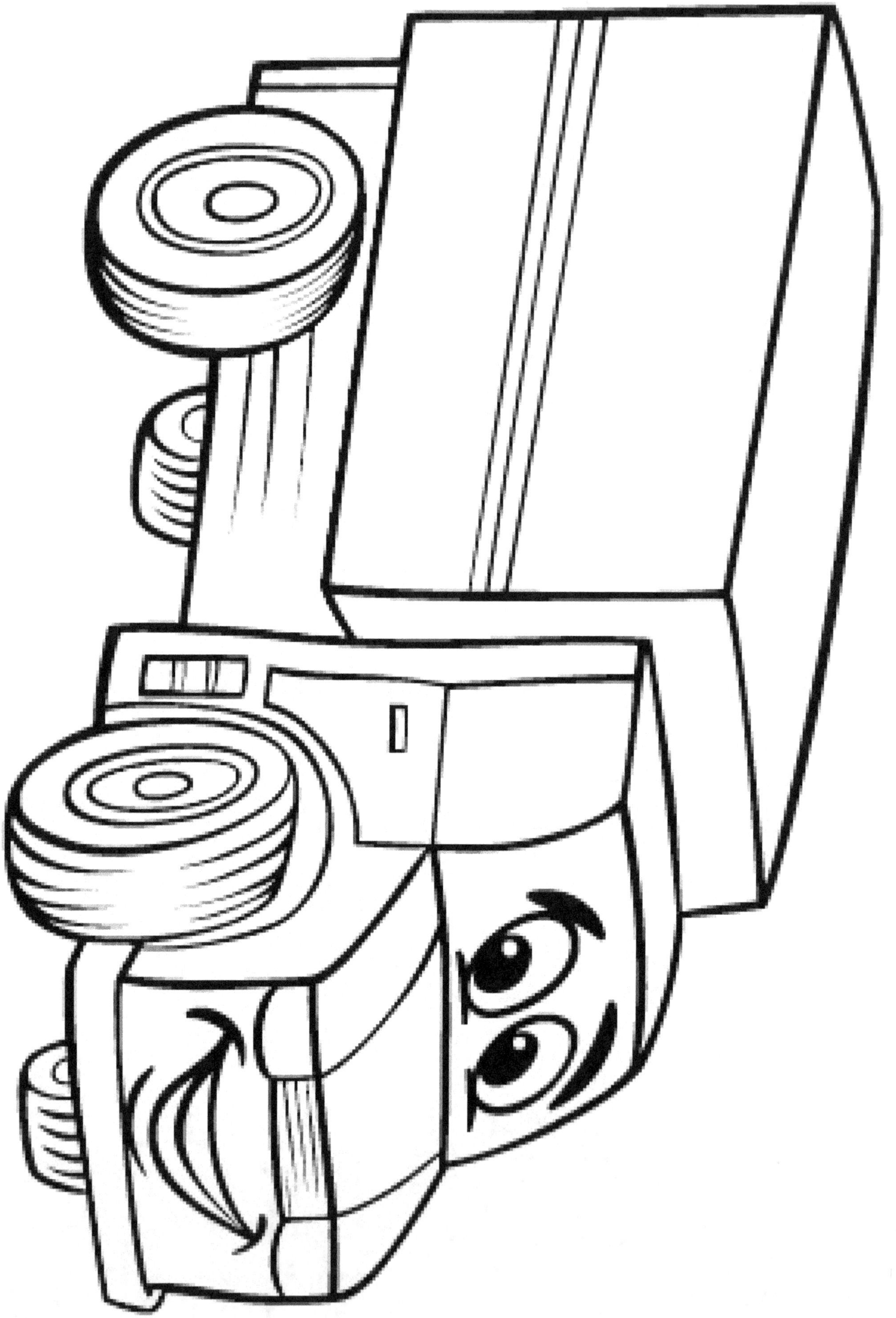

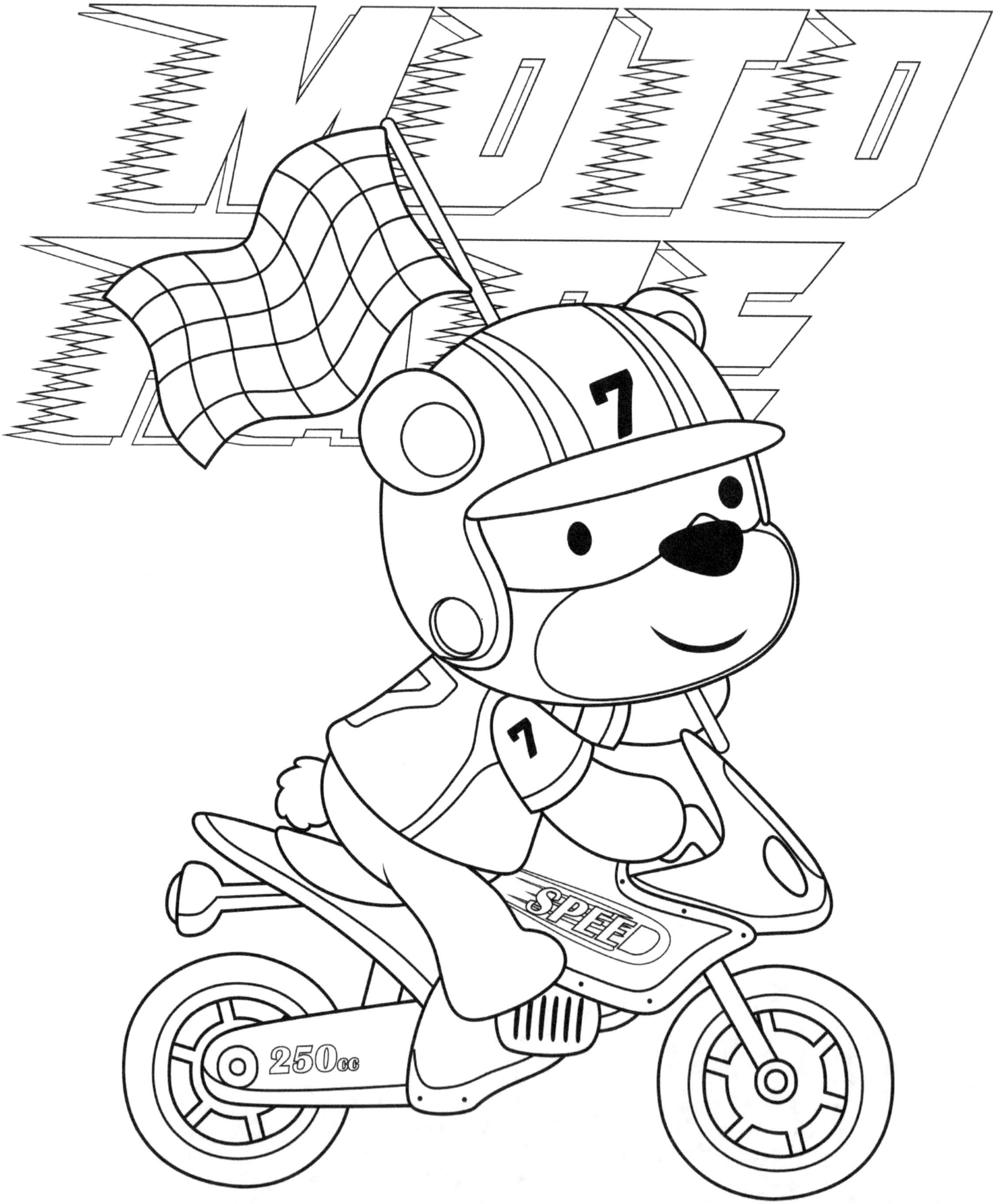
MOTO
7
7
SPEE
250cc

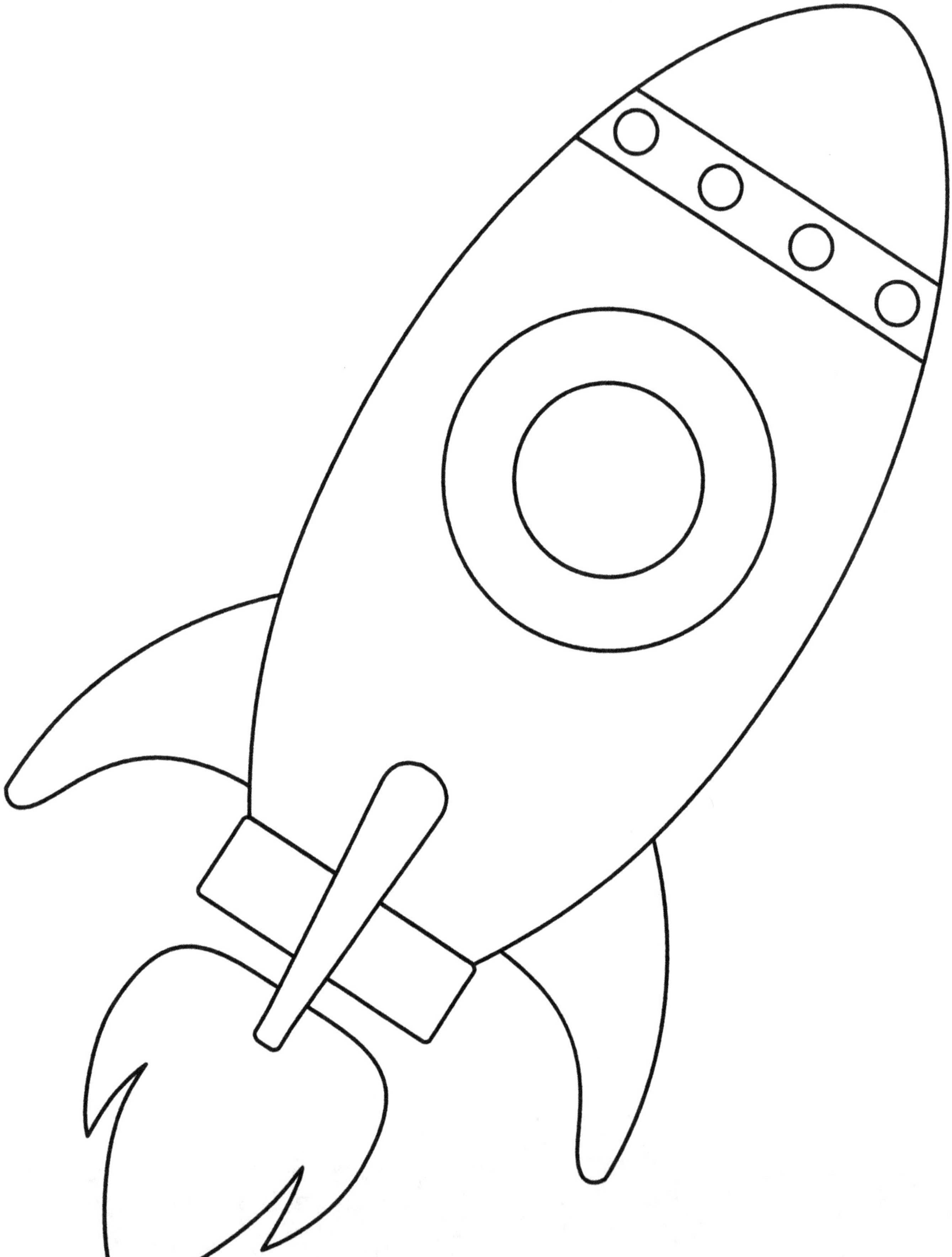

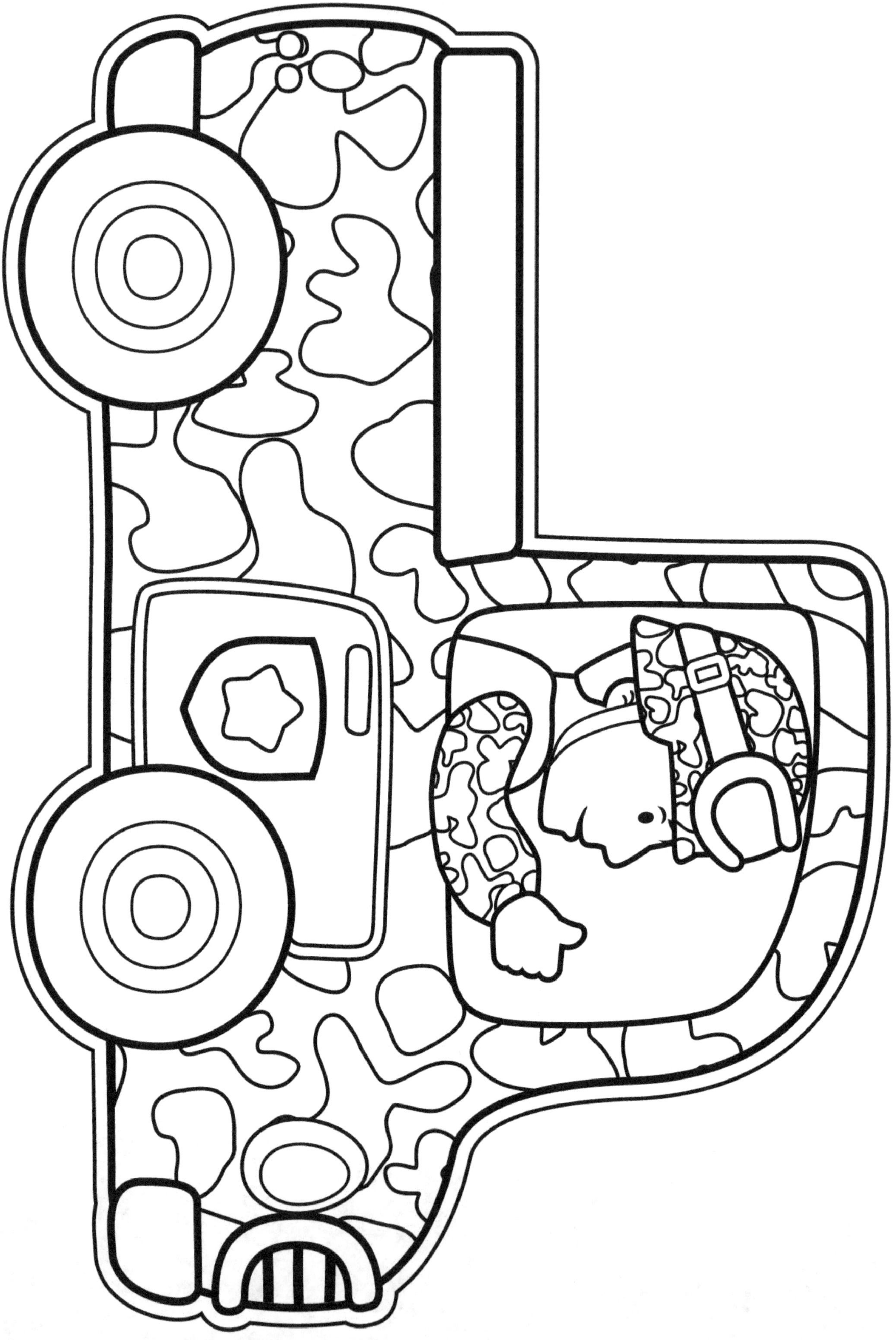

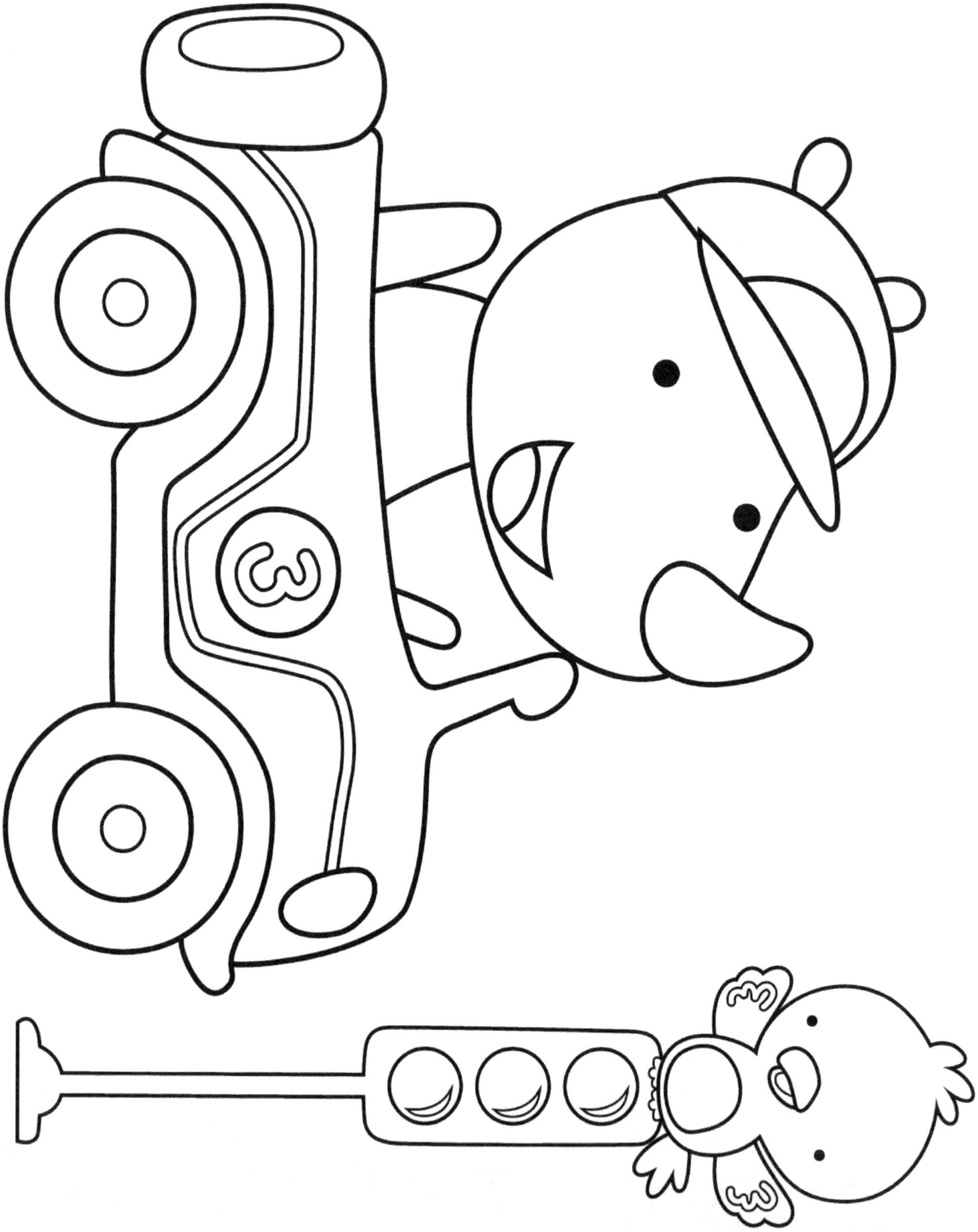
3

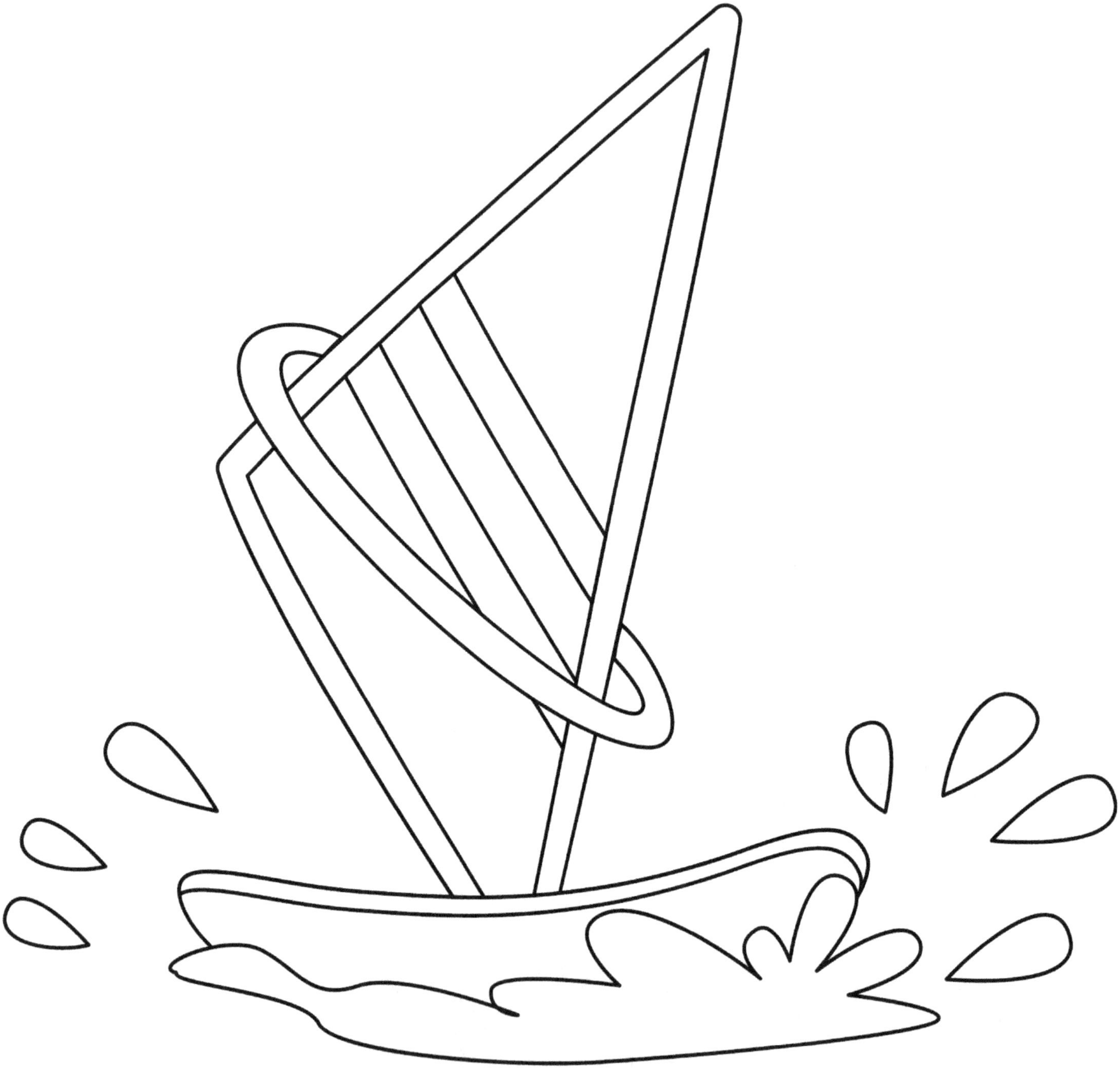

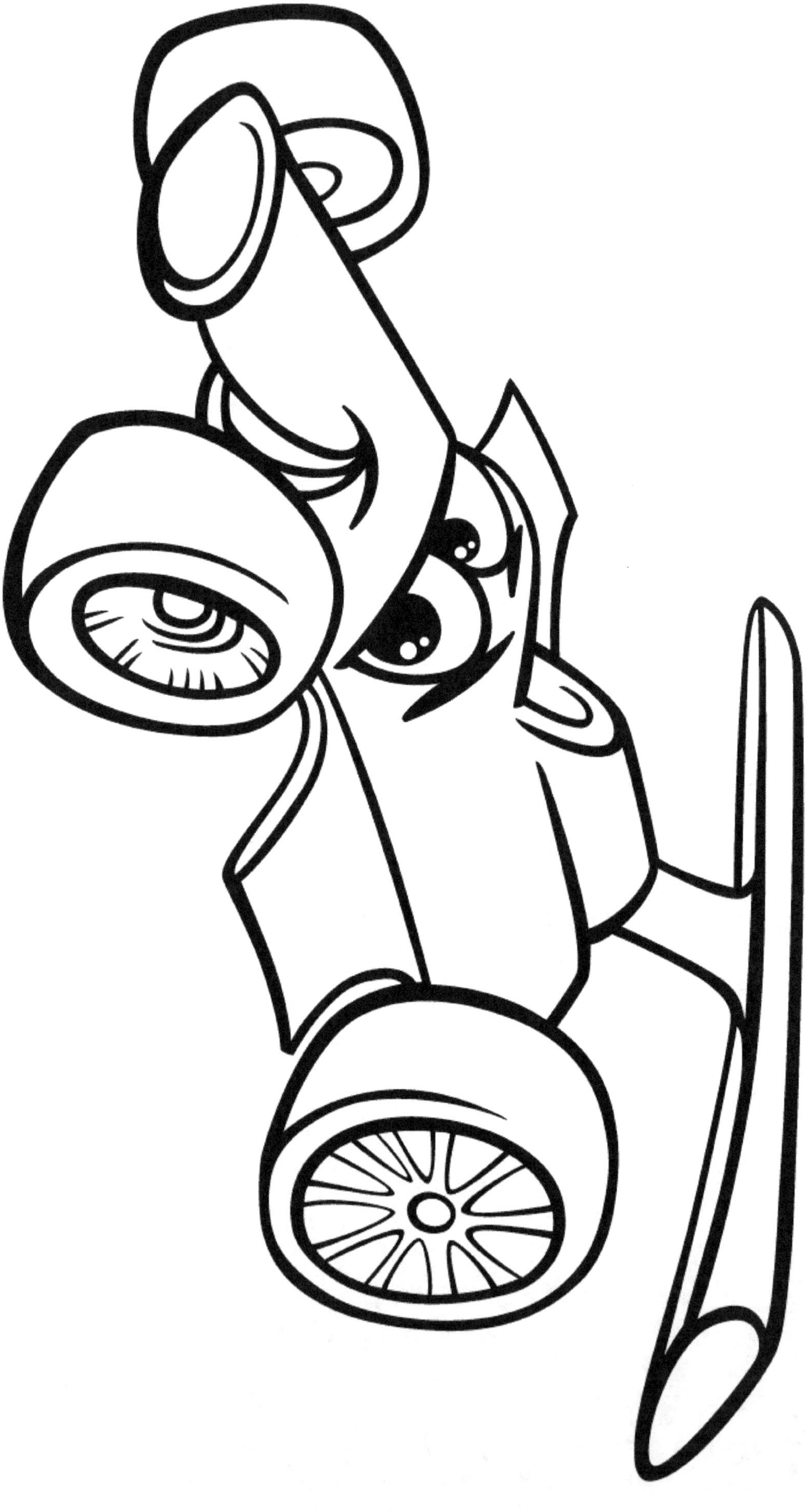

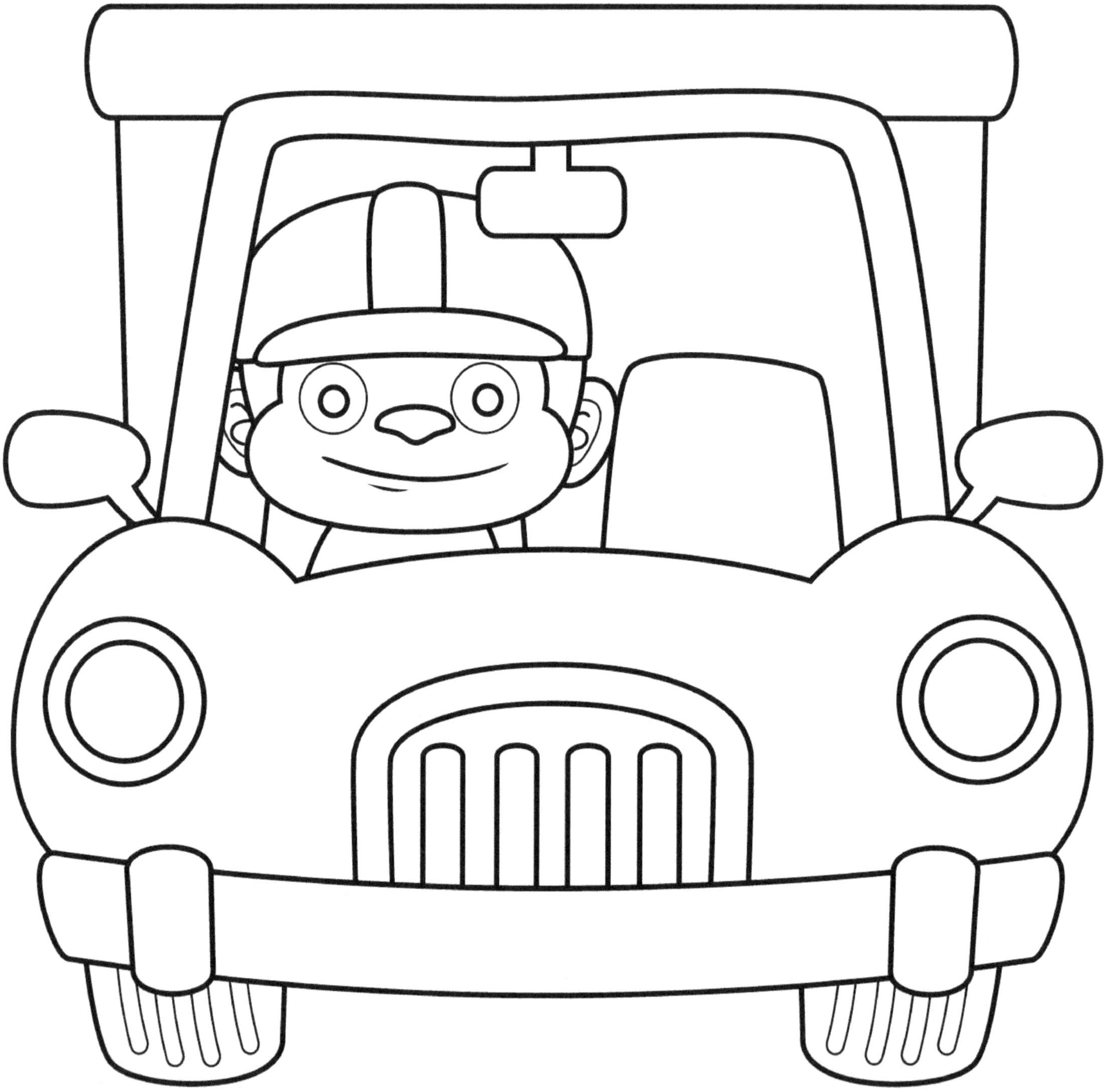

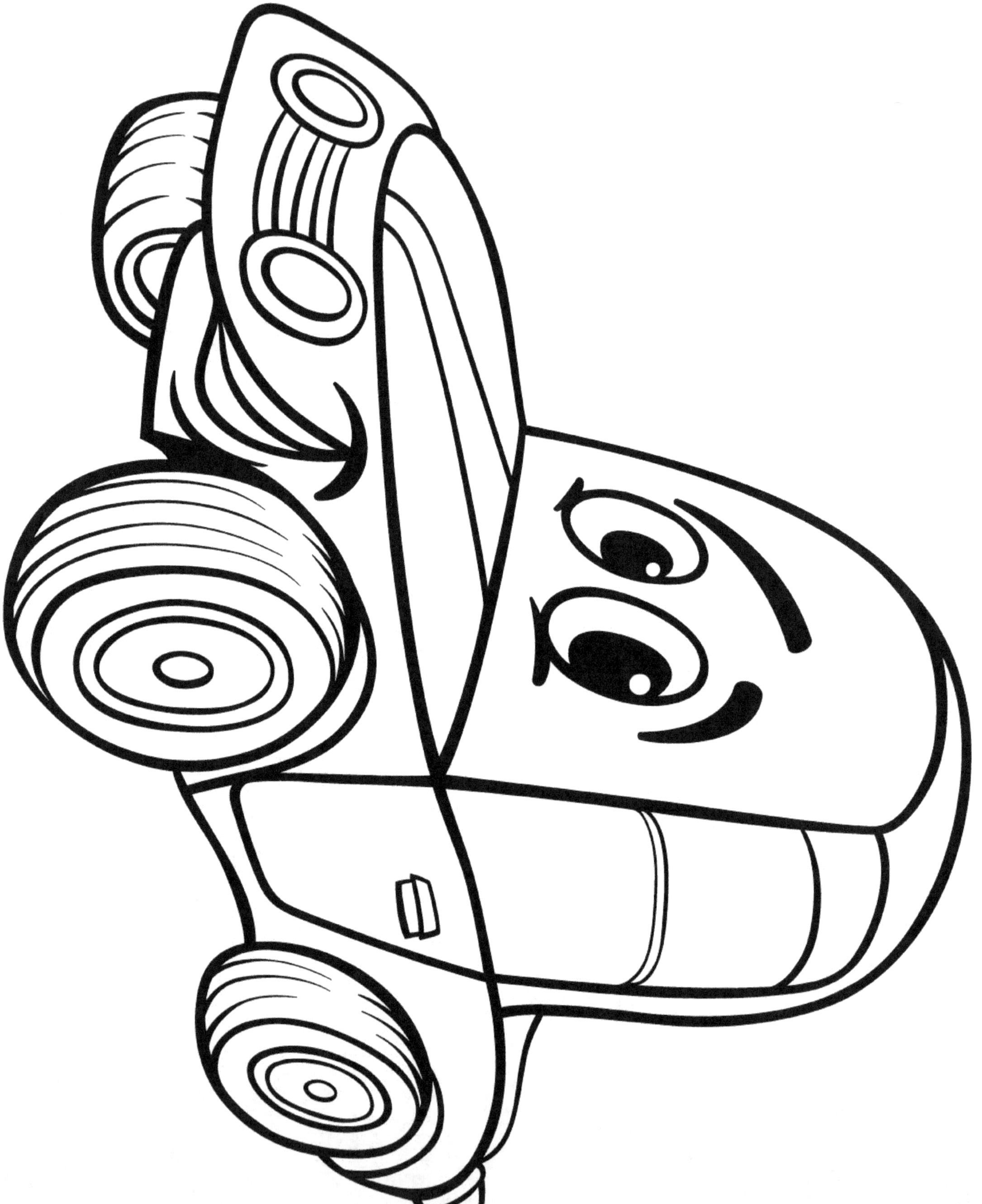

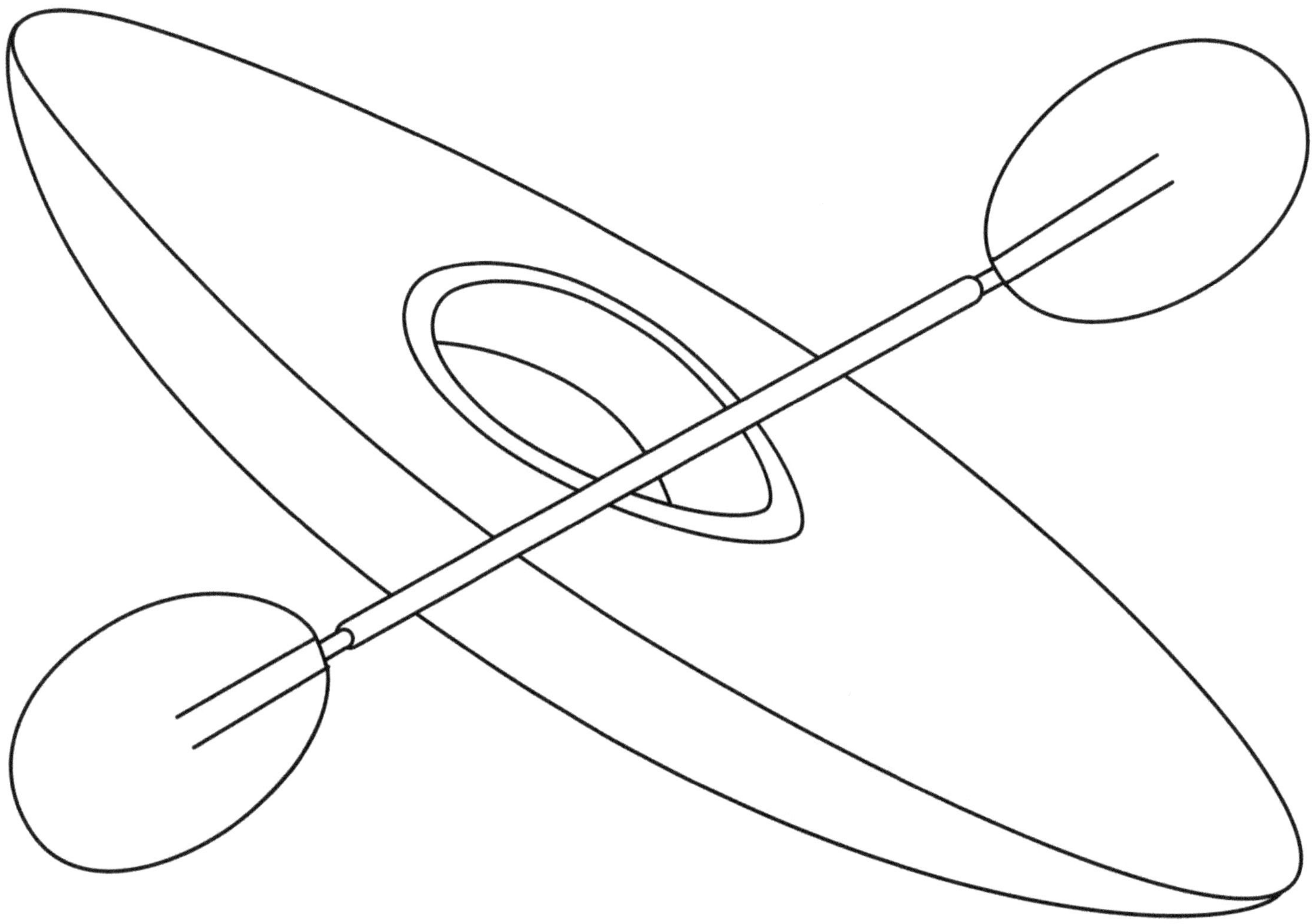

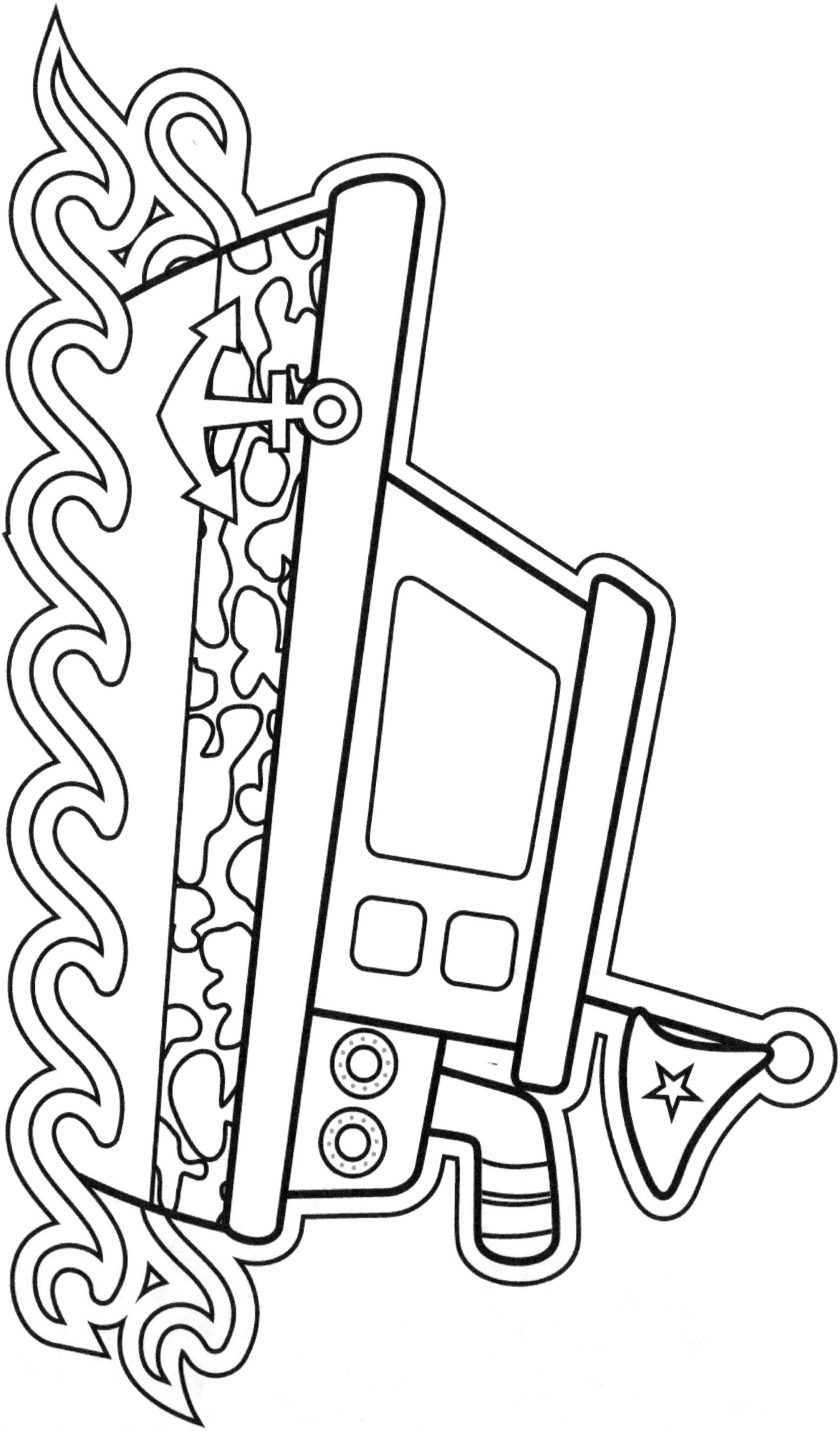

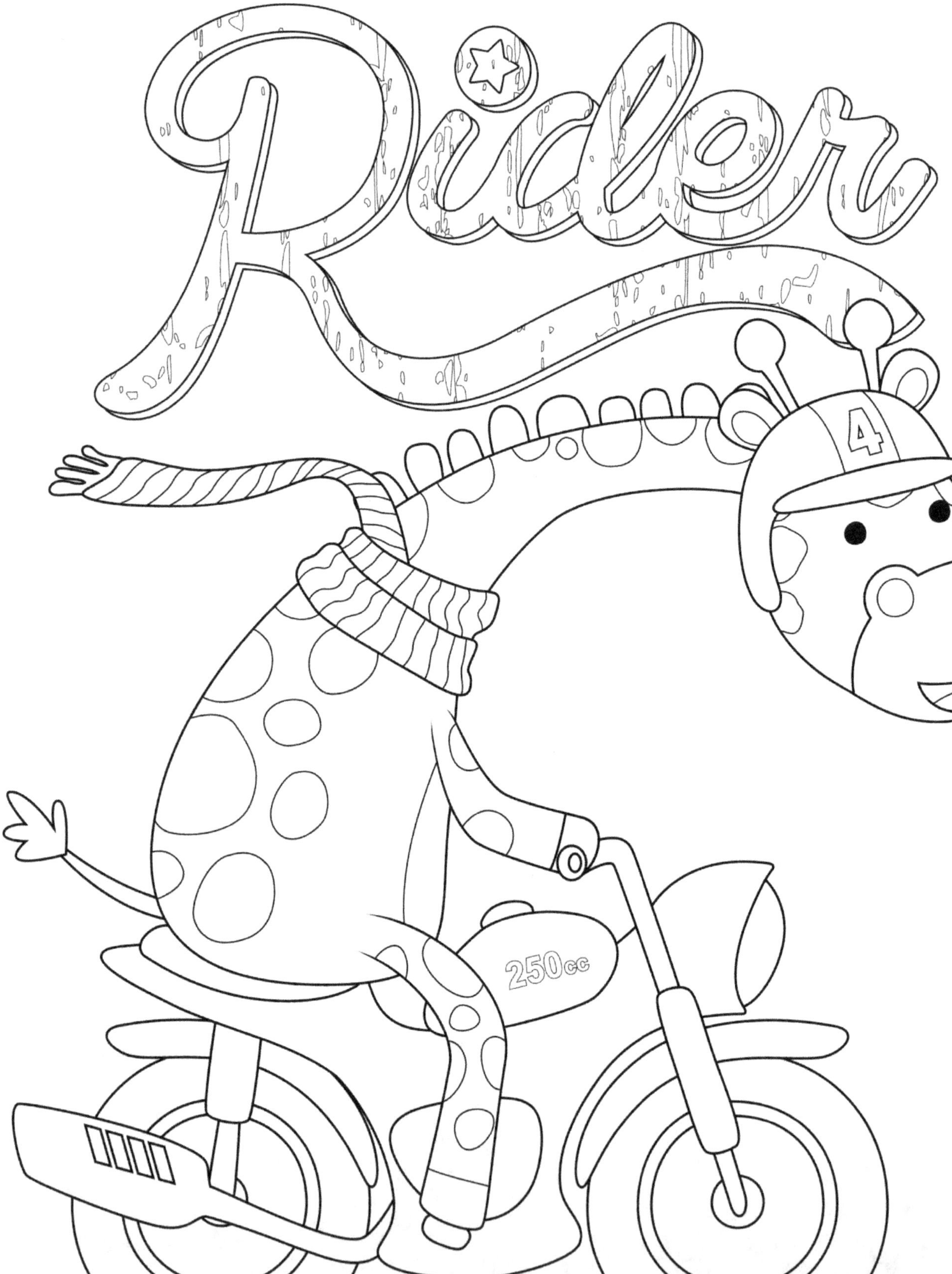
Rider
4
250cc

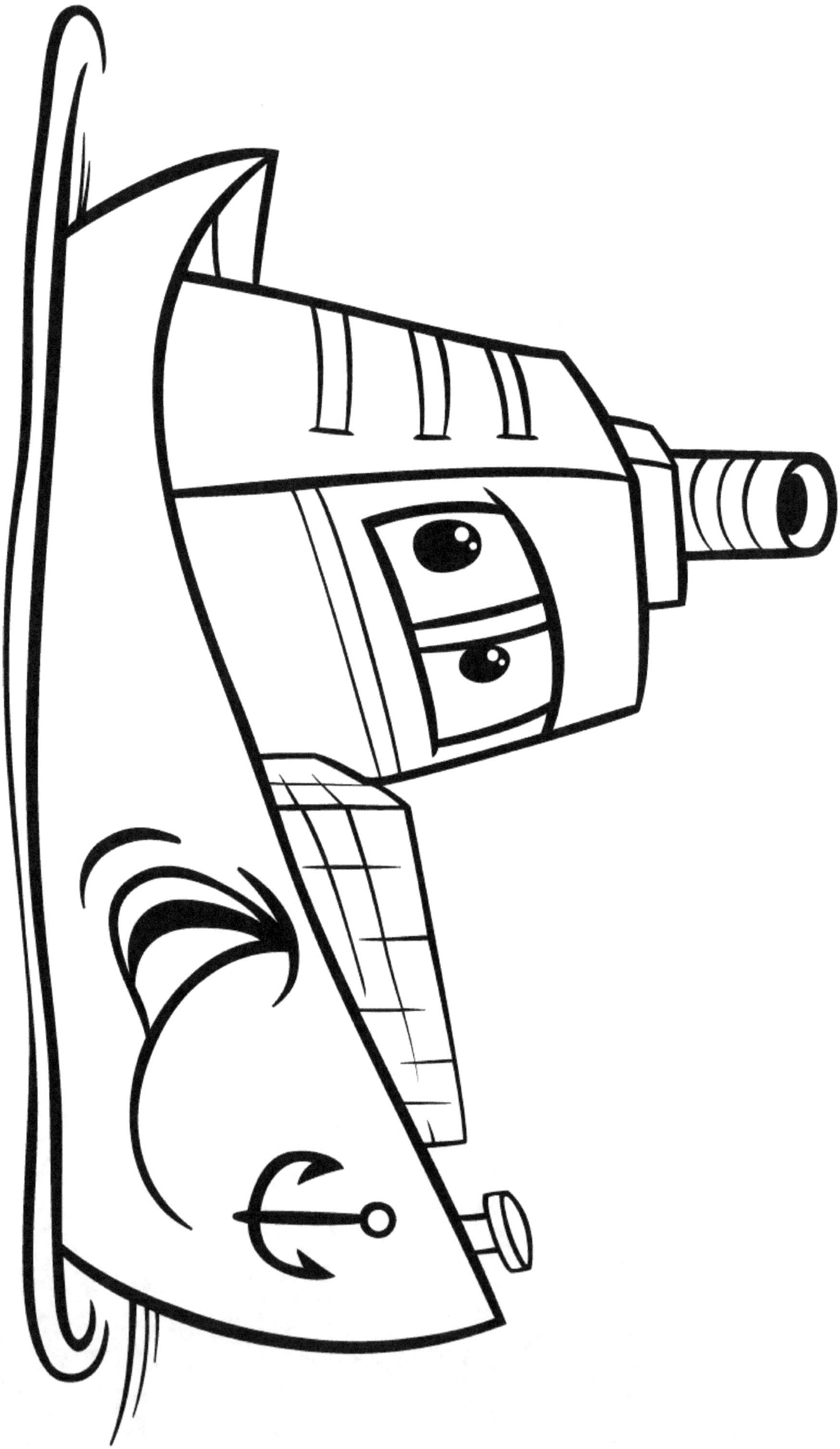

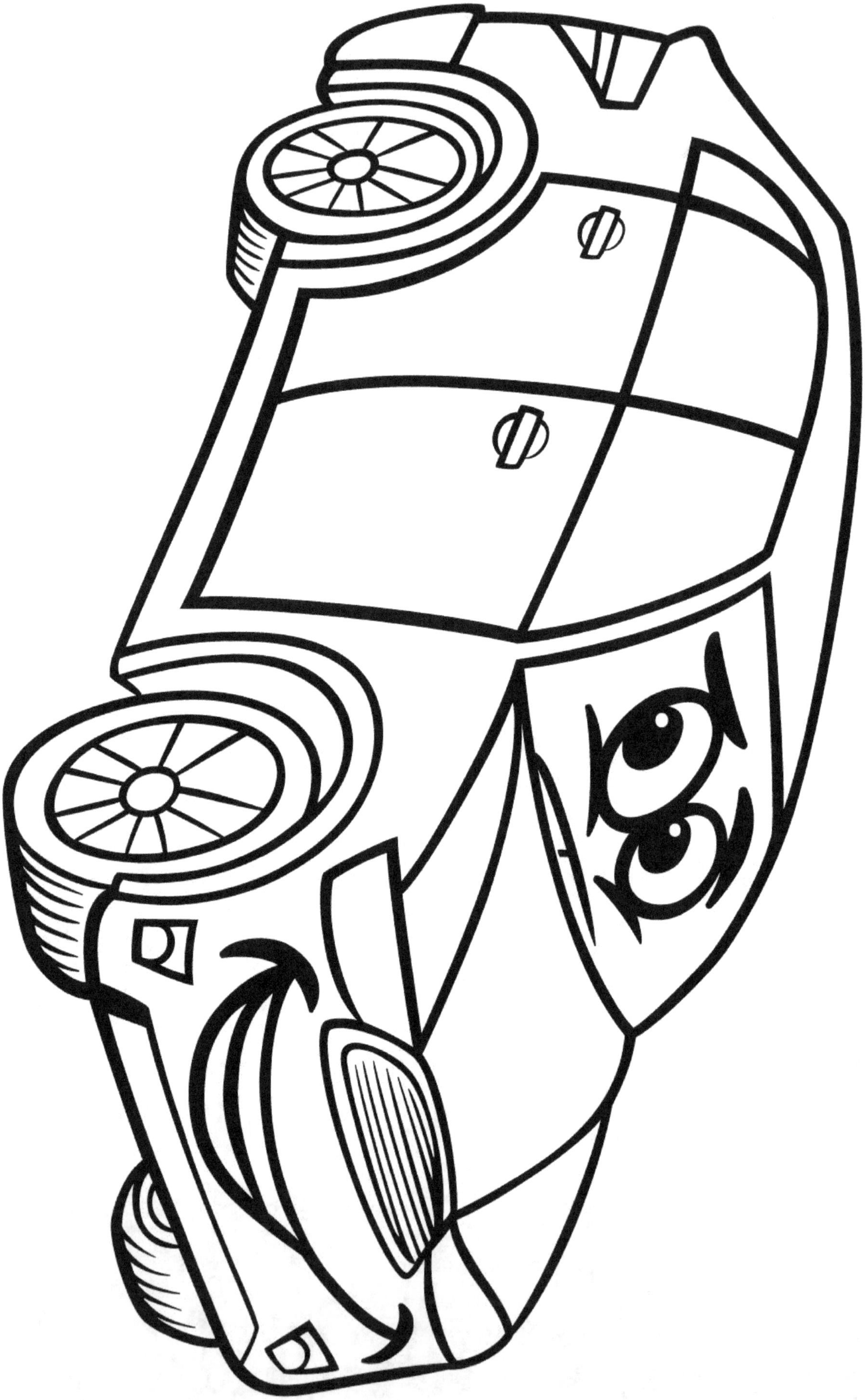

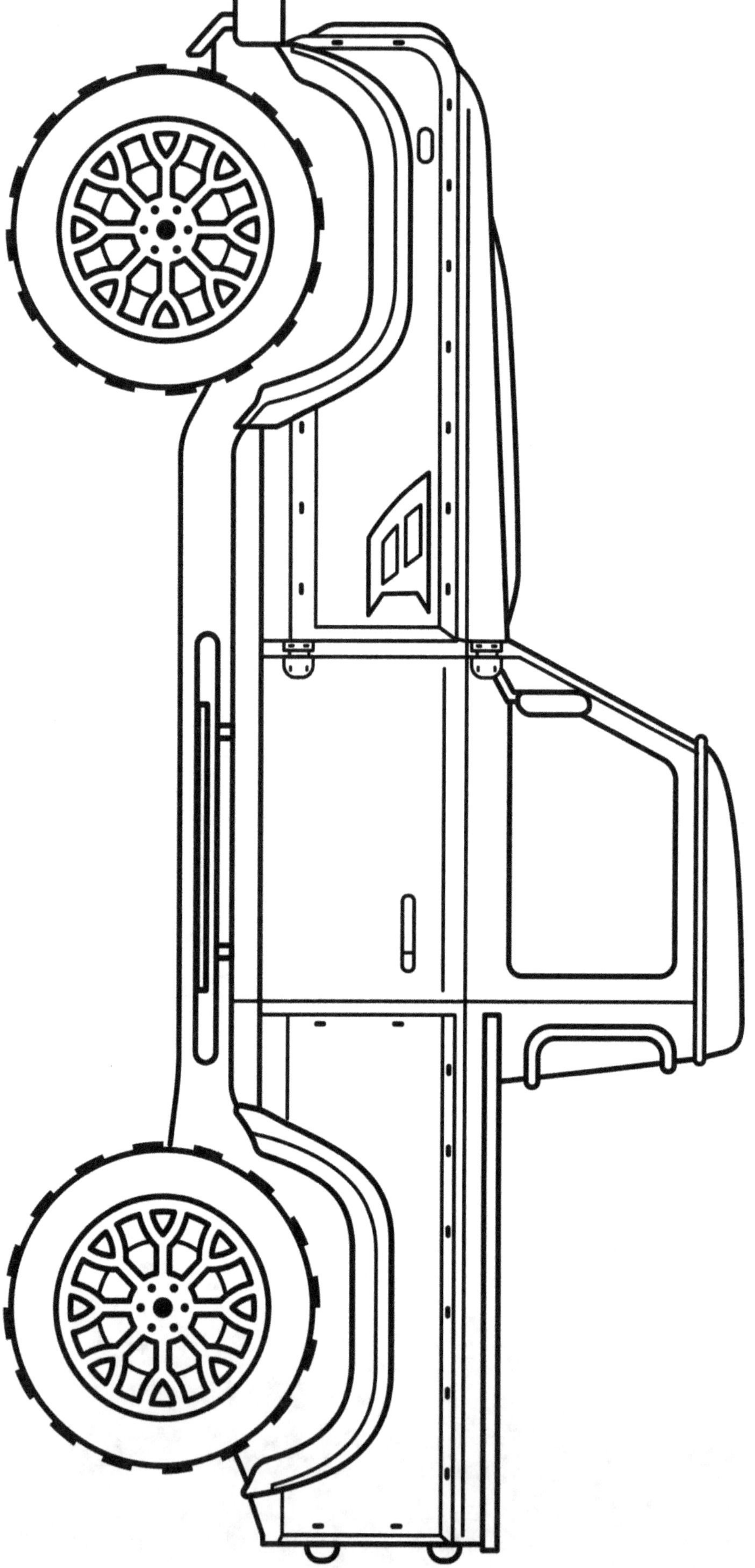

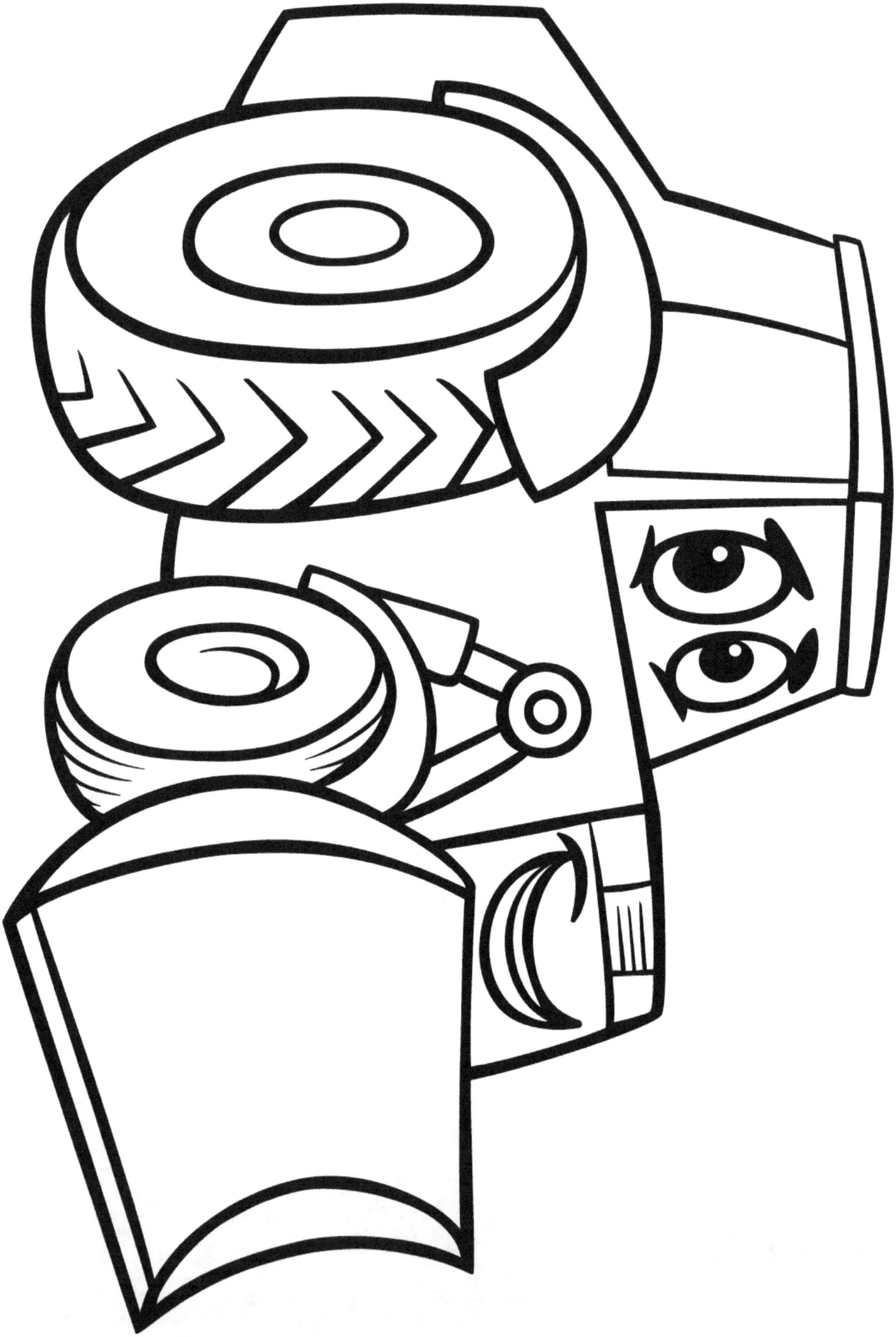

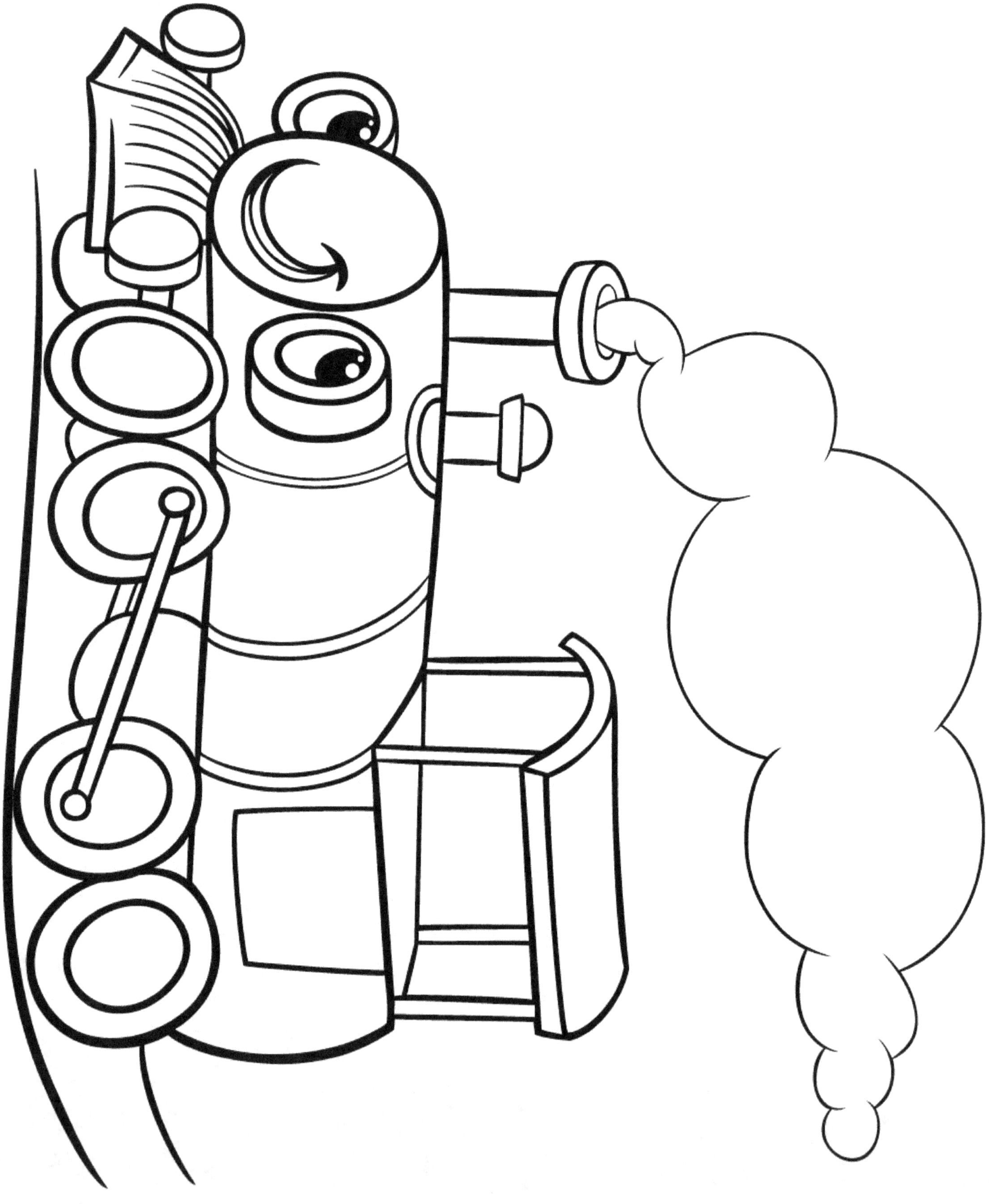

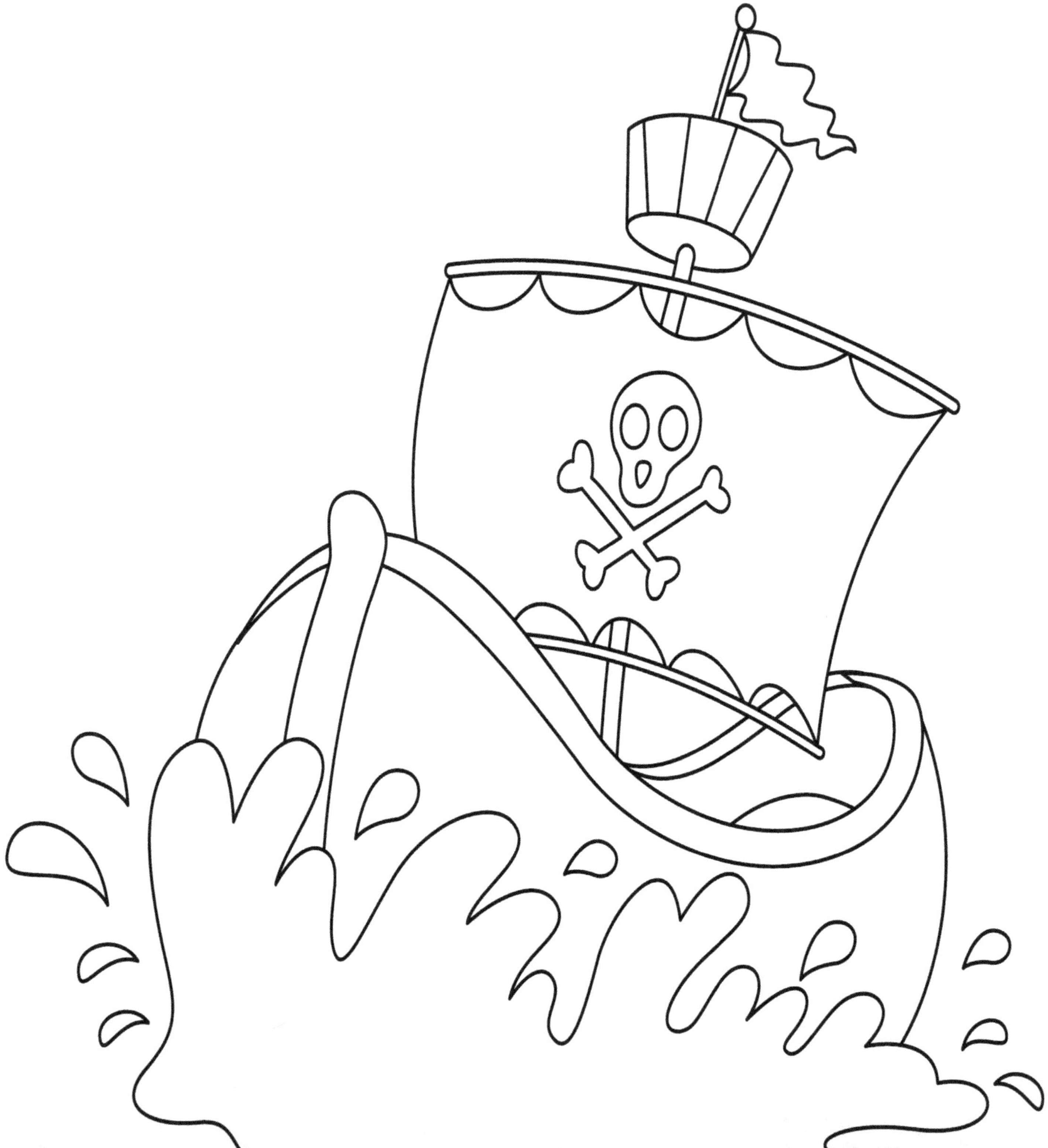

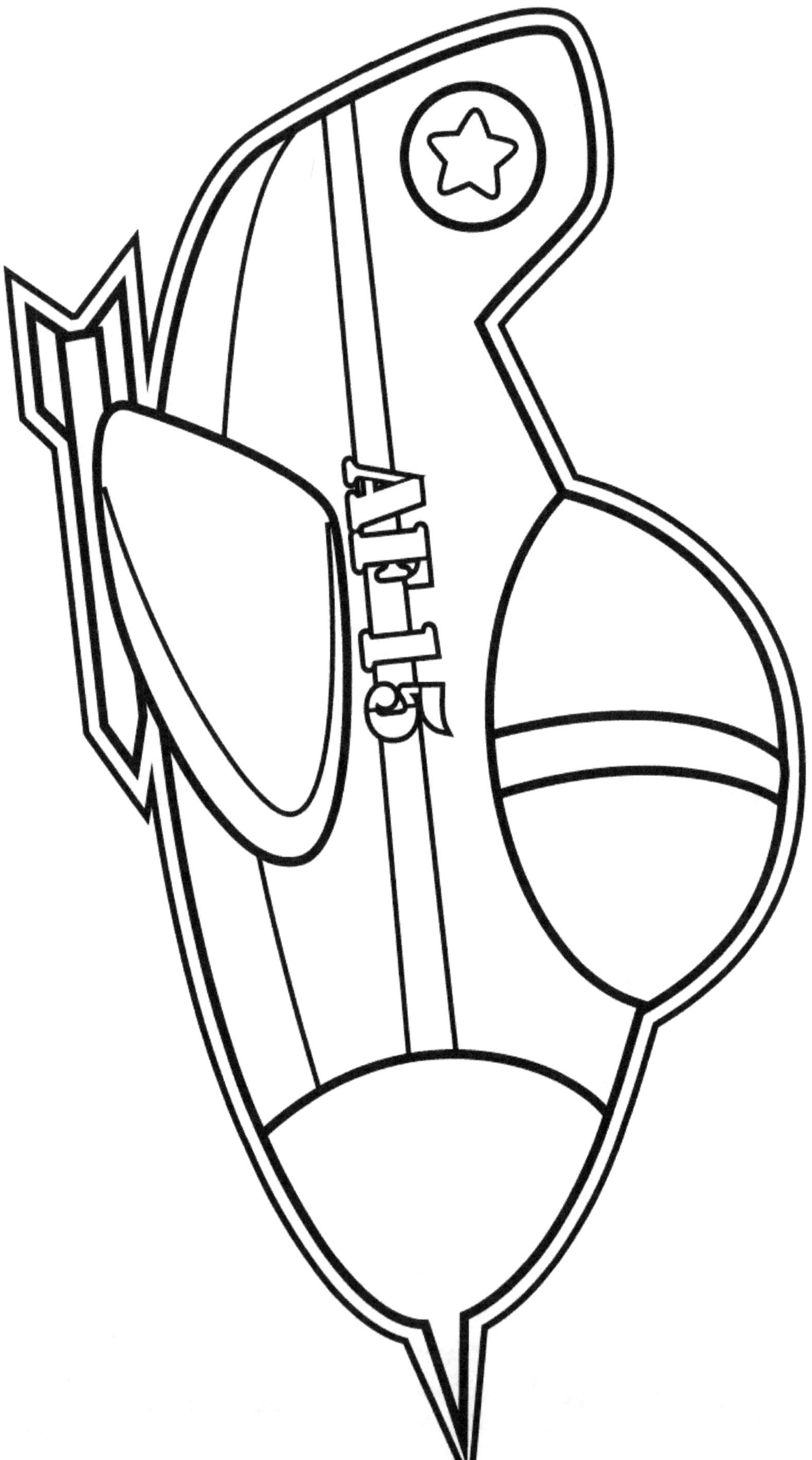
AF15

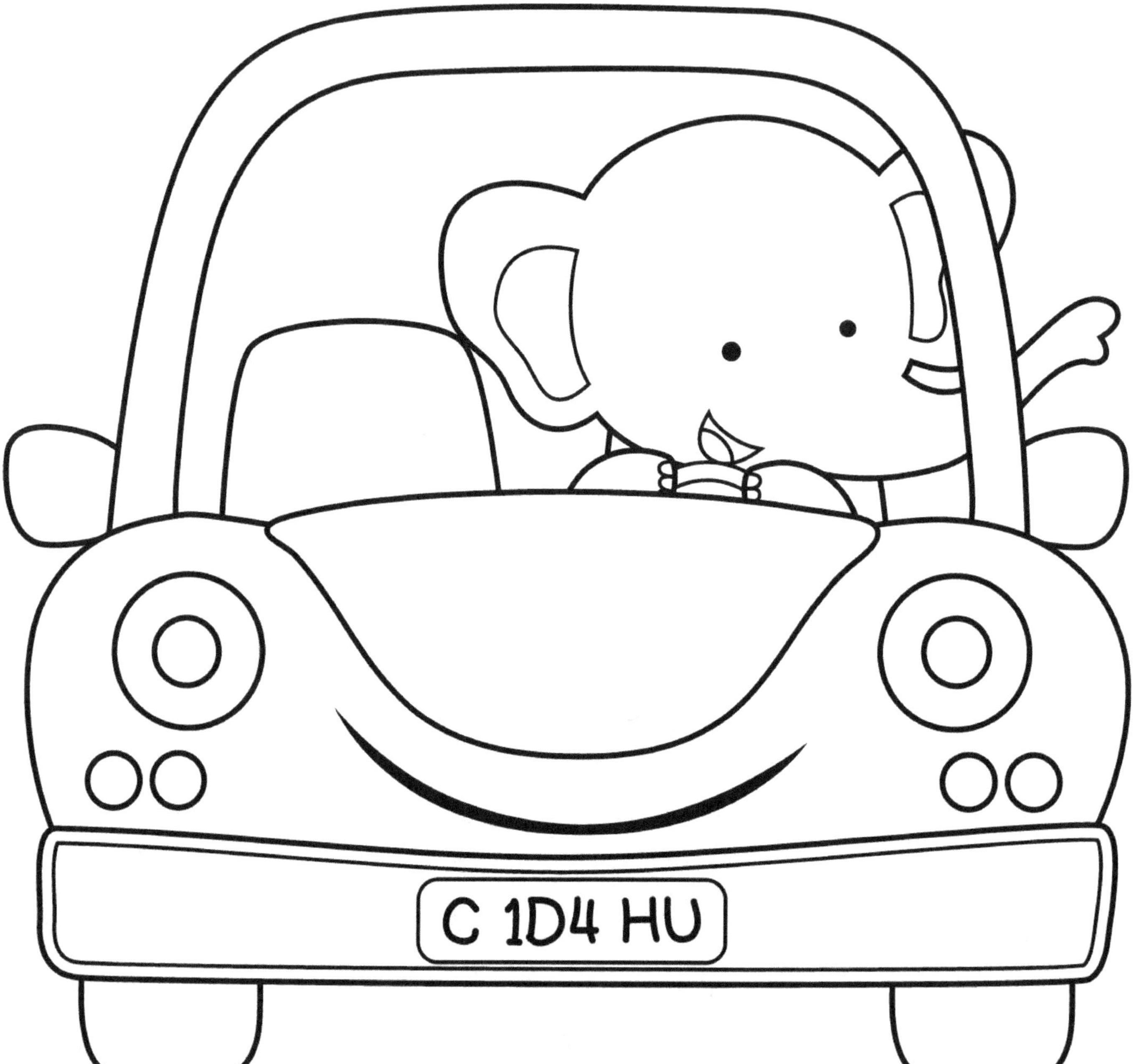
C 1D4 HU

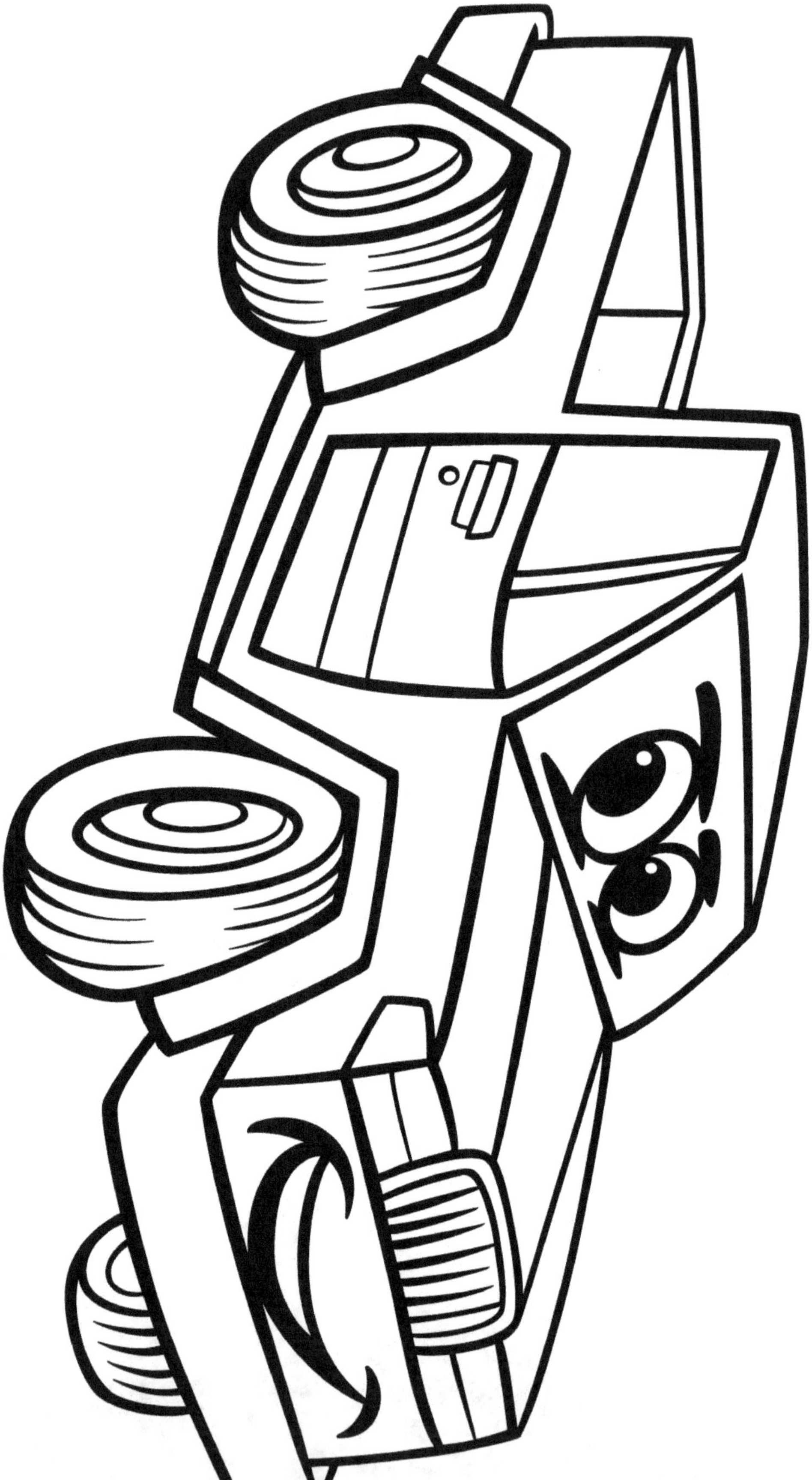

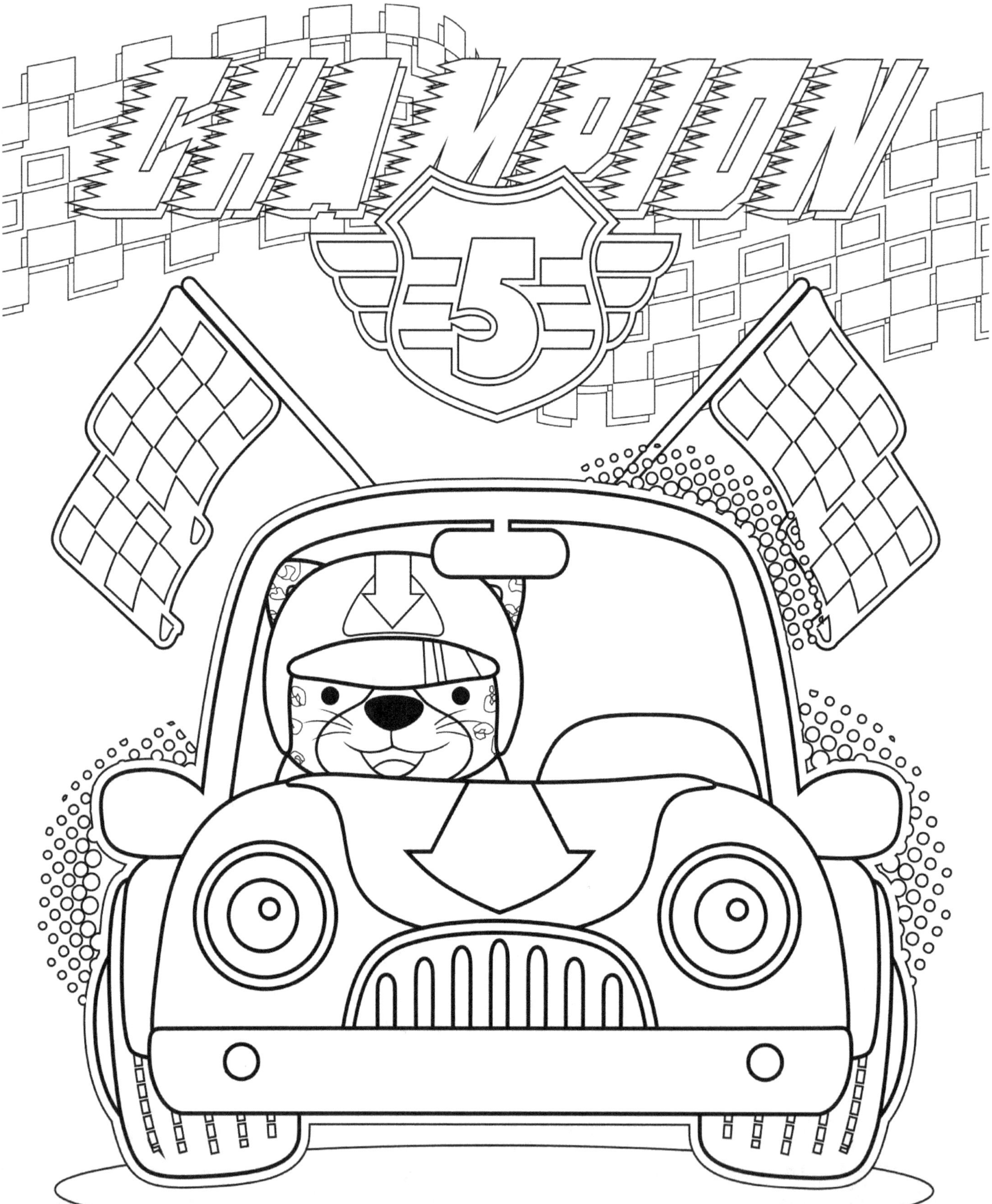
CHAMPION
5

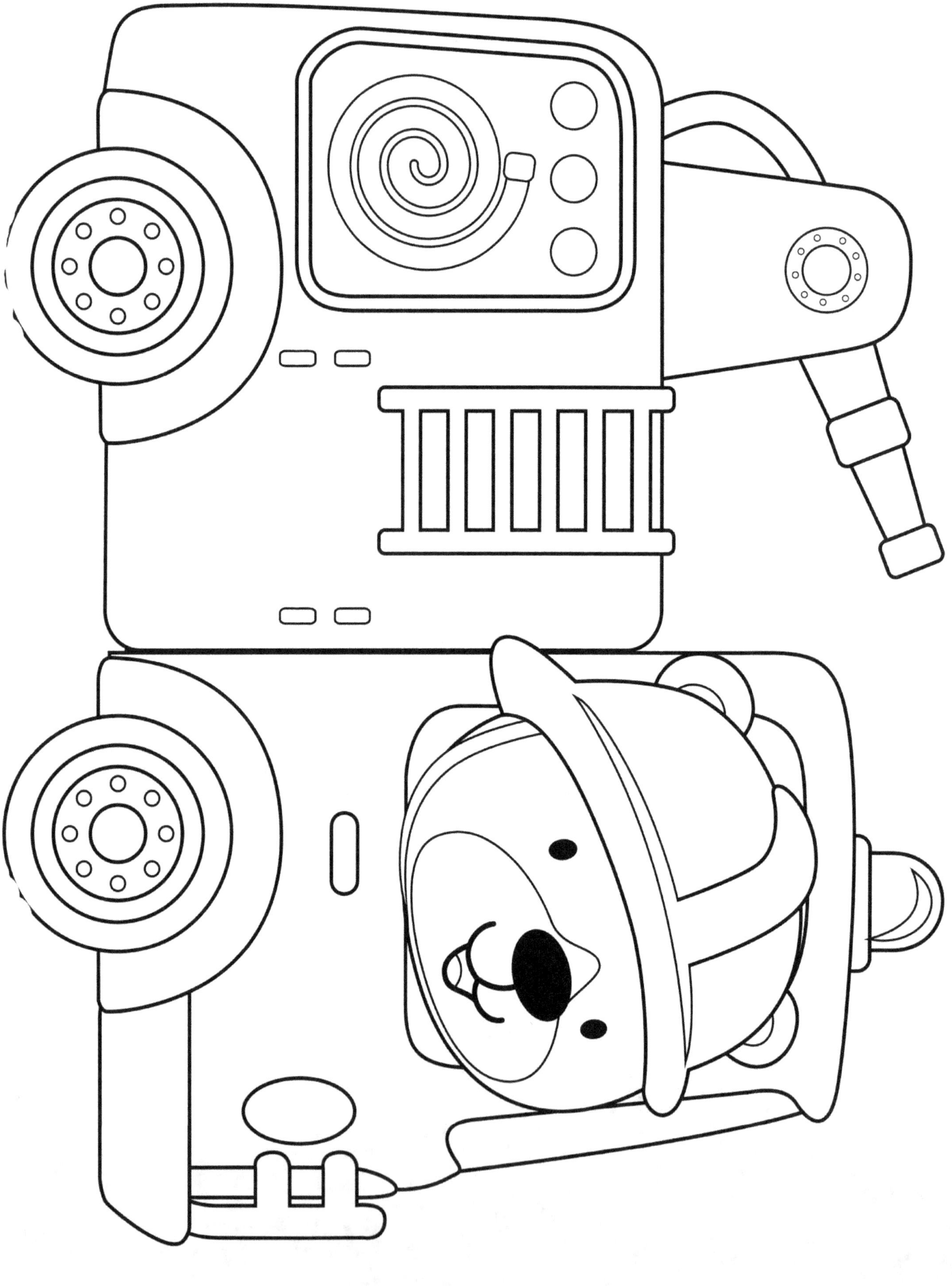

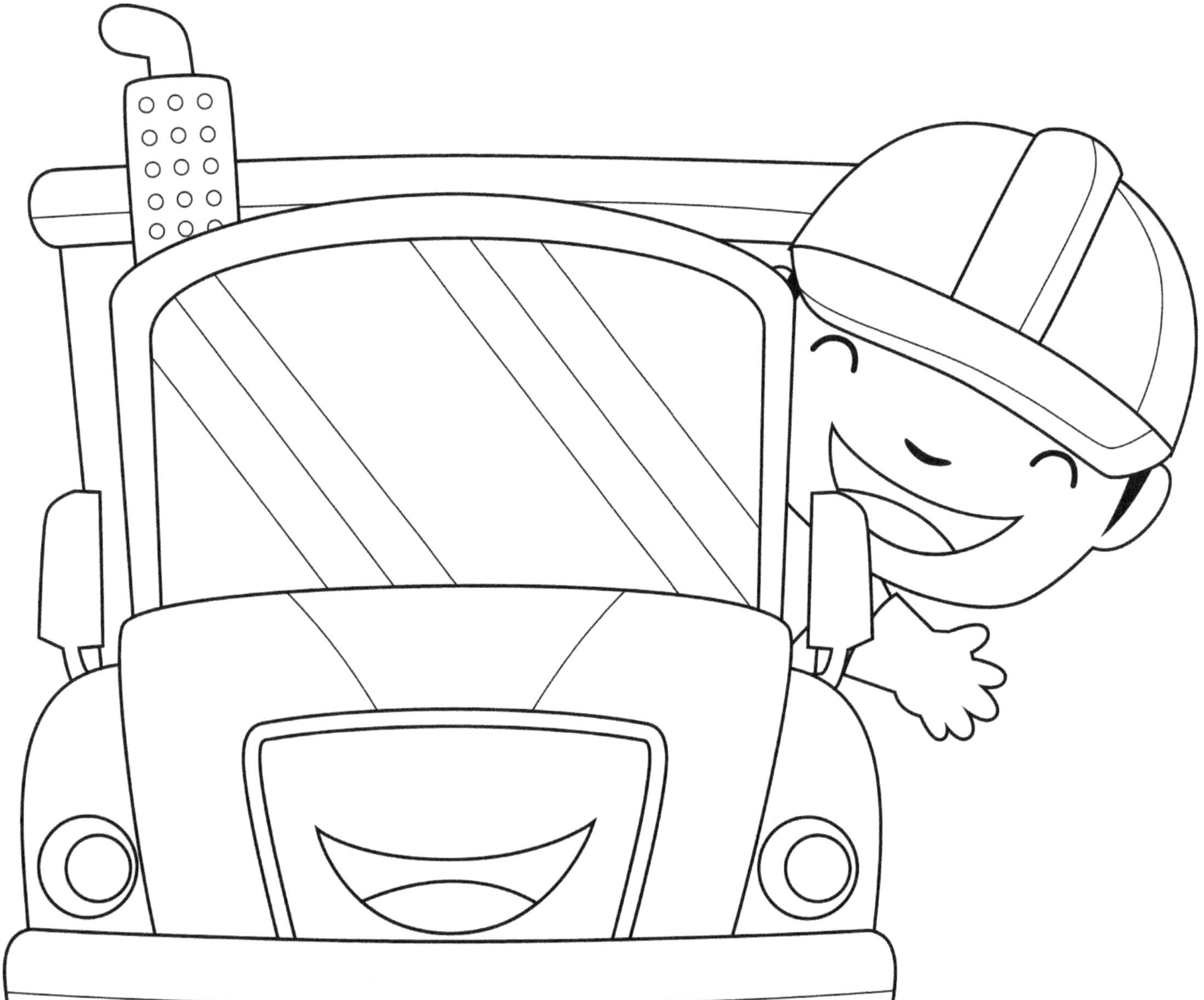

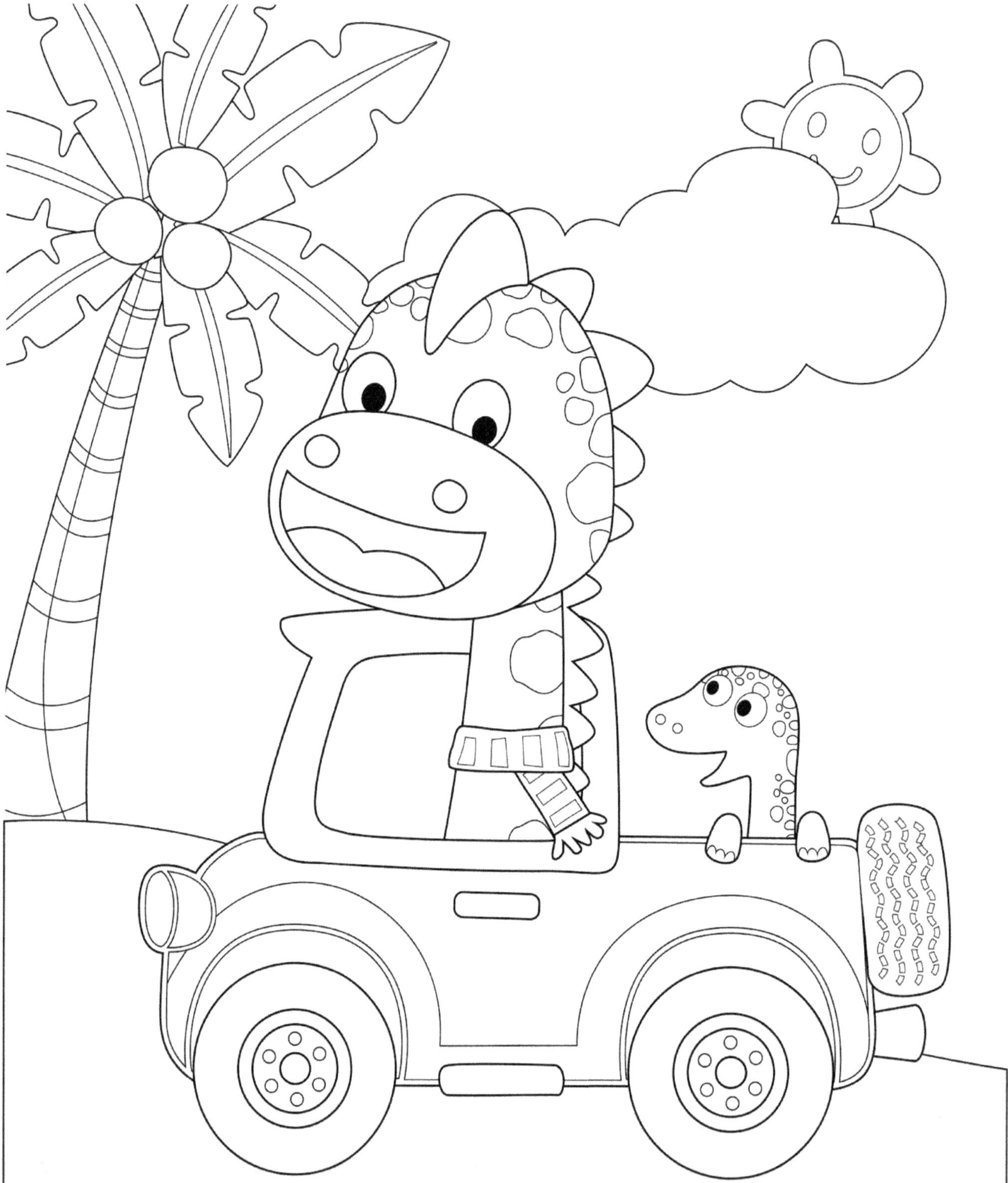

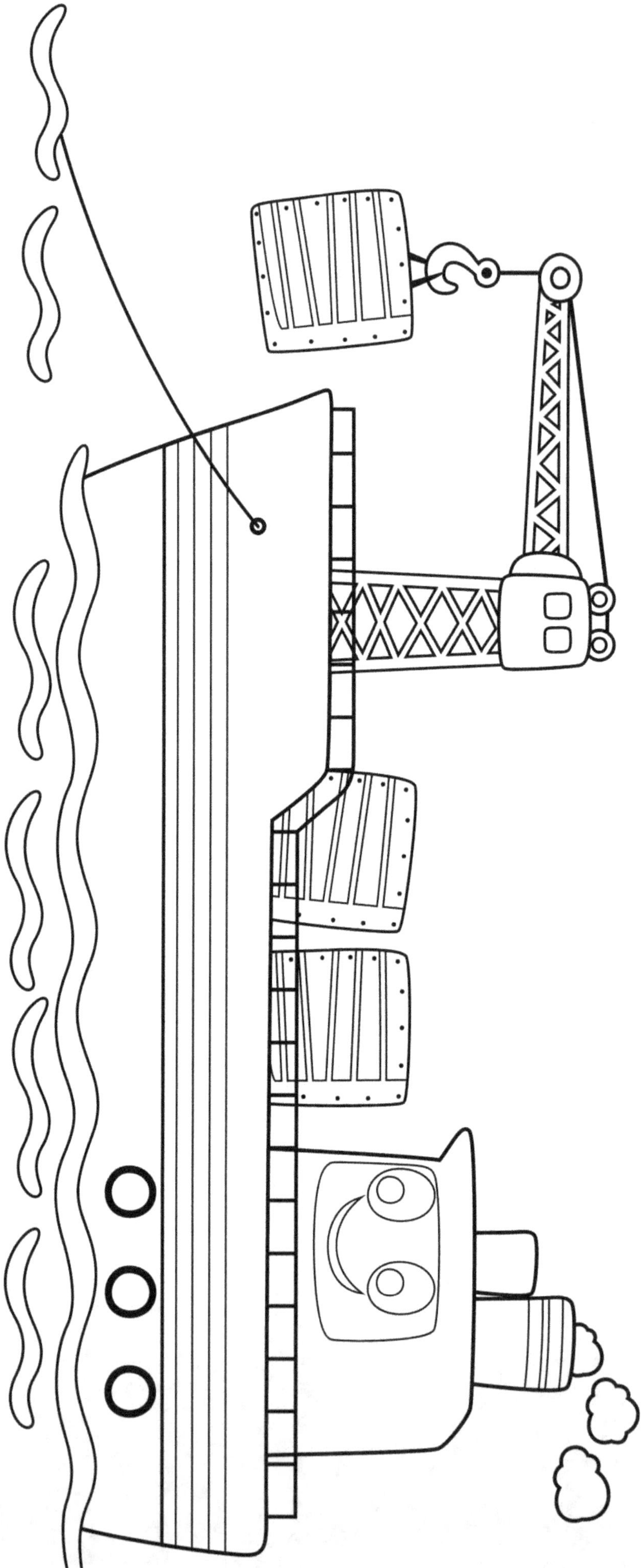

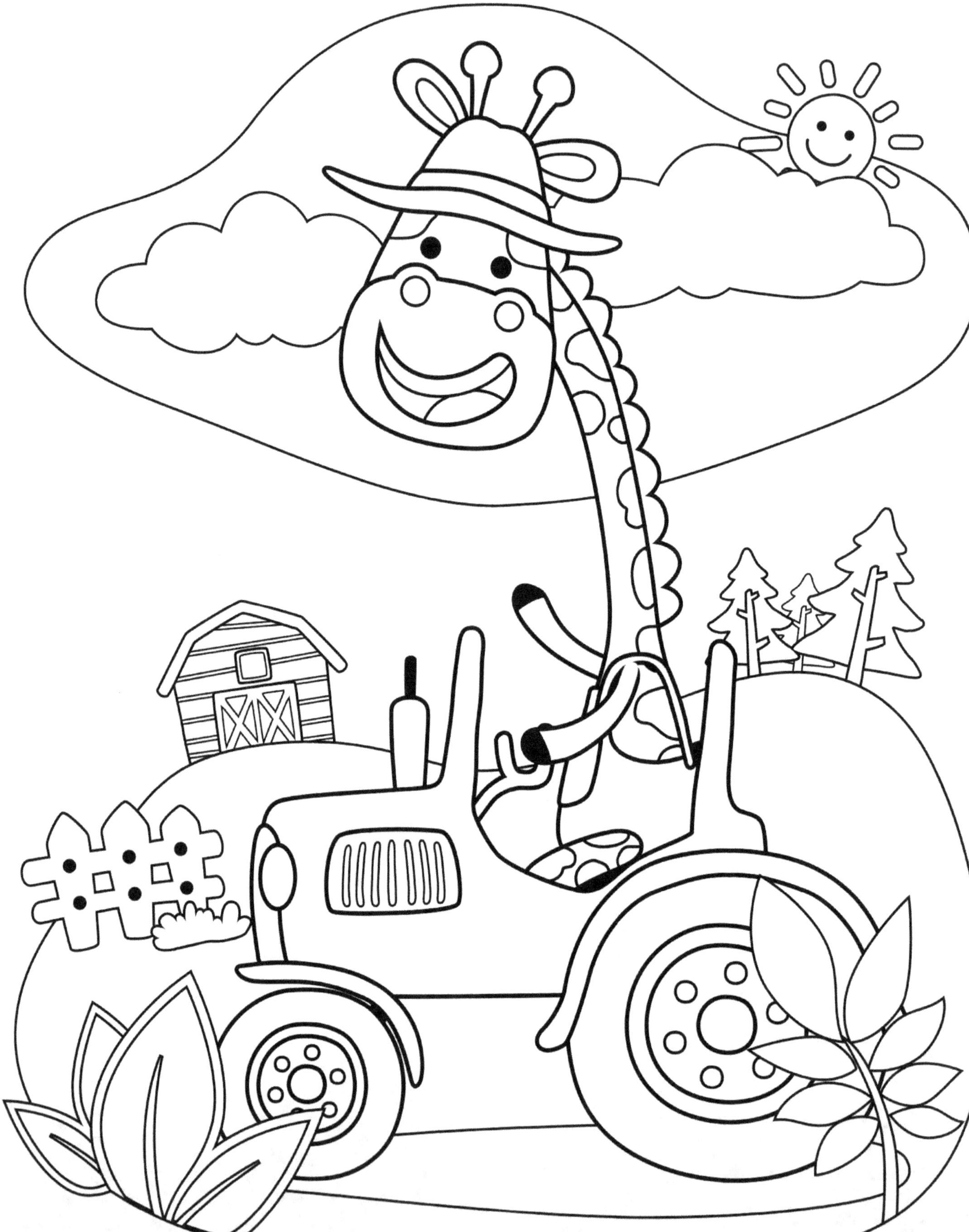

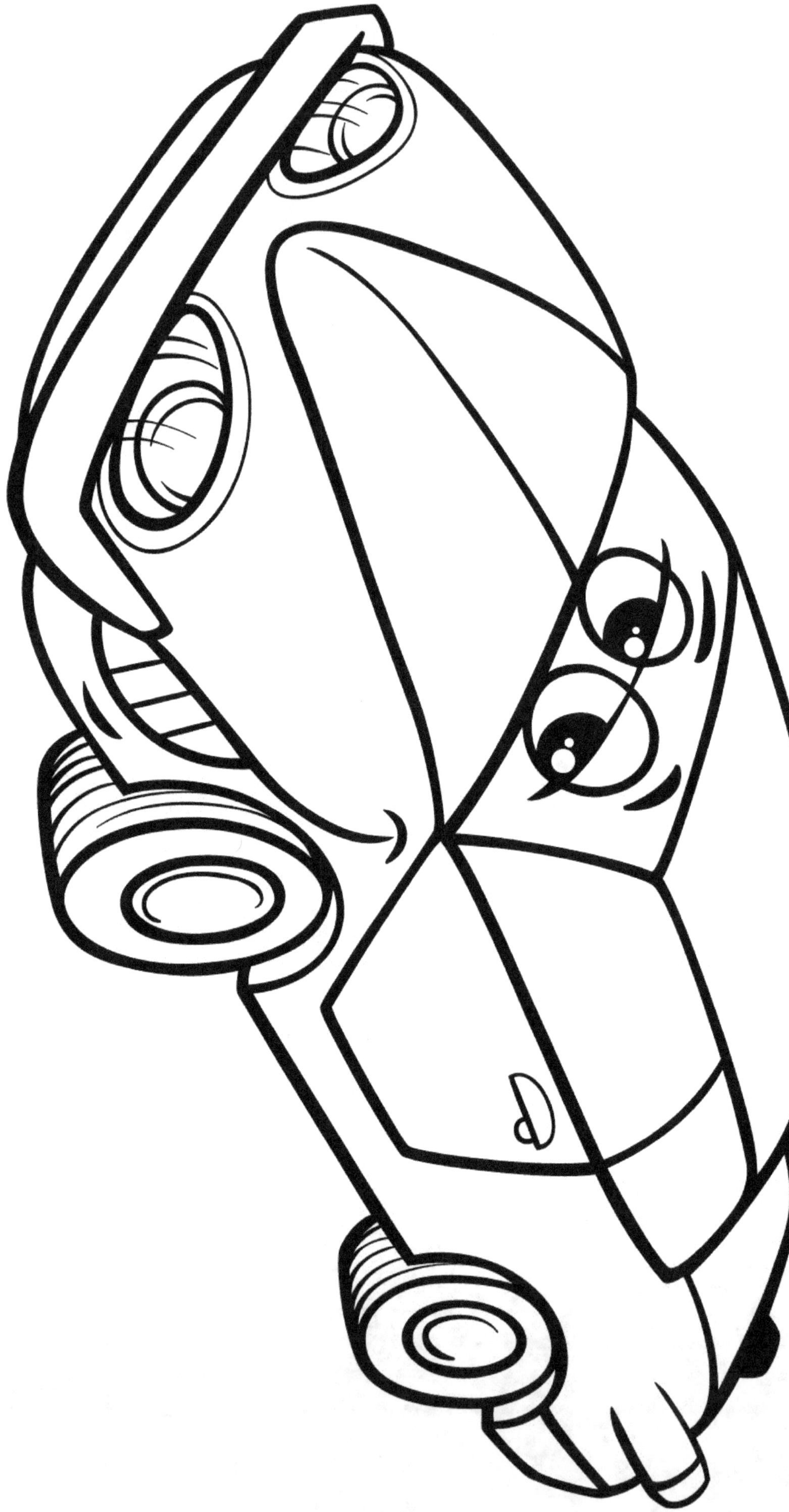

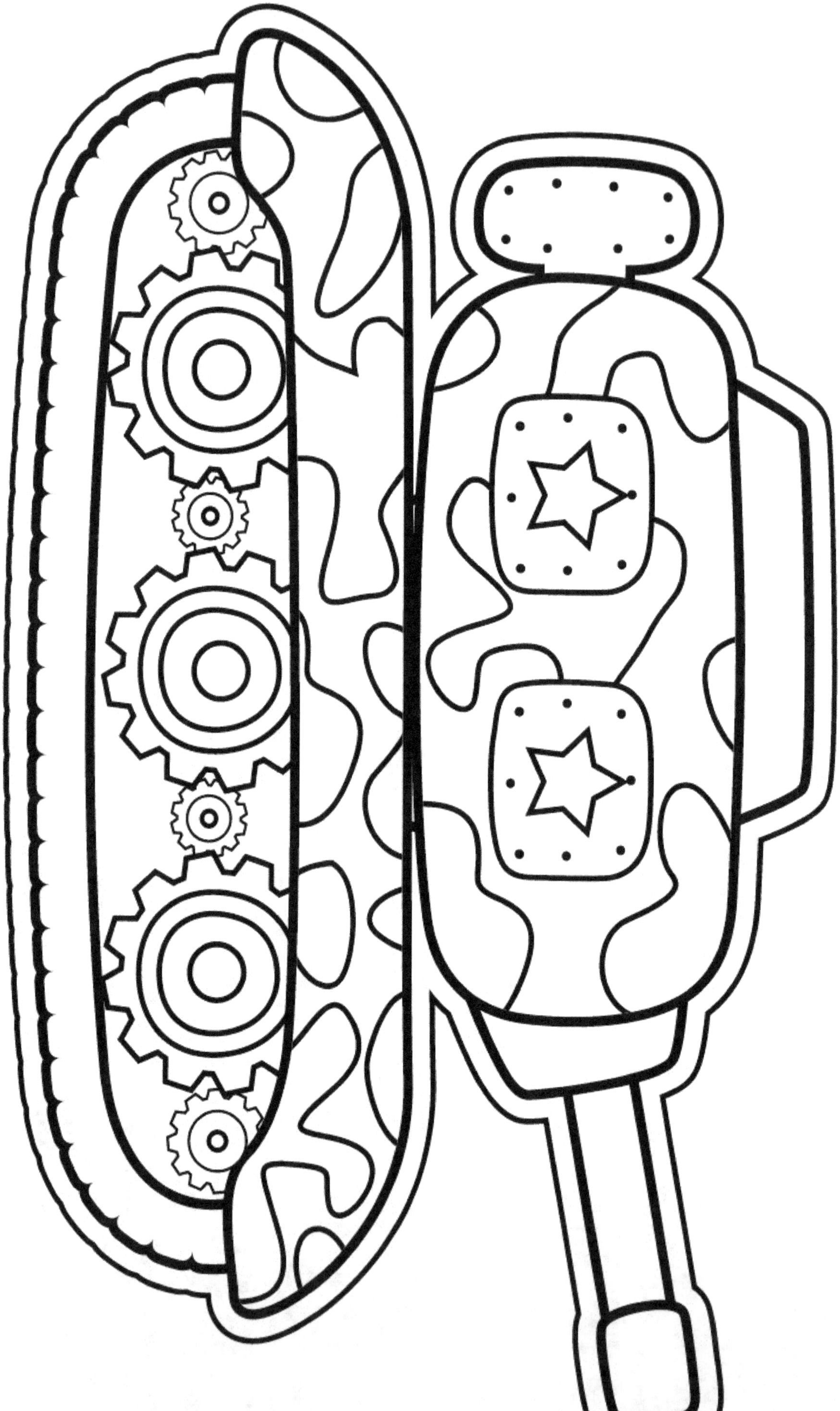

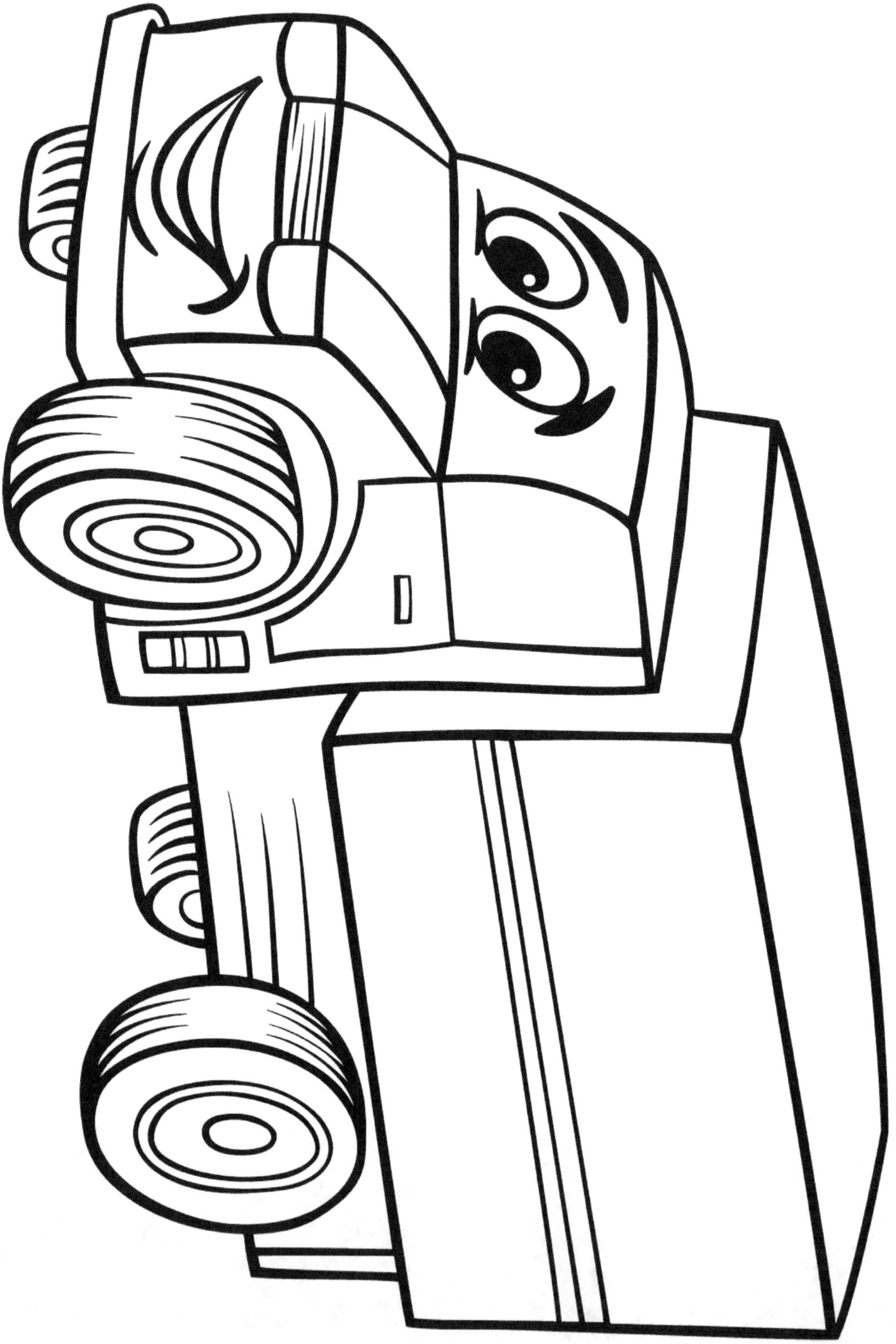

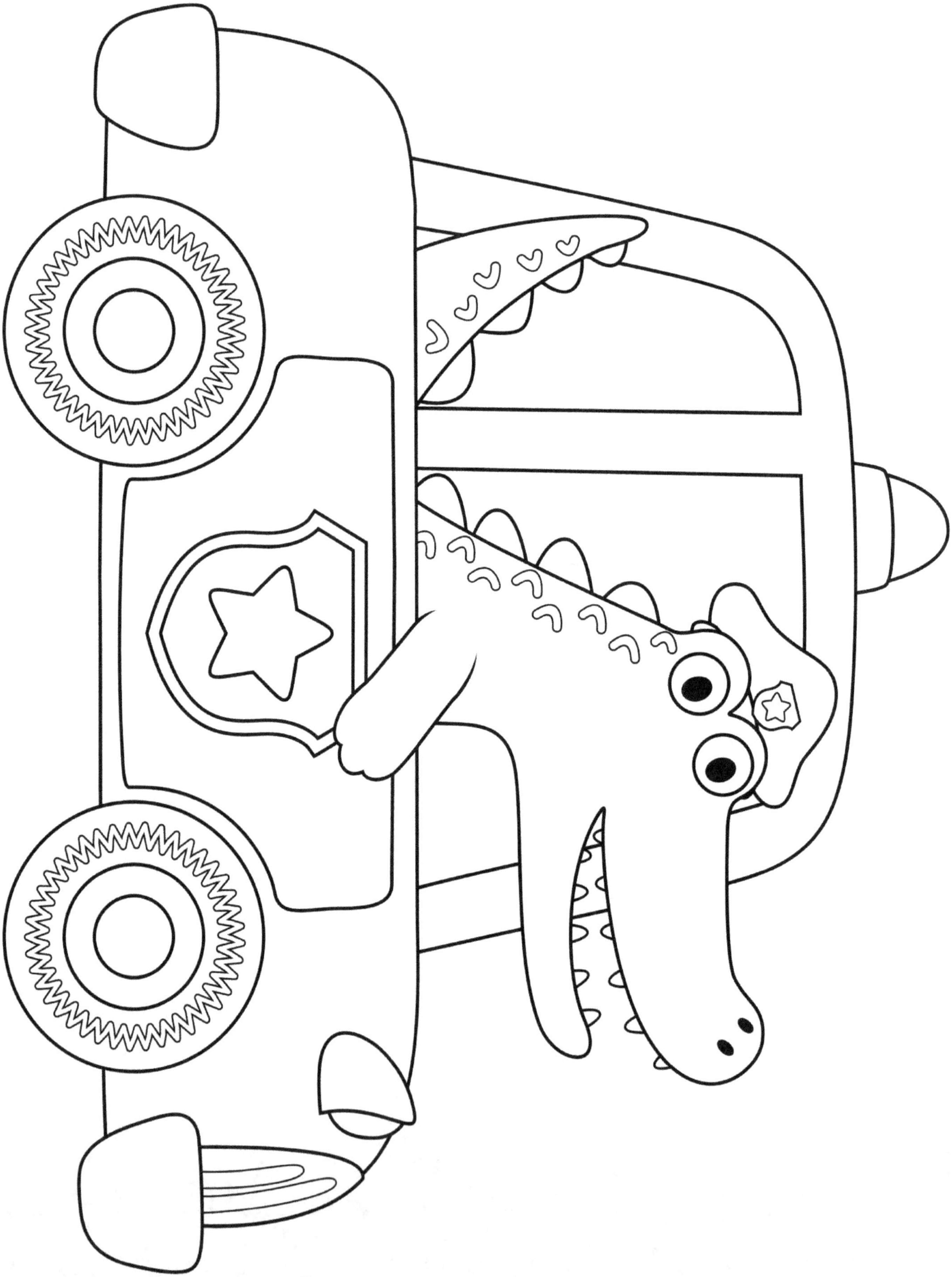

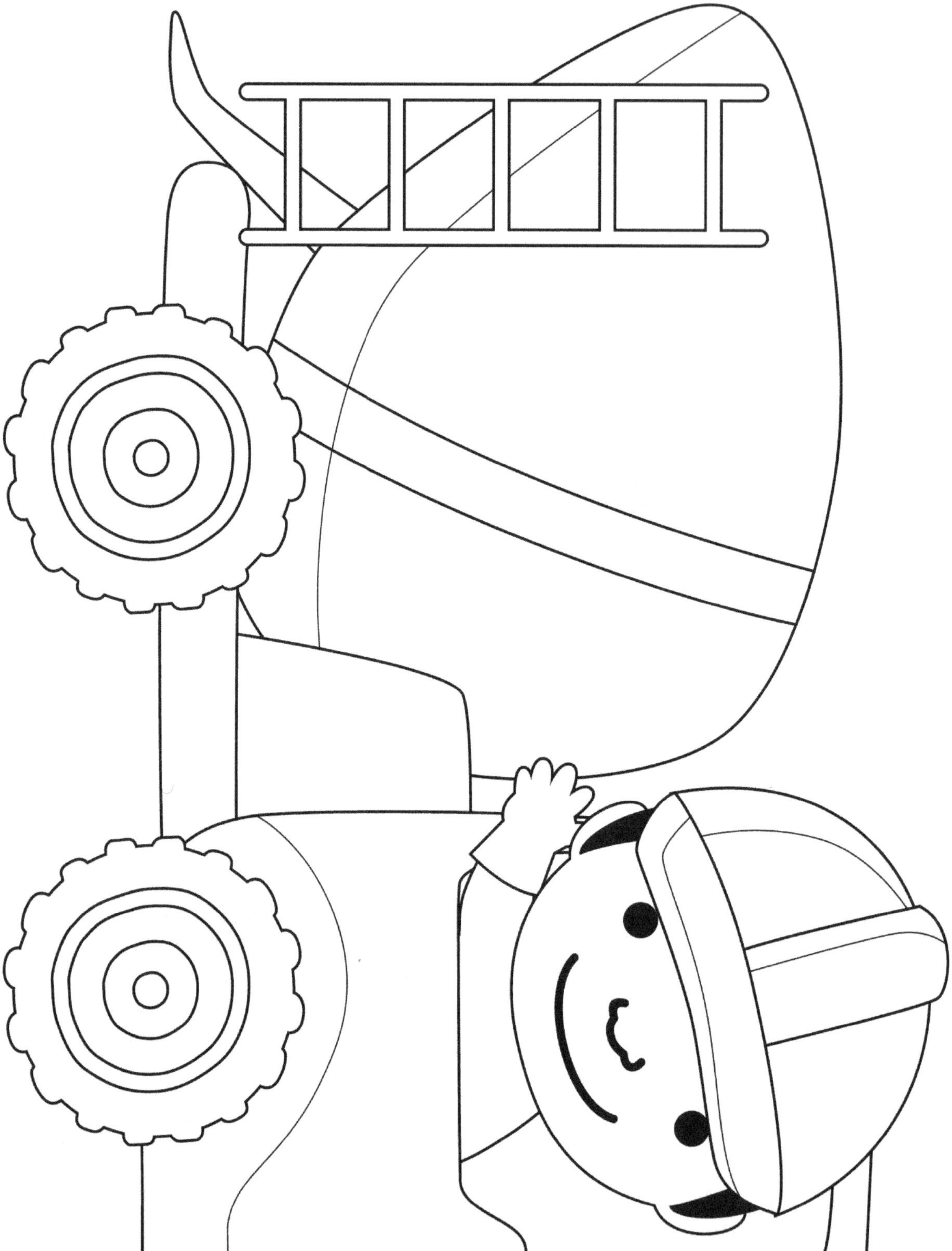

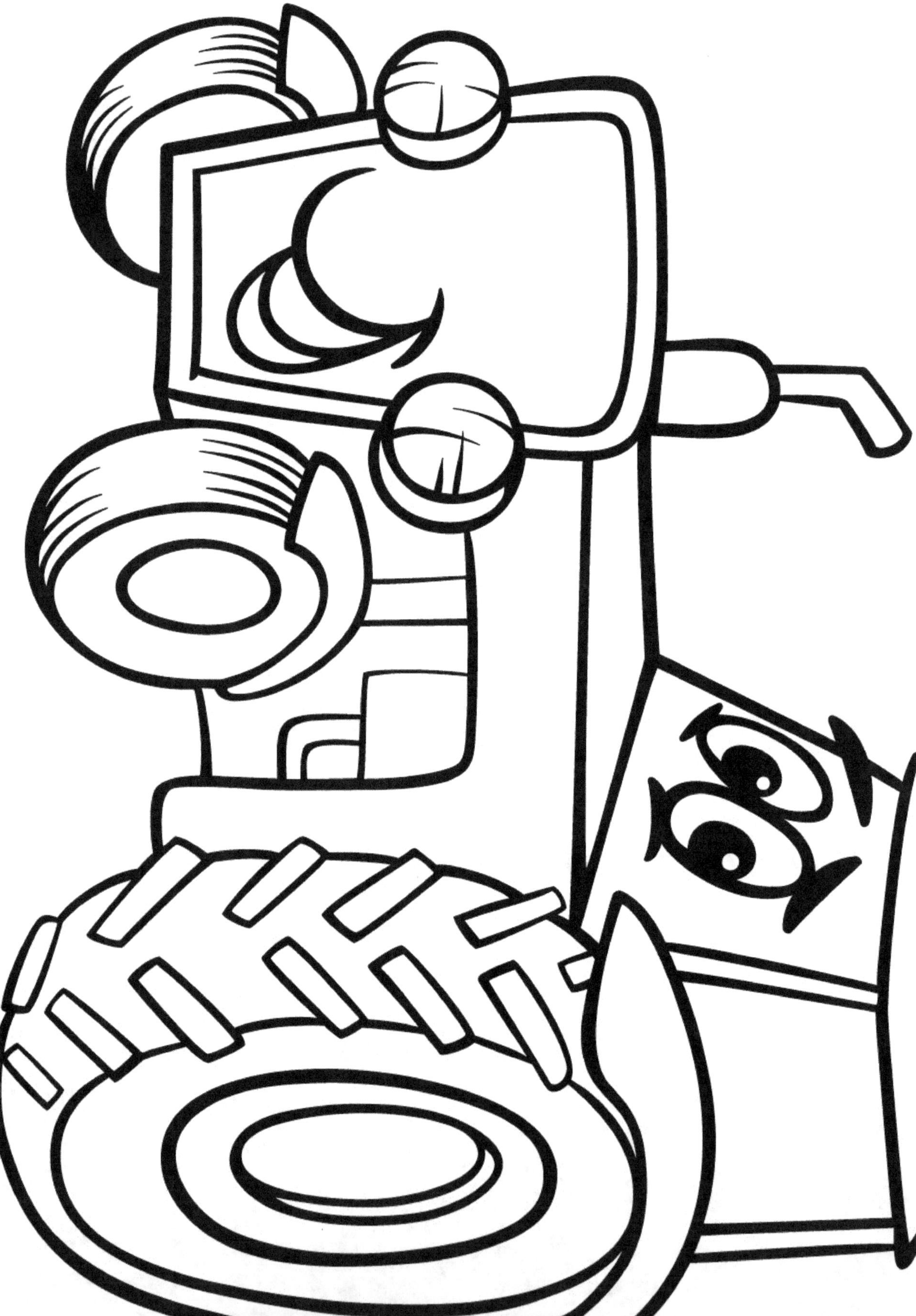

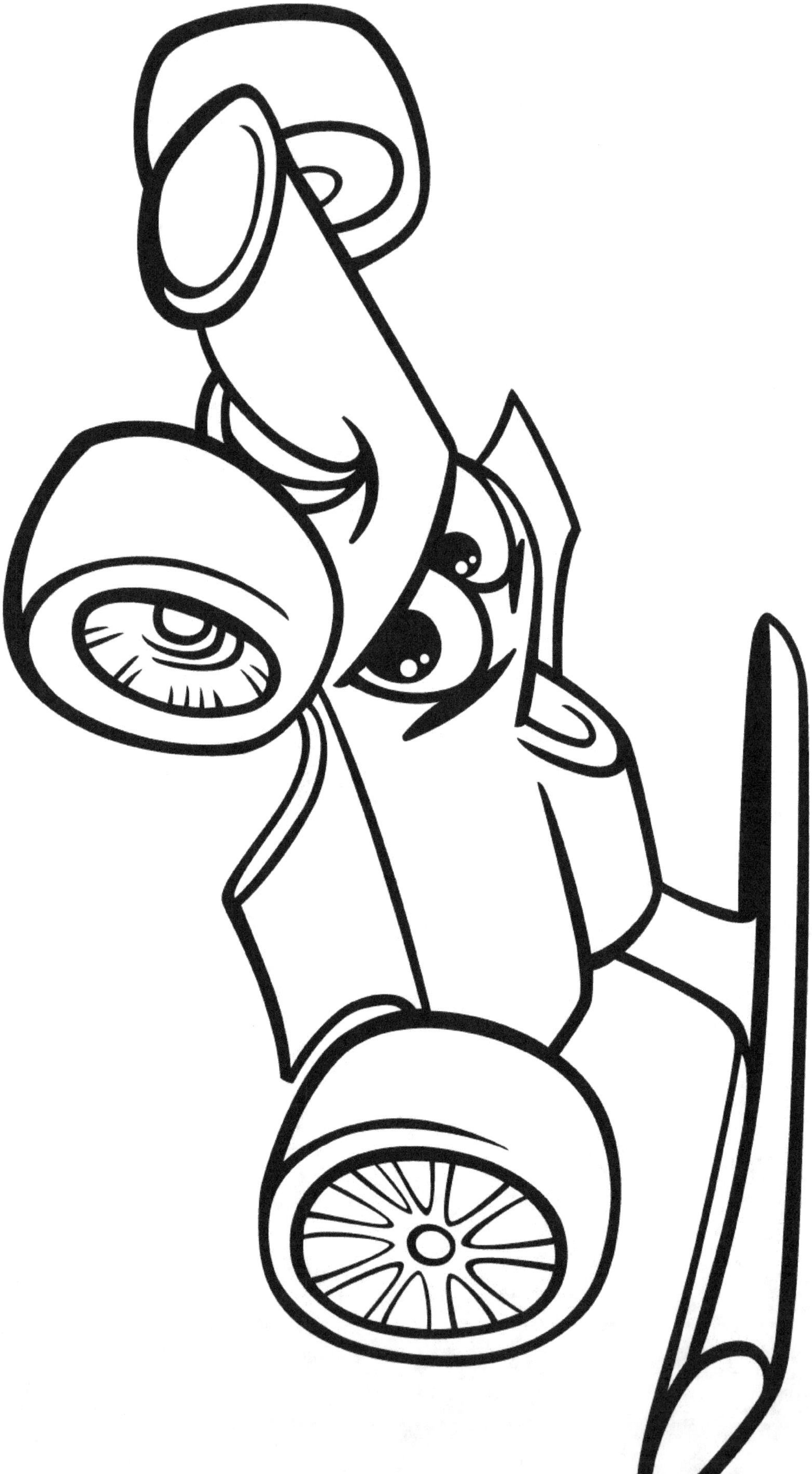

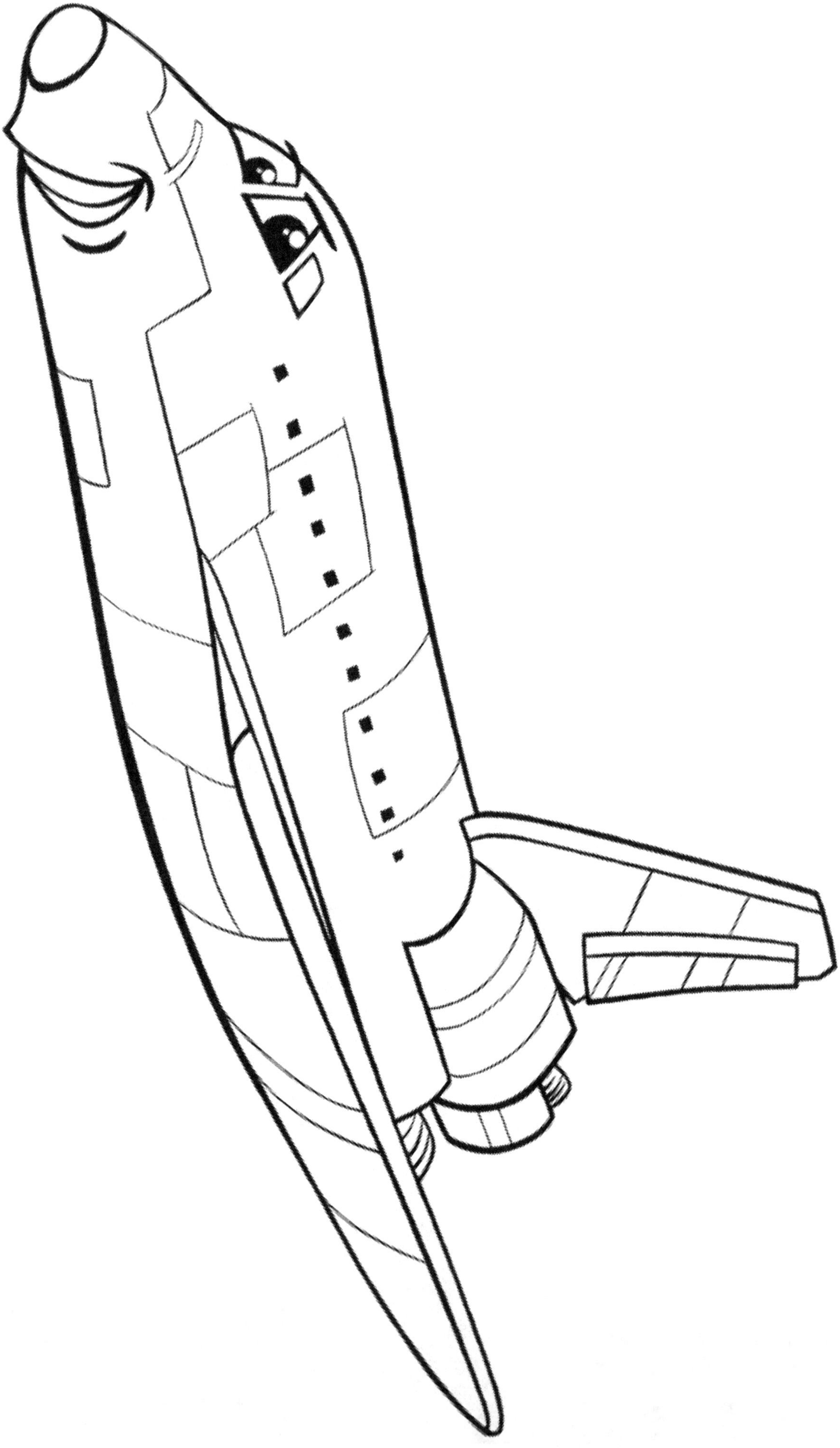

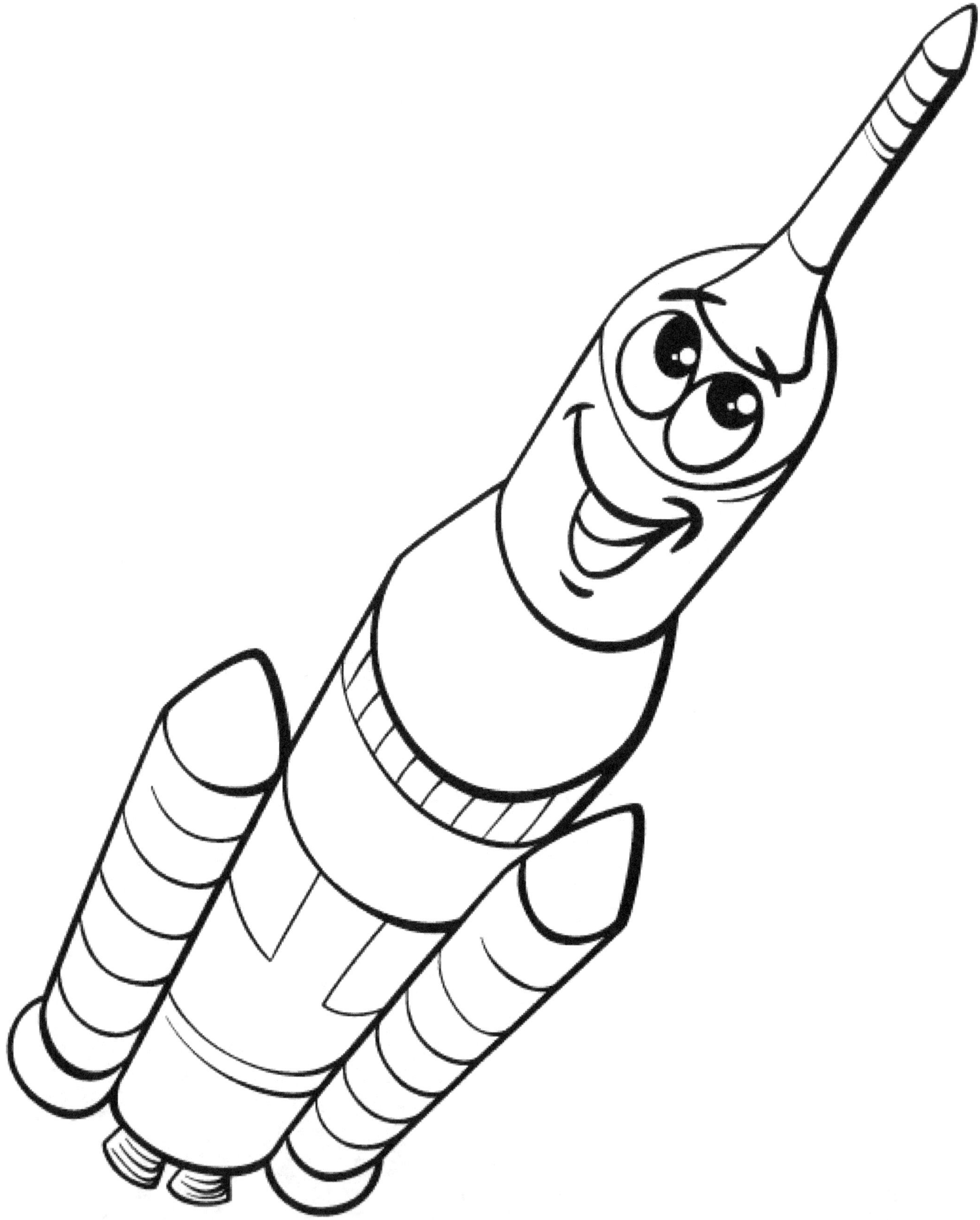

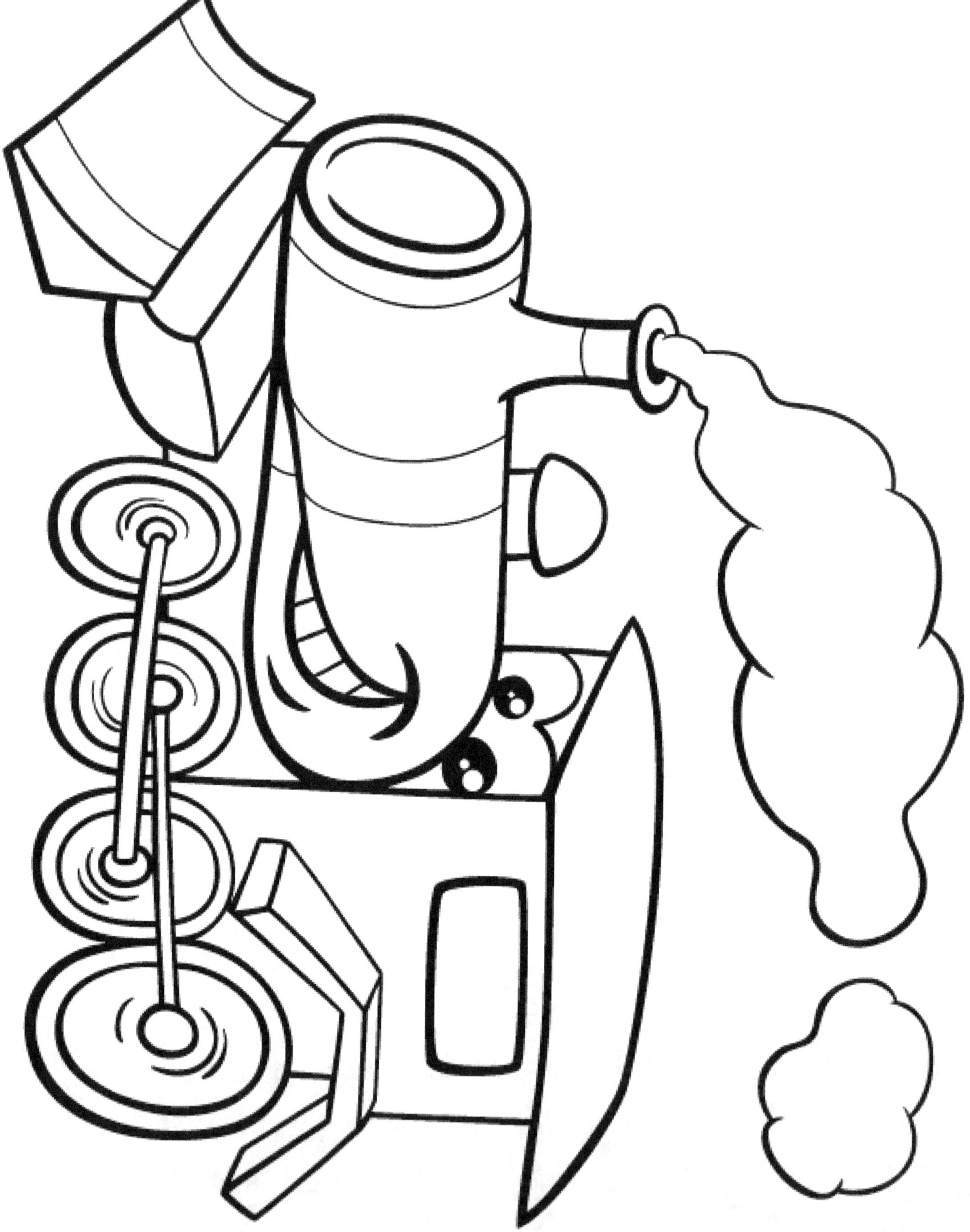

www.ingramcontent.com/pod-product-compliance
Lightning Source LLC
Chambersburg PA
CBHW060413220526
45465CB00008B/2862